Jungar Tuvan Texts

Indiana University Uralic and Altaic Series

Denis Sinor, Editor

Volume 170

JUNGAR

TUVAN

TEXTS

Talant Mawkanuli

Indiana University Bloomington
Research Institute for Inner Asian Studies
2005

Library of Congress Control Number: 2004095057

ISBN: 0-933070-51-9

to Professor György Kara
for his distinguished contribution
in the field of Altaic linguistics

Contents

Abbreviations and Conventions

1. Standard abbreviations and conventions

ABL	ablative
ACC	accusative
ADJ	adjectivelizer/adjectival
ADV	adverbializer
CAUS	causative
COLL	collective
COND	conditional
CONV	converb
COP	copula (copulative particle)
DAT	dative
DERNOM	derived nominal
EMPH	emphatic
EQU	equative
EVID	evidential (particle)
EXSIT	existential
GEN	genitive
IMP	imperative
INSTR	instrumental
INTER	interrogative
LOC	locative
NEG	negative
NEGCOP	negative copula
NEGEXIST	negative existential
PASS	passive
PAST	past (tense)
PL	plural
PNARR	past narrative
POL	polite
POSS	possessive
PRSINDF	present indefinite

PRSPRT	present participle
PSTINDF	past indefinite
PSTPRT	past participle
Q	question marker
REC	reciprocal
REFL	reflexive
RELCL	relative clitic
SG	singular
SUP	superlative particle
1	first person
2	second person
3	third person
-	morpheme boundary
.	separates the parts of a multi-word gloss
( )	optional

2. Language-name abbreviations

The names of languages have usually been written in full, but in some tables they have been abbreviated as follows:

C	Mandarin Chinese
K	Kazak
M	Mongolian
R	Russian
U	Uyghur

Introduction

This collection of Jungar Tuvan texts was selected from a corpus collected by the author during his extensive fieldwork with Jungar Tuvan people in the Jungar-Altay region of the Xinjiang Uygur Autonomous Region of China during the years 1987 through 1995.

The Jungar Tuvan language is a dialect of Tuvan. Tuvan in turn is a Turkic language spoken by slightly more than 200,000 speakers. Jungar Tuvan is spoken by approximately 4,000 people living in the Jungar-Altay region of the Altay Prefecture, Ili Kazak Autonomous District, Xinjiang Uygur Autonomous Region of China. The Jungar Tuva live around Lake Kanas in the Altay Jungar region. Kazakstan lies to the west, Russia to the north and Mongolia to the east. Northeast are the Altay Mountains, south the Ertis River and west the Kaba River. In the 17th century, large numbers of Altay Tuva migrated in all directions, establishing sizable communities within the Altay Jungar region, much of whose ancestral territory also is home to migrating Kazaks and Mongols. Jungar Tuvan is surrounded by the related Kazak language and the unrelated Mongolian language, as well as Chinese to a certain degree.

This book is part of an integrated series in an ongoing project on the Jungar Tuvan language. A grammar and a dictionary are being prepared simultaneously with the texts. A Jungar Tuvan Grammar based on my dissertation is in final stages of preparation, whereas, a Jungar Tuvan-Kazak-English dictionary is still in the early stage of preparation.

The collection includes approximately 37 texts of various types, divided into five loose topics: tales of history and culture, tales of human life/personal experiences, folk tales, songs and blessing, conversations. The word list includes the vocabulary from the texts.

The texts were told (and in part sung) by several informants, Balzhin, Belik, Bermit, Bolat, Chinlinggi, Erkit, Erik, Jinghua, Kadir, Kongir, Mongko, Odun, Omdun, Özetti, Sendish Ergin-ool[1], Serik,

---

[1] Jungar Tuvas usually do not use a last name.

Solungu, Temir, Terbiya, Torgun. All the texts were told in Jungar Tuvan in their entirety with a tape recorder running and the informants did not give me a free translation into Kazak. Later Solunggi and Turgun helped me with a free translation into Kazak.

After the texts were recorded, they were transcribed in a traditional phonemic transcription and Solungu and Turgun helped me with a free translation into Kazak. I then typed the texts after listening repeatedly to the tapes and adding the morphological analysis and the English translation. I also spent a long period of time to clear up some problems in the analysis of the recording and to do some follow-up elicitation. In 2000, I sent a draft of the texts with morphological analysis to Erkit. He checked again and made many corrections. He also kindly provided his own translation into Kazak. The texts have been carefully analyzed over a long period.

The Jungar Tuvan transcription is phonemicized. Each example of text actually consists of three lines: first the Jungar Tuvan in a morphophonemic representation, then a morpheme-by-morpheme gloss, and finally a free English translation are given for each unit of text. Examples are glossed using the abbreviations just presented with the morphological categories present in small capitals and lexical glosses in ordinary type. In the English translation, I have tried to be more faithful to the Jungar Tuvan text than one would normally be if one were simply translating the text into English. Division into lines is generally based on pauses, sometimes producing line of a single clause. Quotation marks are used for reported speech and direct quotations, where appropriate. Additional information necessary for understanding the relevant texts is given in footnotes.

Acknowledgements

First and foremost, I would like to thank the Jungar Tuvan people for welcoming me into their community and their lives. Many people have assisted in my learning and analysis of their language; those who have been the main contributors to this particular work are Erkit, Solungu,

Bermit, Torgun, Bolat, and Kongir. I would like to thank all my informants who provided the data on which this work is based.

I am much obliged to Prof. Dr. Bernard Comrie for his encouragement and help. It was he who first suggested this book project. In 2000, when I sent him a copy of my dissertation entitled "Phonology and Morphology of Jungar Tuva" which includes ten texts and indicated that I had thoughts of revising it for publication, he suggested that I should publish the texts separately. He has gone through the manuscript several times and made many detailed and valuable comments and suggestions.

I am greatly indebted to Prof. György Kara for his continuous encouragement and taking the time to read and comment on various drafts of the manuscript. I would like to express my appreciation to Dr. Ruth I. Meserve for her generous help and constant encouragement, and for proofreading the manuscript. I would like to thank Dr. Martina E. Roos who has taken the time to patiently read and comment on countless versions of this work and has contributed useful insights from her own grasp of the Turkic linguistics. I am indebted to Dr. Larry Clark for detailed and particularly helpful comments and discussions about the specific analyses on earlier drafts of the texts. I want to express my gratitude to Prof. Dr. Lars Johanson for his helpful comments on the texts.

I would like to thank Prof. Sinor, the editor of the Uralic and Altaic Studies Series for his useful comments on the manuscript, as well as his support and encouragement when I was preparing the manuscript for publishing. I gratefully acknowledge financial support received from the Max Planck Institute for Evolutionary Anthropology for the Jungar Tuvan project.

Finally, I would like to thank my wife, Aygul Diyar, my daughter, Dana Talant, and my son Ayaz Talantuli for the support and encouragement which have made this volume possible.

Tales of history and culture

1.1 The Altay Tuva

Narrated by Temir of Kanas Village in September1995

1. *alday-nıŋ žedi gožuun dıba-zı*
    Altay-GEN seven banner Tuva-3POSS

    The Seven Banners of the Altay Tuva

2. *žedi gožuun dıba-nıŋ biri-zi bo taŋdı ooršak*
    seven banner Tuva-GEN one.of-3POSS this Tangdi Oorshak

    Tangdi Oorshak is one of Tuva's seven banners.

3. *ol aldı sumun*
    it six district

    It has six districts.

4. *meereŋ gožuun üš sumun*
    Meereng banner three district

    Meereng banner has three districts.

5. *ak soyan iyi sumun*
    white Soyan two district

    White Soyan has two districts.

6. *kara soyan iyi sumun*
    black Soyan two district

    Black Soyan has two districts.

7. *mončak dört sumun*
Monchak four district

Monchak has four districts.

8. *saruul beš sumun*
Saruul five district

Saruul has five districts.

9. *beesi dört sumun*
Beesi four district

Beesi has four districts.

10. *ol töz-ü   žeerbi aldı sumun bol-ur*
it all-3POSS twenty six   district be-PRSINDF

All together there are twenty-six districts.

11. *žeerbi aldı sumun-nu erte-de   burun čıŋgıs   xaan-nan*
twenty six   district-ACC early-LOC before Chinggis Khan-ABL

soŋgaar o-nu dıba de-p   ınžaŋgaš iyi ambıl dört
after   it-ACC Tuva say-CONV thus   two Ambil four

beesi bir meereŋ bir tayžı   žagır-ıpdır
Beesi one Meereng one Tayzhi rule-PNARR

A long time ago, after Chinggis Khan, then, two Ambil[1], four
Beesi[2], one Meereng[3], and one Tayzhi[4] thus ruled the twenty six
districts calling them Tuva.

---

[1] *Ambil*: governor rank in that time cf. M. Ambil.
[2] *Beesi*: prince of the fourth rank in Manchu times. cf. M. *Bees*

12.　*erte-de　čɪŋgɪs　xaan-nan soŋgaar manžu čin　xaan*
early-LOC Chinggis Khan-ABL after　　Manchu Qing Khan

　ša-a-nda　　　ɪnžaŋgaš dɪba-lar-nɪ　töz-ü-n
time-3POSS-LOC thus　　Tuva-PL-ACC all-3POSS-ACC

　gožuun-ga ülö-pdɪr
banner-DAT divide-PNARR

A long time ago, after Chinggis Khan, during the time of Manchu Qing Khan, they divided all the Tuvas into banners.

13.　*ooson　töz-ü-n　　dɪba-lar-nɪ　alday-nɪŋ žedi gožuun*
after.that all-3POSS-ACC Tuva-PL-ACC　Altay-GEN seven banner

　dɪba-zɪ　de-p　　de ada-an
Tuva-POSS　say-CONV also name-PSTINDF

After that, they also named all the Tuvas the Seven-Banner Tuvas of the Altay.

14.　*altay dɪba gožuun uraŋxaa*
Altay Tuva banner　Uriyangkhai

The Altay Tuva banners are the Uriyangkhai.

15.　*bo alday-nɪŋ žedi gožuun dɪba-zɪ　de-p*
this Altay-GEN seven banner　Tuva-3POSS say-CONV

---

[3] *Meereng*: a rank in the Manchu administration, held by a banner official below the *Zahiragch*, who was a banner official just below the *Tuslagch* who was an assistant to a banner prince. cf. M. *Meeren.*
[4] *Tayzhi*: Taiji, crown prince, and also a title of nobility held by the descendants of Chinggis Khan.

sana-l-ɪr
consider-PASS-PRSINDF

They are considered to be the Seven-Banner Tuvas of the Altay.

16. *aldɪ sumun-nuŋ da bälen-tügön-nüŋ de töz-ü-n*
     six district-GEN also everything-GEN also all-3POSS-ACC

     dɪba de-p   ada-ar
     Tuva say-CONV name-PRSINDF

The six districts and everything else are all called Tuva.

17. *bis-tiŋ nak bo dɪba-nɪŋ bod-u   alday-ga dur-gan*
     we-GEN exact this Tuva-GEN self-3POSS Altay-DAT stand-PSTPRT

     dɪba alday-ga dile-p   bola-p
     Tuva Altay-DAT seek-CONV come.out.this.way-CONV

     gel-be-en
     come-NEG-PSTINDF

We ourselves, I mean these Tuva, are Tuva who had lived in the
Altay. We did not come seeking (= migrating to) the Altay.(i.e.
Tuvas are original inhabitants.)

18. *aldɪ sumun-nuŋ žedi gožuun dɪba-zɪ   bo alday-ga*
     six district-GEN seven banner Tuva-3POSS this Altay-DAT

     dur-gan   dɪba
     stand-PSTPRT Tuva

The Seven-Banner Tuvas of the six districts are the Tuvas who
have lived in the Altay.

1.2 The Clans of Jungar Tuva

Narrated by Sendish Ergin-ool of Akkaba Village in August 1987

1.   *bis-tiŋ bo akkaba-da žurt-tu   dıba de-er*
      we-GEN this Akkaba-LOC people-ACC Tuva say-PRSINDF

      They call the people in this Akkaba of ours Tuva.

2.   *al   bis bo akkaba-da-gı   olur-gan   dıba*
      well   we this Akkaba-LOC-RELCL live-PSTPRT Tuva

      žurd-u-n   mončak da de-er   bis
      people-3POSS-ACC Monchak also say-PRSINDF 1PL

      Well, we also call the Tuva people who live in this Akkaba Monchak[5].

3.   *mında dört sumun de-en   žurt   bar*
      here   four district say-PSTPRT people EXIST

      Here there are people who are called the Four Districts.

4.   *mončak išd-i-nde   dört-ke ülö-n-er*
      Monchak inside-3POSS-LOC four-DAT divide-REFL-PRSINDF

      Monchak is internally divided into four.

5.   *köyük irgit žag dıba šuŋgur de-p   dört-ke*
      Köyük Irgit Zhag Tuva Shunggur say-CONV four-DAT

      ülö-n-er
      divide-REFL-PRSINDF

---

[5] Monchak: The Jungar Tuvas call themselves Tuva (Dıba) or *Monchak*.

They are divided into four (clans) called Köyük, Irgit, Zhag Tuva, and Shunggur.

6. *ınžaŋgaštan o-nu   dört sumun da   de-er   bo*
    therefore   it-ACC four district also say-PRSINDF this

    This is why they also call them (the Monchak) the Four Districts.

7. *köyük-tüŋ išd-i-nde   kara köyük ak   köyük*
    Köyük-GEN inside-3POSS-LOC black Köyük white Köyük

    žanagaš   köyük goŋgutu köyük de-p   ülö-ör
    Zhanagash Köyük Gonggutu Köyük say-CONV divide-PRSINDF

    Within the Köyük they divide them into the Black Köyük, White Köyük, Zhanagash Köyük and Gonggutu Köyük.

8. *baza goŋgutu ırgıt de-p   ayd-ır*
    also Gonggutu Irgit say-CONV say-PRSINDF

    They also say Gonggutu is Irgit.

9. *irgit-tiŋ išd-i-nde   ak   irgıt kara irgıt botbum suk*
    Irgit-GEN inside-3POSS-LOC white Irgit black Irgit Botbum Suk

    möndügöy de-p   ülö-ör
    Möndügöy say-CONV divide- PRSINDF

    Within the Irgit, they divide (them) into the White Irgit, Black Irgit, Botbum, Suk, and Möndügöy.

10. *žag dıba išd-i-nde   kara žag dıba sarıg žag dıba*
    Zhag Tuva inside-3POSS-LOC black Zhag Tuva yellow Zhag Tuva

xadar žag dɪba de-p   üš-ke   ülö-n-er
Kadar Zhag Tuva say-CONV three-DAT divide-REFL-PRSINDF

Within the Zhag Tuva, they are divided into three (clans) called
the Black Zhag Tuva, Yellow Zhag Tuva, and Kadar Zhag Tuva.

11.   *šuŋgur   söök böl-bös*
Shunggur clan   divide-NEGPRSINDF

They do not divide the Shungur clan.

1. 3 My hometown - Akkaba

Narrated by Torgun of Akkaba Village in September1995

1.   *dɪba ulud-u-nuŋ   žalpɪ žagday-ɪ*
Tuva nation-3POSS-GEN general situation-3POSS

The General Situation of the Tuvan Nation

2.   *men bod-um-nuŋ   žurd-um-nuŋ   žönünde-gi*
I   self-1SG.POSS-GEN hometown-1SG.POSS-GEN about-RELCL

žer sug kandɪg ɪyaš daž-ɪ   žönünde bod-um-nuŋ
land water how   tree   stone-3POSS about   self-1SG.POSS-GEN

bil-gen-im-še   siler-ge ayd-ɪp   ber-eyin
know-PSTPRT-1SG.POSS-EQU you.PL-DAT say-CONV give-1SG.IMP

Please let me tell you, according to what I know, about the land
and water (geography), and what kind of trees and stones (nature)
pertain to my own hometown.

3.   *akkaba bis-tiŋ   xaba awdan-ga   kara-ar*
     Akkaba we-GEN Kaba county-DAT belong-PRSINDF

     Akkaba belongs to our Kaba county.

4.   *oo-ŋ   išd-i-nde   terekti awıldık akkaba gıstak*
     it-GEN inside-3POSS-LOC Terekti village   Akkaba small.village

     de-p   ayd-ır
     say-CONV say-PRSINDF

     Within it, they call it Akkaba sub-village (of) Terekti village (of
     Kaba county).

5.   *akkaba-nı   iyi gıstak-ka   ülö-ör*
     Akkaba-ACC two small.village-DAT divide-PRSINDF

     (They) divide Akkaba into two sub-villages.

6.   *biri-zi-n   kazak gıstak   biri-zi-n   mool*
     one.of-3POSS-ACC Kazak small.village one.of-3POSS-ACC Mongol

     gıstak   de-er
     small.village say-PRSINDF

     They call one of them Kazak sub-village and the other Mongol
     sub-village.

7.   *dıba-nıŋ   žan   san-ı   dört žüs-tön   artık*
     Tuva-GEN person number-3POSS four hundred-ABL more

     The population of the Tuvas is more than four hundred.

8.   *kazak-tıŋ žan   san-ı   üš žüs-tön   artık*
     Kazak-GEN person number-3POSS three hundred-ABL more

The population of the Kazaks is more than three hundred.

9.   *akkaba säbet-ke žook*
     Akkaba soviet-DAT near

     Akkaba is close to the Soviets[6].

10. *säbet-tiŋ šegärä-zi-niŋ   üsd-ü-nde*
     soviet-GEN border-3POSS-GEN top-3POSS-LOC

     It is on the Soviet border.

11. *oo-ŋ moyn-u-nda   zän   bar*
     it-GEN neck-3POSS-LOC station EXIST

     There is a (frontier) station on its neck (mountain pass).

12. *zän-niŋ üsd-ü-nde   ulug dag   bar*
     station-GEN top-3POSS-LOC big   mountain EXIST

     Above the (frontier) station, there is a big mountain.

13. *ol dag-nɪ   bolbaday da-a   de-p*
     that mountain-ACC Bolbaday mountain-3POSS say-CONV

     ayd-ɪr
     say-PRSINDF

     They call that mountain Bolbaday Mountain.

14. *oola-p   ɪŋgay on ses kilometir žoru-gan-da*
     ascend-CONV only   ten eight kilometer walk-PSTPRT-LOC

---

[6] In 1995 there were no longer any Soviets, but people still use the term "Soviet" when they refer to Kazakstan.

xanas bar
Kanas EXIST

When you walk only eighteen kilometers down (from there), there is Kanas.

15. *dıba ulud-u   bolbaday da-a-nıŋ*
     Tuva nation-3POSS Bolbaday mountain-3POSS-GEN

     ede-e-nde   kazakstan-nıŋ šegärä-zi-nıŋ
     foot-3POSS-LOC Kazakstan-GEN border-3POSS-GEN

     üsd-ü-nde   akkaba su-u-nuŋ   iyi žü-ü-nde
     upper-3POSS-LOC Akkaba water-3POSS-GEN two side-3POSS-LOC

     ornalaš-kan
     be.located-PSTINDF

     The Tuvan nation is located on both sides of the Akkaba river above the border of Kazakstan at the foot of the Bolbaday Mountain.

16. *murnuu žük bolbaday da-a-nıŋ   ede-e-nde*
     southern side Bolbaday mountain-3POSS-GEN foot-3POSS-LOC

     The south side (of their location) is at the foot of the Bolbaday Mountain.

17. *soŋgu žük kazakstan-nın šegärä-lig*
     northern side Kazakstan-INSTR border-ADJ

     The north side shares a border with Kazakstan.

18. *burun dıba ulud-u   xaba awdan-da-gı   xara oy*
     before Tuva nation-3POSS Kaba county-LOC-RELCL Kara Oy

de-en   žer-ge   dur-gan
say-PSTPRT place-DAT stay-PSTINDF

Before, the Tuva nation lived in a place called Kara Oy in Kaba county.

19.   *ard-ɪ-nan   dɪba ulud-u   göž-üp   akkaba-ga*
back-3POSS-ABL Tuva nation-3POSS move-CONV Akkaba-DAT

gel-gen
come-PSTINDF

Afterwards, the Tuvan nation migrated and came back to Akkaba.

20.   *dɪba gɪstak-tɪŋ   žan   san-ɪ   dört žüs*
Tuva small.village-GEN person number-3POSS four hundred

žeže-niŋ üsd-ü-nde
some-GEN above-3POSS-LOC

The population of the Tuvan sub-village is over four hundred.

21.   *eŋ bašday bar-ɪp   dur-ar-da   aldɪ žüs   žeže*
SUP at.first go-CONV stay-PRSPRT-LOC six   hundred some

käzɪr dört žüs-tüŋ   üsd-ü-nde
now   four   hundred-GEN above-3POSS-LOC

When they first arrived, it was some six hundred. Now, it is over four hundred.

22.   *eŋ bašday bar-ɪp   dur-ar-da   ɪn-dɪg göböy giži*
SUP at.first go-CONV stay- PRSPRT-LOC that-EQU many   person

käzir žügö ebeešte-p   gal-gan   men de
now   why decline-CONV remain-PSTPRT I   also

bil-bes-pen
know-NEGPRSINDF-1SG

I do not know why there were so many people when they first
arrived and now I don't know [why](the population) has declined.

23. *ınžaŋgaš akkaba-da-gı   giži-ler xaba awdan-da-gı*
     so   Akkaba-LOC-RELCL people-PL Kaba county-LOC-RELCL

     xara oy de-en   žer-ge   dur-gan   burun
     Kara Oy say-PSTPRT place-DAT stay-PSTINDF before

     So, the people in Akkaba lived in the place called Kara Oy in
     Kaba county before.

24. *mool-dar-nıŋ žagday-ı   eki ži-ir   žem-i*
     Mongol-PL-GEN situation-3POSS good eat-PRSPRT food-3POSS

     eki dur-gan
     good stay-PSTINDF

     The situation of the Mongols is good. They have good food to eat.

25. *osunda sezen üžünči žıl ıŋgay göž-üp   bar-gan*
     here   eighty third   year only move-CONV go-PSTINDF

     They only moved here in 1983.

26. *göž-üp   bar-ıp   dur-ar-da   ög žibe žok*
     move-CONV go-CONV stay-PRSPRT-LOC house thing NEGEXIST

dur-gan
stay-PSTINDF

When they moved (here) to live, no houses or anything existed.

27.   *osunda ıyaš   gez-ip   ög   gažaa   ga-ap   mal*
      here   wood cut-CONV house enclosure build-CONV livestock

      azıra-p   taraa tarı-p   tın azıra-n-ıp   dur-gan
      raise-CONV grain grow-CONV life raise-REFL-CONV stay-PSTINDF

      Here they subsisted by cutting down trees and building houses and
      pens, tending livestock and farming (growing grain).

28.   *dıba-lar negizinen taraa tarı-p   tın azıra-n-ar*
      Tuva-PL basically   grain grow-CONV life raise-REFL-PRSINDF

      The Tuvas basically get through life by farming (growing grain).

29.   *žamdık biri-zi   malčı-nın   žan ba-ar*
      certain some.of-3POSS herdsman-INSTR life support-PRSINDF

      Some of them support (themselves) as herders.

30.   *baza turmuž-ı ın-dıg   eki   emes*
      also   life-3POSS that-EQU good NEGCOP

      And their life is not so good.

1.4 Distribution of Jungar Tuva

Narrated by Serik of Kaba county in September 1995

1.   *alday ayma-a-nda-gı   dıwa-lar negizinen*
      Altay prefecture-3POSS-LOC-RELCL Tuva-PL   basically

buwuršın awdan-ı   xanas moŋgul   ulut-tug
Buwurshin county-3POSS Kanas Mongolian nation-ADJ

aal-ı-nda   topta-ž-ıp   xonuštan-gan
village-3POSS-LOC amass-REC-CONV settle-PSTINDF

The Tuvas of Altay prefecture[7] are basically settled, concentrated
in the Kanas Mongol ethnic village in the Buwurshin county.

2.   *büdün giži   san-ı   bir mıŋ   beš žüs*
     whole person number-3POSS one thousand five hundred

     on-ža giži
     ten-EQU person

     The total population is about 1,510 something.

3.   *mo-oŋ žedi žüs   on-day giži san-ı   xom*
     this-GEN seven hundred ten-EQU person number-3POSS Kom
     gısta-a-nda   dur-ar
     small.village-3POSS-LOC stay-PRSINDF

     About 710 persons of this population live in Kom village.

4.   *ses žüs-tey   giži san-ı   xanas*
     eight hundred-EQU person number-3POSS Kanas

     gısta-a-nda   dur-ar
     small.village-3POSS-LOC stay-PRSINDF

     About 800 people live in Kanas sub-village.

---

[7] The present Chinese official administrative institutions in Xinjiang are in ascending
order: *kıstak* (cun)'small village', *awıl ~ aal* (xiang) 'village', *awdan* (xian) 'county',
aymak (diqu) 'prefecture', *oblıst* (zhou) 'district' and *rayon* (qu) 'region, province'.

5.   *xaba awdan-ɪ   terekti awɪldɪ-ɪ-nda   akkaba*
      Kaba county-3POSS Terekti village-3POSS-LOC Akkaba

      gɪsta-a-nda   beš žüs   sezen-dey duwa-lar bar
      small.village-3POSS-LOC five hundred eighty-EQU Tuva-PL EXIST

      There are about 580 Tuvas in the Akkaba sub-village of Terekti
      village in Kaba county.

6.   *alday xala-zɪ-nɪŋ   xandagaytɪ alagak de-en   šigi iyi*
      Altay city-3POSS-GEN Kandagayti Alagak say-PSTPRT like two

      awɪldɪ-ɪ-nda   šamanan   bir žüs   aldan beš-tey
      village-3POSS-LOC approximately one hundred sixty five-EQU

      duwa-lar bar
      Tuva-PL EXIST

      There are about 165 Tuvas in the two villages, Kandagayti and
      Alagak in Altay city.

7.   *mo-oŋ aldan beš-tey-i   aldan beš-tey giži*
      this-GEN sixty five-EQU-3POSS sixty five-EQU person
      As far

      san-ɪ   xandagaytɪ-da
      number-3POSS Kandagayti-LOC

      About 65 of them, 65 people are in Kandagayti.

8.   *žüs-tey   žan   san-ɪ   alagak-ta*
      hundred-EQU person number-3POSS Alagak-LOC

      About 100 (people) of the population are in Alagak.

9. *bo iyi awıldık-ta-gı   dıva-lar öndürüs žäne*
    this two village-LOC-RELCL Tuva-PL production and

    malčılıg   gıstak-tar-ı-nda   bıdırandı
    animal-husbandry small.village-PL-3POSS-LOC scattered

    xonuštan-gan
    settle-PSTINDF

    Tuvas in these two villages are scattered over small villages that
    engaged in farming and animal-husbandry.

10. *göktogay awdan-ı-nda   dur-ar   duwa-lar temeki*
    Köktogay county-3POSS-LOC stay-PRSPRT Tuva-PL   Temeki

    awıldı-ı   žäne turgun awıldı-ı-nda   dur-ar
    village-3POSS and Turgun village-3POSS-LOC stay-PRSINDF

    The Tuvas in Köktogay county live in Temeki village and Turgun
    village.

11. *temeki awıldı-ı-nda   žeden örege bar*
    Temeki village-3POSS-LOC seventy family EXIST

    There are seventy families in Temeki village.

12. *gıži san-ı   bir žüs   bežen-deg*
    person number-3POSS one hundred fifty-EQU

    The population is about 150 people.

13. *turgun awıldı-ı-nda   on örögö bar*
    Turgun village-3POSS-LOC ten family EXIST

    There are ten families in Turgun village.

14.   *giži   san-ı   bežen-deg*
person number-3POSS fifty-EQU

The population is about 50 people.

15.   *mo-oŋ   žaštın-da   buwuršın   awdan-ı   šuŋkur*
this-GEN outer-LOC   Buwurshin   county-3POSS Shungkur

awıldı-ı-nda   bir žüs   sezen dört-tey duva-lar bar
village-3POSS-LOC one hundred eighty four-EQU Tuva-PL   EXIST

Beside this, there are about 184 Tuvas in the Shungkur village of
Buwurshin county.

16.   *buwuršın kala-zı-nda   dörtön žedi giži san-ı   bar*
Buwurshin city-3POSS-LOC forty seven person number-3POSS EXIST

There are 47 people in the city of Buwurshin.

1. 5 Tuvas in China

Narrated by Solungu of Akkaba village in September1995

1.   *kazir bo dıba bis-tiŋ   žoŋgo-da men bil-er-de*
now   this Tuva we-GEN China-LOC I   know-PRSPRT-LOC

iyi   mıŋ-ga   žook
two thousand-DAT near

As far as I know, there are now about two thousand Tuvas in our
China.

2.   *bo žoŋgo-ga dur-gan   dıba-lar alday ayma-a-nda*
this China-DAT stay-PSTPRT Tuva-PL Altay district-3POSS-LOC

dur-ar
stay-PRSINDF

These Tuvas who live in China live in the Altay district.

3.   *bo xaba awdan-ɪ-nɪŋ   akkaba gɪsta-a-nda   bar*
     this Kaba county-3POSS-GEN Akkaba small.village-3POSS-LOC EXIST

There are (Tuvas) in Akkaba village of this Kaba county.

4.   *buwuršɪn awdan-ɪ-nɪŋ   xom-ɪ-nda   xanaz-ɪ-nda*
     Buwurshin county-3POSS-GEN Kom-3POSS-LOC Kanas-3POSS-LOC

     bar
     EXIST

There are (Tuvas) in Kom and Kanas (villages) of the Buwurshin county.

5.   *alday awdan-ɪ-nɪŋ   gök sug alagak de-p*
     Altay county-3POSS-GEN blue water Alagak say-CONV

     žer-i-nde   bis-tɪŋ mončak-tar bar
     place-3POSS-LOC we-GEN Monchak-PL EXIST

There are our Monchaks in the place called Gök Sug Alagak of Altay county.

6.   *onsoonda bo göktogay bilen šiŋgil   awdan-dar-ɪ-nda*
     then   this Köktogay and   Shinggil county-PL-3POSS-LOC

     da bar
     also EXIST

Then, there also are Tuvas in these Köktogay and Shinggil counties.

7.   *göktogay-da temeki awıldık de-p   žer bar ında*
Köktogay-LOC Temeki village   say-CONV place EXIST there

mončak-tar bar
Monchak-PL EXIST

There is a place called Temeki village in Köktogay, and there are Monchaks there.

8.   *teginde bis-ti   baškar-ıp   dur-gan   beesi-bis   ol*
formerly we-ACC govern-CONV stay-PSTPRT Beesi-1PL.POSS that

göktogay-da   dur-gan
Köktogay-LOC   stay-PSTINDF

In the past, our governing Beesi lived in that Köktogay (county).

9.   *taŋma moš gaz-ı-nda   mın-dıg dörbölžin taŋma-zı bar*
seal   seal side-3POSS-LOC this-EQU square   seal-POSS EXSIT

Beside the (*moš*) seal, he had a square seal like this.

10.   *kümüs taŋma tut-kan   arzalaŋ tutkıš-tık*
silver   seal hold-PSTINDF lion   holder-ADJ

He had a silver seal that held a lion on it.

11.   *teginde manžu xaan taard-ıp žaza-p   ber-gen*
formerly Manchu khan emboss-CONV make-CONV give-PSTINDF

Formerly, the Manchu Khan embossed and made (the seals).

12.   *mool-dan   gel-gen   tört taŋma bol-gan*
Mongol-ABL come-PSTPRT four seal   be-PSTINDF

There were four seals which came from the Mongols.

13.   *bo xom bilen xanas-ta-gɪ   dur-gan   dɪba-lar bis dɪba*
this Kom with Kanas-LOC-RELCL stay-PSTPRT Tuva-PL we Tuva

emes-pis   de-er-i   mege ol
NEGCOP-1PL say-PRSPRT-3POSS false   it

The Tuvas who live in these Kom and Kanas (villages), when they
say they are not Tuvas, that is (they are) wrong.

14.   *mool-ča   žüge domaktan-bas*
Mongol-EQU why speak-NEGPRSINDF

Why would they not be speaking Mongolian?

15.   *ɪnžalsa žüge dɪba-ša   domaktan-ɪp dur*
but   why Tuva-EQU speak-CONV   stay

But why are they speaking Tuvan ?

16.   *olar dɪba*
they Tuva

They are Tuvas.

17.   *mäselen   o-oŋ   dɪba bol-ɪr-ɪ   dɪl-ga*
for.example it-GEN Tuva be-PRSPRT-3POSS language-DAT

negizdel-ip   ayd-ɪp   dur-men
be.based-CONV say-CONV stay-1SG

For example, I am saying that their being Tuvas is based on language.

18.   *ol   xom-ga   ög-ge   žüge töz-ü   mool-ča*
that Kom-DAT home-DAT why   all-3POSS Mongol-EQU

domaktan-ba-y dɪba-ša   domaktan-ɪp dur
speak-NEG-CONV Tuva-EQU speak-CONV stay

Why are all of them speaking Tuvan at home in Kom, but not Mongolian?

1. 6 Movements of Tuvas in Akkaba

Narrated by Solungu of Kanas Village in September1995

1.   *mɪŋ   tos žüs   bežen sesinči žɪl-dɪŋ   baž-ɪ*
thousand nine hundred fifty   eighth   year-GEN beginning-3POSS

zasɪk   žurt-tuŋ   bütkün mal-dar-ɪ-n   gidis
government people-GEN all   livestock-PL-3POSS-ACC felt

ö-ö   bilen dɪrd-ɪp   a-p   a-p   zorla-p
house-3POSS with drag-CONV take-CONV take-CONV force-CONV

kɪzɪl üyök-ke   göžür-dü
Kɪzɪl Üyök-DAT relocate-PAST

At the beginning of 1958, the government confiscated all the livestock and felt homes of the people and forced them to relocate to Kɪzɪl Üyök.

2.   *ol   gez-de   zor sekiriw de-p   öskörtüw de-p*
that time-LOC big leap   say-CONV reform   say-CONV

büdün akkaba-da-gı   dur-gan   dıba-nı ayda-p
entire   Akkaba-LOC-RELCL stay-PSTPRT Tuva-ACC drive-CONV

olur-ıp kızıl üyök-ke apar-dı
sit-CONV Kizil Üyök-DAT take-PAST

At that time, saying it is the Great Leap Forward and saying it is
reform, they drove away the entire Tuva population that lived in
Akkaba, and took them away to Kızıl Üyök.

3. *soŋ-u-nda   bir ay-nıŋ   išd-i-nde   sook bagay*
    end-3POSS-LOC one month-GEN inside-3POSS-LOC cold   bad

    bol-gan   aldan bičii ool öl-dü
    be-PSTINDF sixty small child die-PAST

    The cold was severe for a month at the end (of this relocation) and
    sixty small children died.

4. *onsoŋ bo bol-bas   ırgin de-p   dedir   žalaŋaš*
    then   this be-NEGPRSINDF EVID say-CONV backward Zhalangash

    de-p   žer-ge   ında äkel-di
    say-CONV place-DAT there bring-PAST

    Later, saying this won't work, they brought them back there to a
    place called Zhalangash.

5. *žalaŋaš   agın sug-lu   žer*
    Zhalangash flow water-ADJ place

    Zhalangash is a place with running water.

6.   *ınga äkel-gen   soŋ-u-nda   bičii eki bol-du*
      there bring-PSTPRT end-3POSS-LOC little good be-PAST

      After they brought them there, it became a little better.

7.   *ınga bir žıl dur-gan   soŋ-u-nda   žurt talaptan-gan*
      there one year stay-PSTPRT end-3POSS-LOC people request-PSTPRT

      soŋgaar dedır   göž-ür-üp   akkaba-ga äkel-di
      after   backward move-CAUS-CONV Akkaba-DAT bring-PAST

      After they had lived there for a year and after the people had made
      an appeal, they moved them back and brought them to Akkaba.

8.   *al   aldan iyinči žıl-ga   gel-ir-de   oy bo dıba*
      well sixty second year-DAT come-PRSPRT-LOC oh this Tuva

      šiwžinžuyi de-p   söwet bilen žaštıgı mool-ga
      revisionist   say-CONV soviet with   outer   Mongolia-DAT

      öd-üp   ba-ar   de-p   mege ayd-ıp bis-tiŋ
      cross-CONV go-PRSPRT say-CONV lie   say-CONV we-GEN

      dıba-lar-nı ayda-p   olur-up bo xara oy de-p
      Tuva-PL-ACC drive-CONV sit-CONV this Kara Oy say-CONV

      žer-ge   äkel-gen
      place-DAT bring-PSTINDF

      Well, coming to 1962, they made false statements, saying hey,
      these Tuvas are revisionists and they will cross over to the Soviets
      and to Outer Mongolia; they began to drive our Tuvas away and
      brought them to this place called Kara Oy.

9.   *xara oy-ga äkel-gen soŋ-ɪ-nda ol žer-de on*
     Kara Oy-DAT bring-PSTPRT end-3POSS-LOC that place-LOC ten

žɪl-ga žook dur-gan
year-DAT near stay-PSTINDF

After they had brought them to Kara Oy, the (Tuvas) lived almost ten years in that place.

10. *bir mɪŋ tos žüs sezen iyinči žɪl akkaba*
     one thousand nine hundred eighty second year Akkaba

žer-i-ŋge žurt bod-u-nuŋ talab-ɪ
place-3POSS-DAT people self-3POSS-GEN demand-3POSS

boyunča göž-üp bar-dɪ
according move-CONV go-PAST

In 1982, the people moved back to their Akkaba country on their own demands.

1. 7 Education

Narrated by Solungu of Kanas Village in September1995

1.   *okuw agartuw bilim al-ɪr iyi-i-nde*
     study education knowledge take-PRSPRT aspect-3POSS-LOC

About Education and Learning

2.   *öt-kön-de alday uraŋxay-lar-ɪ-n mool*
     pass-PSTPRT-LOC altay Uriyangkhai-PL-3POSS-ACC Mongol

tab-ɪ-na   *gɪr-gɪz-ip*   *baškar-gan*
class-3POSS-DAT enter-CAUS-CONV rule-PSTINDF

In the past, they ruled the Uriyangkhais of Altay by classifying them as Mongols.

3.   *ɪnžaŋgaš bir mɪŋ   tos žüs   üžünči žɪl-dar-ɪ*
therefore one thousand nine hundred thirtieth year-PL-3POSS

moŋguliya-nan arnawlɪ bilim-nig   giži-ler gɪyde-p
Mongolia-ABL   special   knowledge-ADJ person-PL call-CONV

xom xanas šigi dɪva-lar-nɪŋ göböy ornalaš-kan
Kom Kanas like Tuva-PL-GEN many be.settle-PSTPRT

žer-i-ŋge   bičii semiyä-de šagɪn mektep až-ɪp
place-3POSS-DAT small family-LOC small school   open-CONV

bir bölüm duva anɪyag-dar-ɪn   ööröt-kön
one part   Tuva young.people-PL-3POSS-ACC teach-PSTINDF

Therefore in the 1930s, they invited specially designated knowledgeable people (teachers) from Mongolia and opened small family schools in places like Komɪ and Kanas where Tuvas were concentrated, (and) had them teach one part of the Tuvan youngsters.

4.   *bir mɪŋ   tos žüs   dörtönšü žɪl-dan bašta-p*
one thousand nine hundred fortieth   year-ABL begin-CONV

alday-da-gɪ   gomindaŋ   ökümöd-ü   arnawlɪ
altay-LOC-RELCL Guomindang government-3POSS special

giži-ler   ööröd-üp   xom xanas akkaba šigi žer-ler-de
person-PL teach-CONV Kom Kanas Akkaba like place-PL-LOC

orus   mekteb-i-nen   birleš-tir-ip   mool
Russian school-3POSS-INSTR unite-CAUS-CONV Mongol

dıl-ı-nda   bastawıš mektep-ter-i-n
language-3POSS-LOC elementary school-PL-3POSS-ACC

aš-kan
open-PSTINDF

From the 1940s onwards, the Guomindang government in the Altay educated special people, and along with the Russian school, opened elementary schools in the Mongolian language in places like Kom, Kanas and Akkaba.

5.   *soŋ bir mıŋ   tos dörtön žedinči žıl-dan bašta-p   bo*
     then one thousand nine forty   seventh year-ABL begin-CONV this

     mektep dapžı-p   nomšu-ur   ool-dar san-ı
     school   develop-CONV study-PRSPRT child-PL   number-3POSS

     göböy-üp   arnawlı mektep bo-p
     increase-CONV special   school   become-CONV

     kur-ul-gan
     establish-PASS-PSTINDF

Later on, from 1947 onwards, this school has developed and the enrollment of students has increased. It was established as a special school.

6.   *kazir duva-lar möŋ   xonuštan-gan žer-de   üš*
     now   Tuva-PL heavily settle-PSTPRT   place-LOC three

bastawɪš mektep iyi toluksuz-orta mektep bar
elementary school two junior.middle   school   EXIST

Now there are three elementary schools and two junior middle
schools in the places where Tuvas are settled (and) concentrated.

7.   *mektep-tiŋ nom-u   mool   dɪl-ɪ-nda*
school-GEN instruction-3POSS Mongol language-3POSS-LOC

ber-il-er
give-PASS-PRSINDF

The instructional language of the school is given in the Mongolian
language.

8.   *dɪva ool-dar-ɪ   toluk-orta   mektep-ti alday xala-zɪ*
Tuva child-PL-3POSS senior.middle school-ACC Altay city-3POSS

birinči orta   mekteb-i-nde   nomšu-ur
first   middle school-3POSS-LOC study-PRSINDF

Tuvan children get senior high school education at the Number 1
Middle School in the city of Altay.

9.   *mu-nuŋ bir bölüm šuunžɪ nätiyže-zi   eki*
this-GEN   one part   exam   result-3POSS good

bol-gan-nar-ɪ   örlö-p   öörü mektep-ter-ge bar-ɪp
be-PSTPRT-PL-3POSS go.up-CONV high school-PL-DAT go-CONV

nomšu-ur
study-PRSINDF

Some of the those who get better grades in their exams continue
and go to college to study.

10.   *baštawıš mektep-te duva ool-dar-ı   mool*
elementary school-LOC Tuva child-PL-3POSS Mongol

dıl-ı-n   eki bil-be-en-dik-ten
language-3POSS-ACC good know-NEG-PSTPRT-DERNOM-ABL

üžünči dörtünči kılas-ka žed-ir   nom-nu mugalım
third   fourth   grade-DAT reach-PRSPRT lesson-ACC teacher

tuva dıl-ı-ŋga   ·   aŋnar-ıp   ool-dar-ga
Tuva language-3POSS-DAT translate-CONV child-PL-DAT

tüsün-dür-üp   be-er
understand-CAUS-CONV give-PRSINDF

In elementary school, because of the fact that the Tuvan children
do not know the Mongolian language well, the teachers translate
the lessons into the Tuvan language up to third and fourth grade to
make the children understand.

11.   *bastawıš bit-tir-gen-nen   soŋgaar dıva ool-dar-ı*
elementary end-CAUS-PSTPRT-ABL after   Tuva child-PL-3POSS

mool   dıl-ı-ŋga   bir xur   xanıg bo-p
Mongol language-3POSS-DAT one over.all fluent be-CONV

gal-ır
remain-PRSINDF

After finishing elementary school, Tuvan children have become
much more fluent in the Mongolian language.

12.   *toluk orta-ga   ba-ar-da   mool*
senior.middle.school-DAT go-PRSPRT-LOC Mongolian

ool-dar-ı-nan   *birge*   *nomšu-ur*
child-PL-3POSS-INSTR together study-PRSINDF

When they go to senior middle school, they will study together
with Mongolian children.

13.   *duva-lar berekelig tırıššaŋ*   *žurt* *bol-gan-dık-tan*
Tuva-PL amicable hard.working people be-PSTPRT-DERNOM-ABL

baška bod-u-nun   *kadı*   *olur-gan*   *köršülös*
other self-3POSS-INSTR together live-PSTPRT neighboring

ulut-tar-ı-nıŋ   *dıl*   *bičik-ter-i-n*   *šuluun*
nation-PL-3POSS-GEN language script-PL-3POSS-ACC fast

öörön-üp   al-ır
learn-CONV take-PRSINDF

Because the Tuvas are amicable and hardworking people, they
quickly learn the languages and scripts of other nationalities who
live side by side with them.

14.   *käzir duva-lar dur-gan*   *žer-de*   *žerlik giži-ler* *gırgan*
now   Tuva-PL live-PSTPRT place-LOC local   person-PL old.man

žaš   di-beyin   *mool*   *kazak duva dıl-ı-n*
young say-NEGCONV Mongol Kazak Tuva language-3POSS-ACC

teŋ   goldan-ır
equal use-PRSINDF

Now, in places where the Tuvas live, the local people no matter
whether they are old or young use the Mongolian, Kazak and
Tuvan languages equally.

15.   *žäne mool   kazak biži-i-n   toluk biči-p paydalan-ıp*
       and   Mongol Kazak script-3POSS-ACC fully   write   use-CONV

       al-ır
       take-PRSINDF

       They also are able to use the Mongolian and Kazak scripts
       (written languages) freely.

1. 8 The Tuvan Language

Narrated by Solungu of Akkaba Village in September1995

1.   *amdı bo   dıba žönnün ayt-kan-da   dıba   dıl*
      now   this Tuva as.far.as say-PSTPRT-LOC Tuvan language

      öskör-e   ba-ar-ı   šındık
      change-CONV go-PRSPRT-3POSS truth

      Now, speaking about this Tuvan language, it is true that Tuvan is
      changing.

2.   *öskör-e   ba-ar-ı   bis-tiŋ bo   dıba dıl   tek*
      change-CONV go-PRSPRT-3POSS we-GEN this Tuva language only

      bo akkaba-nıŋ išd-i-nde   ög-nüŋ   išd-i-ŋge
      this Akkaba-GEN inside-3POSS-LOC house-GEN inside-3POSS-DAT

      gene domaktan-ır-bıs
      only speak-PRSINDF-1PL

      It is changing (because) we only speak this Tuvan language of
      ours in this Akkaba and at home.

3   *kogam-ga   ün-ör-de   iš   ažılda-ar-da   kazak-ša*
society-DAT enter-PRSPRT-LOC work do-PRSPRT-LOC Kazak-EQU

materiyal gel-er-de   kazak-ša   domaktan-ır-bıs
material   come-PRSPRT-LOC Kazak-EQU speak-PRSINDF-1PL

When we go into society or when we are at work, we speak Kazak
when it comes to Kazak subject matter.

4.   *onun ıŋgay awdan ürümži žeže žer-ge   bar-gan-da*
then   always county Ürümchi some place-DAT go-PSTPRT-LOC

xanzu-ša domaktan-ır bol-ba-za   kazak-ša   da
Han-EQU   speak-PRSPRT be-NEG-COND Kazak-EQU also

güž-ü-nen   gal-ır
might-3POSS-ABL be.left-PRSINDF

Then they always have to speak Chinese when they go to places
like the county (town) or Ürümchi, since Kazak has no status
(there in Ürümchi) either.

5.   *al   am bis mool-ša   nomšu-p dur-bus*
well now we Mongol-EQU read-CONV stay-1PL

Well, now we are studying Mongolian.

6.   *išti mool-dıŋ   xudma üzü-ü-n   nomšu-p*
inner Mongol-GEN Hudma letter-3POSS-ACC study-CONV

mool-ša   nomšu-p   dur-bus
Mongol-EQU study-CONV stay-1PL

We are studying the *Hudma* (Inner Mongolian) script and we are
studying Mongolian.

7.   *bis-tɪŋ mool-ša   nomšu-un ool-ubuz   tek*
     we-GEN Mongol-EQU study-PSTPRT child-1PL.POSS only

     mektep-tɪŋ išd-i-ŋge   gene domaktan-ɪr
     school-GEN inside-3POSS-DAT only speak-PRSINDF

     Our children who study Mongolian only speak it at school.

8.   *ol ool-dar-ga awdar-ɪp   gene nomšu-d-ur-bus*
     that child-PL-DAT translate-CONV only learn-CAUS-PRSINDF-1PL

     We only teach those children by translating (from Mongolian into Tuvan).

9.   *onson bol-gan-nan   gedeer on-u ganžaar de-ze-ger*
     after   be-PSTPRT-ABL after it-ACC how.much say-COND-2PL

     After all this, what can you say about it (how much can you expect from them) ?

10. *kogam-ga ün-gön-nen   gedeer ö-ö-ŋge*
     society-DAT go.out-PSTPRT-ABL after   home-3POSS-DAT

     bar-gan-nan   gedeer dɪba dɪl   domaktan-ɪr
     go-PSTPRT-ABL after   Tuva language speak-PRSINDF

     They speak Tuvan after (when) they go back out into society and go home.

11. *ada-eyi-zi-nen   olar mool-ša   domaktan-gan*
     grandparents-3POSS-INSTR they Mongol-EQU speak-PSTPRT

     bilen mool-ša   bil-bes   ol
     with Mongol-EQU know-NEGPRSINDF that

Even though they want to speak with their grandparents in Mongolian, they (the grandparents) don't know Mongolian.

12. *baxšı-lar-ı   ool-dar-ga mool-ša   domaktan-gan bile*
teacher-PL-3POSS child-PL-DAT Mongol-EQU speak-PSTPRT   with

   ög-gö   bar-gan   soŋda olar ganžaar de-ze-ger
home-DAT go-PSTPRT after   they how.much say-COND-2PL

   dɪba-ša   domaktan-ɪr
Tuva-EQU speak-PRSINDF

Even though their teachers speak to the children in Mongolian, no matter what you say (to them), after they go home they speak Tuvan.

13. *am ulug giži   bol-sa   öörüg-den bir materiyal xužat*
now big person be-COND above-ABL one material   document

   gel-se   ol kazak-ša
come-COND it Kazak-EQU

Now, as for the adults, if an official document comes from above (the government), it is in Kazak.

14. *o-oŋ bilen bis-ter kazı-p   bil-e   sal-ır-bis*
it-GEN with   we-PL read-CONV know-CONV put-PRSINDF-1PL

   ödö aar
very difficult

Even if we read it and understand it, it is very difficult.

15. *bir giži   bol-ur   užun bod-ubus-tuŋ   dɪba*
one person be-PRSPRT for   self-1PL.POSS-GEN Tuva

ult-ubus-tu   sakta-p   gal-ɪr   užun
nation-1PL.POSS-ACC preserve-CONV remain-PRSPRT for

mool-ša   öörön-ür-übüs   kerek irgin
Mongol-EQU learn-PRSPRT-1PL.POSS need   EVID

It would seem that we have to learn Mongolian in order to be
people, in order to preserve our own Tuvan ethnic identity. (said
sarcastically)

16. *onson kogam-ga ülöz-üp   žor-ur   užun sösžok*
     then   society-DAT follow-CONV walk-PRSPRT for   definitely

     kazak-ša bil-ir   kerek irgin
     Kazak-EQU know-PRSPRT need EVID

     Also, it would seem that we definitely have to know Kazak in
     order to follow along into society. (also said sarcastically)

17. *ulug iyik-ten a-b   ayt-kan-da   memleket-tiŋ*
     broad aspect-ABL take-CONV say-PSTPRT-LOC state-GEN

     dɪl-ɪ   xanzu bol-gan užun xanzu-ša   öörön-er
     tongue-3POSS Han   be-PSTPRT for Chinese-EQU learn-PRSPRT

     kerek dur
     need EMPH

     Speaking from a broad perspective, we have to learn Chinese
     because Chinese is the state language.

18. *al ürümži-ge   bar-za   oygur dɪl-ɪ-n*
     well Ürümchi -DAT go-COND Uyhgur language-3POSS-ACC

bil-be-ze   *de bol-bas*
know-NEG-COND also be-NEGPRSINDF

Well, if someone goes to Ürümchi, it won't do if s/he doesn't know the Uyghur language.

19.   *ɪnžaŋgaš käzɪr men bod-um   ülögörü   mončak*
therefore now I   self-1SG.POSS for.example Monchak

dɪl   bil-er-men   mool dɪl
language know-PRSINDF-1SG Mongol language

bil-er-men   kazak dɪl   bil-er-men
know-PRSINDF-1SG Kazak language know- PRSINDF-1SG

xansu-ša bil-er-men
Han-EQU know- PRSINDF-1SG

Therefore, now, taking my own example, I know Monchak, I know Mongolian, I know Kazak, (and) I know Chinese.

20.   *oygur dɪl-ɪ   da bičii-bičii öörön-üp*
Uygur language-3POSS also gradually learn-CONV

žor-ur-men
walk-PRSINDF-1SG

I am also learning the Uygur language little by little.

21.   *žügö de-ze-ŋ   ürümži-ge   bar-gan-da   oygur-ša*
why say-COND-2SG Ürümchi-DAT go-PSTPRT-LOC Uyghur-EQU

domaktan-ba-za-ŋ kazak dɪl   domaktan-sa-ŋ
speak-NEG-COND-2SG Kazak language speak-COND-2SG

olar baza taard-ıp   žaktır-bas   žagday   bar
they also   rebuke-CONV like-NEGPRSPRT circumstance EXIST

If you ask why, (it is because) if you do not speak Uyghur when you go to Ürümchi, [and] if you speak Kazak, there will be a situation where they (will) rebuke and not like you.

22.   *o-oŋ bilen bis-ti   mın-dıg mın-dıg da žagday bar*
it-GEN with   we-ACC this-EQU this-EQU also situation EXIST

kazak-ša domaktan-sa-ŋ olar oy koŋkabay de-er
Kazak-EQU speak-COND-2SG they hey Kongkabay say-PRSINDF

Moreover, we have experienced such kinds of situations where they will say to you "Hey Kongkabay[8]" if you speak Kazak.

23.   *oygur-ša domakdan-za-ŋ eki gö-ör*
Uygur- EQU speak-COND-2SG good consider-PRSINDF

They will like you if you speak Uygur.

24.   *ol iyik-nen gel-gen-de   bis-ter mıysalı am ol*
that aspect-ABL come-PSTPRT-LOC we-PL for.example now that

žer-ge   gel-gen-de   ärkandık ädet-te   pukara-nıŋ
place-DAT come-PSTPRT-LOC any.kind   situation-LOC mass-GEN

bod-u   da üš tür-lüg dıl   bil-er   gerek
self-3POSS also three kind-ADJ language know-PRSPRT necessary

When it comes to that aspect, when for example we now come to that place (and) in all sorts of situations, the common people have to know three different languages.

---

[8] *Kongkabay*: a derogatory term used by Uygurs when they refer to Kazaks.

25.   *mončakta-za   o-nu bod-u   burun-nan*
speak.Monchak-COND it-ACC self-3POSS before-ABL

   bil-er
   know-PRSINDF

   As far as speaking Monchak, one knows it already.

26.   *onsoŋ kazak bilen xansu dıl   bil-er   gerek*
also   Kazak with Han   language know-PRSPRT necessary

   Also, one has to know Kazak and Chinese.

27.   *žamdıg biri-zi   mool   dıl   bil-bes   ulug*
certain one.of-3POSS Mongol language know-NEGPRSINDF big

   amtan-nar-nıŋ keybiri-si   gene bil-er
   people-PL-GEN some.of-3POSS only know-PRSINDF

   Some of them don't know Mongolian. Only some of the older
   people know it.

1. 9 The changing language and cultures

Narrated by Solungu of Kanas Village in September1995

1.   *dıba žönnön gel-gen-de   bežen žežerči žıl geŋ*
Tuva about   come-PSTPRT-LOC fifty   some   year Geng

   at-tıg   bir giži   gel-gen
   name-ADJ one person come-PSTINDF

   Talking about Tuva, someone named Geng came in the1950s.

2. *sezen birinči žɪl-dar suŋ at-tɪg   bir giži   gel-gen*
    eighty first   year-PL Sung name-ADJ one person come-PSTINDF

    Someone named Song came in the 1981.

3. *ol baza dɪba-nɪŋ   žorun žozun-u-n*
    he also   Tuva-GEN customs.and.habits-3POSS-ACC

    beedil-i-n   zertte-p   gel-gen
    condition-3POSS-ACC research-CONV come-PSTINDF

    He came here to do research on Tuvan customs, habits and
    conditions.

4. *men-že al-gan-da   bis-tiŋ dɪba žalpɪ al-gan-da*
    I-EQU   take-PSTPRT-LOC we-GEN Tuva general take-PSTPRT-LOC

    käzir dɪba-nɪŋ bo žook-ta-gɪ   dɪba-nɪŋ keybir
    now   Tuva-GEN this recent-LOC-RELCL Tuva-GEN some

    dɪl-dar-ɪ   kazak-ka öskör-gön
    language-PL-3POSS Kazak-DAT change-PSTINDF

    According to me (I think), when taking into account our Tuvan in
    general, some (aspects) of the Tuvan language have now changed
    towards Kazak, lately.

5. *žügö de-ze   memeleket azat   bol-gan-nan   gedeer*
    why say-COND country   liberation be-PSTPRT-ABL after

    guŋšo   gur-ul-gan-nan   gedeer kazak-tar-nan
    commune establish-PASS-PSTPRT-ABL after   Kazak-PL-INSTR

    gadɪ   žor-guš-tan   olar-dɪŋ turmuš-tɪg äded-i
    together walk-CONV-ABL they-GEN life-ADJ   custom-3POSS

öndürüs   barız-ı-nda-gı   domaktan-ır
production course-3POSS-LOC-RELCL speak-PRSPRT

dıl-dar-dıŋ   barı töz-ü   kazak dıl-ı-ŋga
language-PL-GEN all   all-3POSS Kazak language-3POSS-DAT

öskör-gön
change-PSTINDF

"Why is that? Because since the liberation of the country, and the establishment of the commune, they have been living together with the Kazaks, and in general their (the Tuva's) customs (life style) and the language (specific lexicon) they speak during the production process have been totally changed into Kazak.

6.   *al   amdı öskör-beyin   dur-gan   dıl   gaysı*
      well now   change-NEGCONV stay-PSTPRT language which

      de-se-ger   dıba-nıŋ burun-gı   könö dıl-ı
      say-COND-2PL Tuva-GEN before-RELCL old   language-3POSS

      Well, if you ask which parts (aspects) of the language have not been changed, (I would say that) it is Tuva's old language of long ago.

7.   *birinči mädeniy dıl-dar*
      first   cultural   language-PL

      First, it is the cultural languages (lexical terms pertaining to the culture).

8.   *iyi üšinči din-niy   dıl-dar*
      two third   religion-ADJ language-PL

      Second and third are the religious languages (terms).

9.   *bo gadarlı   at   san   esim-i*
     this together.with name number noun-3POSS

     Along with these are nouns and numerals.

10. *xanzu miŋči duŋči de-er*
     Han   mingci dongci say-PRSINDF

     The Chinese call them mingci (nouns) and dongci (verbs.)

11. *olar öskör-bö-dü*
     they change-NEG-PAST

     They didn't change.

12. *baška iš-žüzündük žagday-da   bo men käzir*
     other   practical   situation-LOC this I   now

     bod-um   da öskör-d-üp   ayd-ıp   olur-men
     self-1SG.POSS also change-CAUS-CONV say-CONV sit-1SG

     As a matter of fact, I myself too am now speaking while changing
     it (the language.)

13. *öskör-be-di   de-en   sös bo bod-u   da kazak*
     change-NEG-PAST say-PSTPRT word this self-3POSS also Kazak

     söz-ü   emes   pe
     word-3POSS   NEGCOP Q

     Isn't even the word *öskör-* "to change" itself Kazak ?

14. *ınžangašta bo mın-dıg žäyit*
     therefore   this this-EQU situation

     Therefore, this is the situation.

15. *al   bis-tiŋ dıba bo mool-dan   gandıg   park-ı*
     well we-GEN Tuva this Mongol-ABL what.kind difference-3POSS

     bar   gandıg ayırmašılı-ı   bar de-en-de   mool
     EXIST what.kind divergence-3POSS EXIST say-PSTPRT-LOC Mongol

     de-en-niŋ   bo bis-tiŋ dıba-nıŋ ädet gurpu onsonda
     say-PSTPRT-GEN this we-GEN Tuva-GEN custom habits here

     bo dın-niy   iyik-ten   šažın   žütülgü   iyik-ten
     this religion-ADJ aspect-ABL religious consciousness aspect-ABL

     a-b   ayt-kan-da   mool-ga   dööy
     take-CONV say-PSTPRT-LOC Mongol-DAT alike

     Well, when talking about what kind of differences and divergence
     exist between (our) Tuvan and (this) Mongolian, (I would say)
     they resemble the Mongol with regard to the habits and customs,
     and they (Tuvas and Mongols) are identical when we talk about
     the religious aspect and religious consciousness.

16. *ged-er   kep iyik-ten a-b   ayt-kan-da*
     wear-PRSPRT clothes aspect-ABL take-CONV say-PSTPRT-LOC

     da   mool-ga   dööy
     EMPH Mongol-DAT alike

     They also resemble the Mongol with regard to the clothing (that)
     they wear.

17. *dööy emes   žer-i   kaysı de-en-de   dıba-nıŋ*
     alike NEGCOP place-3POSS which say-PSTPRT-LOC Tuva-GEN

     bo dıl-ı   dööy emes
     this language-3POSS alike NEGCOP

If you ask what are the differences? (I would say) the languages
are not the same.

18. *dıba gıži   dıl   kazak til   de-er   emes pe*
Tuva person language Kazak language say-PRSINDF NEGCOP Q

Don't (you know that) the Tuvas say *dil* "language," and the
Kazak *til* "language"?

19. *al   am   ınžalgaštan bis-tiŋ mool-ga   dıl-ı   teŋ*
well now therefore   we-GEN Mongol-DAT language-3POSS same

emes
NEGCOP

Well, therefore, our language is not the same as the Mongolian.

20. *bis-tiŋ dıba-nıŋ negizinin göb-ü   dörtön žeže*
we-GEN Tuva-GEN basically   many-3POSS forty   some

pırasent-i   dıba dıl
percent-3POSS Tuva language

Basically, more than forty percent of our Tuvan is Tuvan.

21. *könö türk   sestema-zı-nda-gı   dıba dıl*
old   Turkic system-3POSS-LOC-RELCL Tuva language

(It) is the Tuvan language that belongs to the old Turkic system.

22. *mool-ga   okša-ar-ı   negizinen on beš-ten*
Mongol-DAT resemble-PRSPRT-3POSS basically   fifteen-ABL

on ses pırasent gana
eighteen percent   only

The parts that are the same as Mongolian are basically fifteen to eighteen percent only.

23.   *kazak dıl-ı-ŋga*   *ülösör-lör-ü*   *üžön*
Kazak language-3POSS-DAT convergent-PL-3POSS thirty

prasent-tıŋ üsd-ü-nde
percent-GEN above-3POSS-LOC

Some thirty percent (or) more converges with the Kazak language.

24.   *ol da dörtön pırasent-tig*
that also forty   percent-ADJ

That is also like forty percent.

25.   *bo mın-dıg mın-dıg öskölü-ü*   *bar*
this this-EQU this-EQU   particularity-3POSS EXIST

It has these kinds of particularities.

26.   *ne mool da emes ne kazak da emes ne*
what Mongol also NEGCOP what Kazak also NEGCOP what

oygur da emes o-oŋ išd-i-nde   *oygur dıl*
Uygur also NEGCOP it-GEN inside-3POSS-LOC Uygur   language

da bar
also EXIST

It's neither Mongolian nor Kazak, nor is it Uygur either. It also has (elements of the)Uygur language.

27.   *mäselen   buluŋ-nı   oygur buluŋ de-ze   bis de buluŋ*
for.example corner-ACC Uygur corner say-COND we also corner

de-er-bis
say-PRSINDF-1PL

For example, if the Uygur say: *buluŋ* (corner) we also say: *buluŋ* (corner.)

28.   *argamžɪ-nɪ oygur argamžɪ de-ze   bis de   argamžɪ*
      lasso-ACC   Uygur lasso   say-COND we   also lasso

      de-er-bis
      say- PRSINDF-1PL

      The Uygur say *argamžɪ* (lasso), we say *argamžɪ* as well.

29.   *inek-ti   oygur inek de-ze   bis de   inek de-er-bis*
      cow-ACC Uygur cow say-COND we also cow say- PRSINDF-1PL

      The Uygur say *inek* (cow), we say *inek* as well.

30.   *dööy de   dɪl-dar-ɪbɪs   bar*
      alike   also language-PL-1PL.POSS EXIST

      We have languages (vocabularies) like that too.

31.   *keybir at   dɪl-dar-ɪ-nda   al   me-eŋ göz*
      some   name language-PL-3POSS-LOC well I-GEN eye

      karaz-ɪm-nan   ayt-kan-da   bis-tiŋ dɪba
      point.of.view-1SG.POSS-ABL say-PSTPRT-LOC we-GEN Tuva

      dɪl   öde erte-de bol-gan   dɪl
      language very early-LOC be-PSTPRT language

(With respect to) some (of the) language (nouns), well, in my opinion, (I would say that) our Tuva is an very ancient language.

1. 10 Religion

Narrated by Bermit of Akkaba Village in July 1987

1. *duwa-lar budda lama   din-i-ŋge   sen-er*
   Tuva-PL Buddhist Lama religion-3POSS-DAT believe-PRSINDF

   The Tuvans believe in the religion of Lamaism and Buddhism.

2. *olar-nıŋ din-niy   senim-i   güštük*
   they-GEN religion-ADJ believe-3POSS strong

   Their religious belief is strong.

3. *käzır-ge žed-ır   lama baxšı   xam-nar bar*
   now-DAT reach-PRSPRT Lama shaman.healer shaman-PL EXIST

   Up to now, they have lamas, shamans and shaman healers.

4. *xam-nar-ı   žalgaž-ıp   gel-e   žid-ır*
   shaman-PL-3POSS continue-CONV come-CONV lie-PRSINDF

   Their shaman healers remain.

5. *lama baxšı-lar-ı   duva-lar-nıŋ bod-dar-ı-nıŋ*
   Lama shaman-PL-3POSS Tuva-PL-GEN self-PL-3POSS-GEN

   šagaa   owaa dagıır gadarlıg ulug meyram-nar-ı-nda
   New Year cairn.worship etc.   big   holiday-PL-3POSS-LOC

bod-dar-ɪ-nıŋ   sald-ɪ   boyunša   din-niy
self-PL-3POSS-GEN customs-3POSS according.to religion-ADJ

äreket-ter   iste-p   nom nomšu-ur
performance-PL do-CONV book read-PRSINDF

Lamas and shaman healers do religious performances and pray at
the Tuva's own major holidays (such as) New Year's, cairn
(*owaa*) ceremonies, etc as ritual performance ceremonies and so
on, according to their own customs.

6.   *žäne žok   bol-gan   amtan-nar-ga nom*
      and   NEGEXIST be-PSTPRT people-PL-DAT book

nomšu-p   žerle-er
read-CONV bury-PRSINDF

They also pray for the deceased and bury them.

1. 11 Worshiping Altay

Narrated by Jinghua of Akkaba Village in September1995

1.   *men bo bir akkaba-nıŋ alday dagɪ-ır*
      I   this one Akkaba-GEN Altay sanctify-PRSINDF

žibe-zi-n   xoožıla-p ber-eyin   ä
thing-3POSS-ACC tell-CONV give-1SG.IMP okay

Ok, let me talk about how the Akkaba people perform the rites for
the Altay[9].

---

[9] Altay: refers to Tangir "sky" or "heavens"

2.   *bis bis-tiŋ dört sumun dɯba-bɯs-ta   alday*
      we we-GEN four district Tuva-1PL.POSS-LOC Altay

      dagɯ-ɯr
      sanctify-PRSINDF

      We, among the Tuva(s)of our Four Districts, sanctify the Altay.

3.   *alday dagɯ-ɯr-da   ol žay-nɯŋ   baškɯ*
      Altay sanctify-PRSPRT-LOC that summer-GEN beginning

      ay-ɯ-nda   alday žer su-um   de-p   o-nu
      month-3POSS-LOC Altay land water-1SG.POSS say-CONV it-ACC

      owaa dagɯ-p   ɯ-ŋga žem-niŋ deeži-zi-n
      sacred.side.sanctify-CONV it-DAT food-GEN seed-3POSS-ACC

      be-er
      give-PRSINDF

      When sanctifying the Altay (God), at the first month of the
      summer, they will perform a ritual (erect an owaa) praising my
      (our) Altay land and water, and offer the seeds of food crops.

4.   *ol alday-ga o-nu žüge be-er   de-ze   bis bir*
      that Altay-DAT it-ACC why give-PRSINDF say-COND we one

      žɯl-dɯn eki ün-dü-büs   žɯl gɯš-tan   eki
      year-ABL good go.out-PAST-1PL year winter-ABL good

      ün-dü-büs   amdɯ munuun munaar bir žay-ɯn
      go.out- PAST-1PL now   from.this on   one summer-INSTR

      eki köŋüldüg öt-küz-ör-büs
      good happy   pass-CAUS-PRSINDF-1PL

If you ask why they give that to the Altay (God), (it is) because we passed through the year well, we passed through the year and winter well, and from now on, we would pass through the summer time happily.

5. *baza mal   žime semis bol-sun taraa arba elbek*
    and livestock thing fat   be-3IMP   wheat barley plentiful

    bol-sun de-p   alday-ga žalbar-tın-ıp   žem žibe-niŋ
    be-3IMP say-CONV Altay-DAT beg-PASS-CONV food thing-GEN

    deeži-zi-n   apa-ar-bıs
    seed-3POSS-ACC deliver-PRSINDF-1PL

    We will bring the seeds of the food to the Altay to beg him, we will beg of the Altay "May the livestock be fat (healthy) and may the wheat and barley be abundant."

6. *ınža-p   alday dagı-p   ba-ar-da   ulug bičii*
    do.so-CONV Altay sanctify-CONV go-PRSPRT-LOC old   young

    er   žügär töz-übüs   ba-ar-bıs
    male female all-1PL.POSS go-PRSINDF-1PL

    When we go to sanctify the Altay, old and young, male and female, all of us would go.

7. *orta ba-ar-da   žem-niŋ deeži-zi-n   baza*
    there go- PRSPRT-LOC food-GEN seed-3POSS-ACC and

    keybiri-ler mal   soy-up   a-p   ba-ar
    some.of-PL animal slaughter-CONV take-CONV go-PRSINDF

    When they go there, they bring the seeds of food and some of them slaughter an animal and bring it there.

8.   *o-nu žaštaar apar-gan-nan   gedeer töz-ü*
     it-ACC outside deliver-PSTPRT-ABL after   all-3POSS

     žɪg-ɪl-ɪp   a-p   že-er
     gather-PASS-CONV take-CONV eat-PRSINDF

     After having taken it (food) outside, all of them will gather
     together and eat.

9.   *baza bäygi-ge   at   sal-ɪr*
     and   horse.race-DAT horse put-PRSINDF

     They will also have a horse race.

10. *dɪba-nɪŋ bɪs-tɪŋ dɪba-bɪs-tɪŋ   burun-nan beer*
     Tuva-GEN we-GEN Tuva-1PL.POSS-GEN before-ABL since

     kalɪptas-tɪr-ɪp gel-e   žɪt-kan üš ulug
     form-CAUS-CONV come-CONV lie-PSTPRT three great

     meyram-i-n   üš   naadɪm de-er
     festival-3POSS-ACC three Nadim   say-PRSINDF

     They call the Tuva's, our Tuvas's three great festivals, which were
     established long ago, the Three Nadim[10].

11. *naadɪm kün-ü   birinči böge   sal-ɪr   iyinči at*
     Nadim   day-3POSS first   wrestler put-PRSINDF second horse

     bäyge-zi-n   sal-ɪr   baza erkin böge
     horse.race-3POSS-ACC put-PRSINDF and   free   wrestler

---

[10] *Nadim*: a Tuvan traditional festival.

güreš-tir-er   *üš*   *oyun öt-küz-ür*
wrestle-CAUS-PRSINDF three game pass-CAUS-PRSINDF

On the Nadim day, they (will) hold three games: first, they have a
wrestling tournament, second, they have a horse-race, and (then)
they hold a free (volunteer) wrestling contest.

12.   *onun gedeer alday žer su-ubuz-ga*   *žalbar-ıp*
      then   after   Altay earth water-1PL.POSS-DAT beg-CONV

      baxšı-lar ol   alday žer su-u-ga   *žem-niŋ*
      shaman-PL that Altay earth water-3POSS-DAT food-GEN

      deeži-zi-n   ber-gen-nen   gedeer ulug bičii xaduŋma
      seed-3POSS-ACC give-PSTPRT-ABL after   old   young relatives

      töz-ü   olur-up a-p   dur-up   ol žem-niŋ
      all-3POSS sit-CONV take-CONV stay-CONV that food-GEN

      deeži-zi-n   ži-ir
      seed-3POSS-ACC eat-PRSINDF

      After that, we will beg our earth and water of the Altay, and after
      the shamans have given the seeds of the foods to the earth and
      water of the Altay, the old and young, relatives, all will sit down
      and eat those seeds of the food together.

13.   *onun bodal-ga   al-gan   ög-lör-ge   bar-gaš*
      then   intention-DAT take-PSTPRT house-PL-DAT go-CONV

      baxšı-lar orda bar-ıp   bičii nom žibe-zi-n
      shaman-PL there go-CONV little book something-3POSS-ACC

      nomšu-p ber-geš   žozun gıl-gaš-tan   ol žem
      read-CONV give-CONV ritual do-CONV-ABL that food

žime-niŋ   deeži-zi-n   že-er
thing-GEN seed-3POSS-ACC eat-PRSINDF

Then, they will go to the designated houses and the shamans will go there and chant some small scriptures there, and after chanting and performing rituals, they will eat the food seeds.

14.   *baza bäygi-de   at   gel-gen   ög-lör-ge   bar-ıp*
       and   horse.race-LOC horse come-PSTPRT house-PL-DAT go-CONV

       bičii žozun gıl-ır
       some ritual   do-PRSINDF

       And they will go to the houses where the horses at the race have come from and perform an augury.

15.   *baza böge   güreš-ken   giži-ler-ge   šaŋ   ın-dıg*
       and   wrestler wrestle-PSTPRT person-PL-DAT reward that-EQU

       žime-zi-n   be-er
       thing-3POSS-ACC give-PRSINDF

       And they will give rewards and such to those people who wrestled.

16.   *baza o-nu žug-dur-ar   de-p   ool-dar da*
       and   it-ACC wash-CAUS-PRSINDF say-CONV child-PL also

       ba-ar
       go-PRSINDF

       Children also go there thinking that they may throw a party.

17.   *ol kün-ü   bis-tiŋ dört sumun ulug bičii xaduŋma*
       that day-3POSS we-GEN four district old   young relatives

töz-ü   öörüškülüg dur-ur
all-3POSS joyful   stay-PRSINDF

On that day, all relatives (people), the old and young and all relatives in our Four Districts are joyful.

18. *on-u bıs alday dagıır de-p   ayd-ar-bıs*
it-ACC we Altay worship say-CONV tell-PRSINDF-1PL

We call it worshiping Altay.

19. *mool-ča   ooba   dagıır de-p   ayd-ar-bıs*
Mongol-EQU sacrificial sanctify say-CONV tell- PRSINDF-1PL

In Mongolian, we call it sacrificial worship.

1. 12 Tuvan traditional marriage

Narrated by Jinghua of Akkaba Village in September1995

1. *bis-tiŋ dört sumun-nuŋ burun-nan beer kalıptaz-ıp*
we-GEN four district-GEN   before-ABL since form—CONV

gel-e   žıt-kan   kazir-gi emes buruŋ-gu   bo
come-CONV lie-PSTPRT now-RELCL NEGCOP before- RELCL this

bir turmuš-tug iyi-i-nde-gi   bir žibe-zi-n
one life-ADJ   aspect-3POSS-LOC-RELCL one thing-3POSS-ACC

men ayd-ıp   ber-eyin
I   tell-CONV give-1SG.IMP

Let me tell (you) one thing in the life of our Four Districts which has been passed on since early time, not of the present but of the past.

2. *gɪžɪ-ler-nɪŋ   ool be-er   ool užun ganžap*
    person-PL-GEN child give-PRSINDF child for   how

    domakta-ž-ɪr   ool ganžap doy   žaza-ar   ool
    speak-REC-PRSINDF child how   wedding make-PRSINDF child

    ganža-ar   gɪl-ɪr-ɪ-n   men ayd-ɪp
    how.it.does-PRSPRT do-PRSPRT-3POSS-ACC I   tell-CONV

    ber-eyin
    give-1SG.IMP

Let me tell (you) how people give (marry their) child, how (they) speak to each other (an arrange engagement on behalf of the children), how they arrange the wedding, and what (their) children do.

3. *birak käzir-gi   kogam-da buruŋ-gu kogam-ga*
    but   now-RELCL society-LOC before-ADJ society-DAT

    okša-bas   de-dir
    resemble-NEGPRSINDF say-EMPH

It is not the same in today's society as in the past society, so they say.

4. *men bɪl-gen-im-še   o-nu ayd-ɪp   ber-eyin*
    I   know-PSTPRT-1SG.POSS-ADV it-ACC tell-CONV give-1SG.IMP

Let me tell (you) as much as I know (about it.)

5. *buruŋ-gu   bis-tiŋ   dıba-lar mın-dıg de-dir*
    before-RELCL we-GEN Tuva-PL this-EQU say-EMPH

It is said that our Tuvas were like this in the past.

6. *ada-iye-zi   boda-p   o-nu   bir ög-de   bir*
    parents-3POSS think-CONV s/he-ACC one house-LOC one

urug bo-za   baza biri-de   bir eržet-ken   ogl-u
girl   be-COND and   one.of-LOC one grow-PSTPRT son-3POSS

bo-za   o-nu   dagın ada-iye-zi
be-COND he-ACC again parents-3POSS

danı-š-tır-ıp   me-eŋ ogl-um-ga   bo urug deŋ
know-REC-CAUS-CONV I-GEN   son-1SG.POSS-DAT this girl   equal

bol-ur   irgin de-p   xuda düž-ör   irgin
be-PRSINDF EVID say-CONV in-law come.down-PRSINDF EVID

The parents would think, if there is a girl in one family and there
is a grown-up boy in another, their parents would next introduce
them to each other if this girl would be equal to (matches) their
son, and they would arrange an engagement (betrothal).

7. *oson ganžaar dagın xuda bo-p   ol giži-ge*
    then   how   again in-law become-CONV that person-DAT

ada-iye-zi   žöp ayt-sa   urug-dar-ı-ŋga
father-mother-3POSS right say-COND girl-PL-3POSS-DAT

ayd-ır   irgin
say- PRSINDF EVID

What's going to happen next about becoming an in-law? If her parents say "Right" to that person, they will tell their daughter (about it).

8. *osonda urug-dar-ı   o-oŋ   ada-iye-zi-niŋ*
    then   girl-PL-3POSS it-GEN father-mother-3POSS-GEN
    dıl-ı-nı   kupta-ar   ganžaar de-en-de
    language-3POSS-ACC agree-PRSINDF how   say-PSTPRT-LOC

    me-eŋ ada-iye-m   men-i er žed-ir-di
    I-GEN   parents-1SG.POSS I-ACC man reach-CAUS-PAST

    mın-dıg ulug gıl-dı   er-niŋ   eŋ deŋ-i-ge
    this-EQU big   make-PAST man-GEN most equal-3POSS-DAT

    žed-ir-ir
    reach-CAUS-PRSINDF

At that time, girls would accept their parents' word. Why is that? (Because they would think:) "My parents brought me up, they made me (grow) this big, they made me reach/become the best of the best.

9. *ol užun men ada -iye-m-niŋ   dıl-ı-n*
    that for I   father-mother-1SG.POSS-GEN language-3POSS-ACC

    al-ır-men   de-p ol ada-iye-zi-niŋ
    take-PRSINDF-1SG say-GEN he father-mother-3POSS-GEN

    söz-ü   bodal-ı-nča   orta   ba-ar   irgin
    word-3POSS thought-3POSS-ADV that.place go-PRSINDF EVID

Therefore, (she thinks that) I should listen to my parents' words and she would go there like her parents wished, conforming to her parents' word.

10. *de-en   bilen ol   žalıı   bilen urug bir*
say-PSTPRT with   that young.man with   girl   one

biri-zi-n   tanı-bas   da   äwöli
one.of-3POSS-ACC know-NEGPRSINDF EMPH even
gör-be-en   de   irgin
see-NEG-PSTINDF EMPH EVID

However, that young man and the girl would not know each other,
and not even have seen each other.

11. *osunda ol bol-ur   ba bol-ur   de-p   iyi*
then   that be-PRSINDF Q   be-PRSINDF say-CONV two

ada-iye   eki bol-gan de-ze   aas   belek
father-mother good be-PSTPRT say-COND mouth bride.price

ayd-ır
say-PRSINDF

Then, one (would ask:) "Is it okay?" and (the other would
answer:) "Yes, it's okay." and they would verbally tell the
betrothal gift (bride-price) if both parents thought it was good.

12. *osunda dagın ak   gud-ar   dagın goržun   šay xadax*
then   again white pour-PRSINDF again saddle.bag tea gift

apa-ar   irgin
deliver-PRSINDF EVID

Then, next they pour white (offer drinks) and they would bring a
saddle-bag with teas and gifts.

13. *goržun   šay xadax apa-ar-da   bis-tiŋ buruŋ-gu*
saddle.bag tea gift   deliver-PRSPRT-LOC we-GEN before-RELCL

dıba-lar ganžaar šay xadax de-p   žime-ler-i-n
Tuva-PL how   tea gift   say-CONV thing-PL-3POSS-ACC

be-er   irgin
give- PRSINDF EVID

When they deliver the saddle-bag with teas and gifts our Tuvas of the past gave (would give) things like tea and gifts.

14.   *e baza šay dörüü dekpe šay de-p   žime-ler-i-n*
     oh and   tea dörüü brick tea say-CONV thing-PL-3POSS-ACC

     apa-ar   irgin
     bring-PRSINDF EVID

     Oh, and they would bring things like teas, *dörüü* brick tea.

15.   *käzir-gi   xogam-da bis-te goržun   ın-dıg mın-dıg*
     now-RELCL society-LOC we-LOC saddle.bag that-EQU this-EQU

     de-p   žüme žok
     say-CONV thing NEGEXIST

     In today's society (nowadays,) we don't have such things as saddle-bags.

16.   *dekpe šay apar-a   al-za   ol gezde bol-ur   irgin*
     brick tea deliver-CONV able-COND that time be-PRSINDF EVID

     At that time it would be okay if you were able to bring dekbe tea.

17.   *birakta olar-nıŋ urug-lar-ı   bilen ool-dar-ı   men*
     however they-GEN daughter-PL-3POSS with son-PL-3POSS I

tanı-ba-dı-m   mo-nu gör-be-di-m   de-beyin
know-NEG-PAST-1SG this-ACC see-NEG-PAST-1SG say-NEGCONV

orta gayta ada-iye-zi-niŋ   dıl-ı
there instead father-mother-3POSS-GEN language-3POSS

boyunča orta ba-ar   irgin
according.to there go-PRSINDF EVID

However, on the contrary, their daughter and their son would go there according to their parents' words instead of saying: "I did not know or I did not see him."

18. *keyin gel-e   olar-nıŋ söz-ü   boyunča   sen orta*
     later   come-CONV they-GEN word-3POSS according.to you there

     eki bol-ur-sen   de-p   ınža-za   ol bir ög
     good be-PRSINDF-2SG say-CONV do.so-COND she one family

     bo-p   kelešek-te bir ın-dıg eki bir ög   bo-p
     be-CONV future-LOC one that-EQU good one family be-CONV

     olar-nıŋ ašı-enži-zi   bo-p   urug-tarıg-lıg bir
     they-GEN descendant-3POSS be-CONV children-ADJ   one

     ög   bol-ur   irgin
     family be-PRSINDF EVID

     Later on, just as their parents had said: "You will be well there and will have a family. This will be such a good family in the future and you will be their descendent," they would become a family with children.

19. *birakta käzir-gi   kogam-da ın-dıg emes*
     but   now-RELCL society-LOC that-EQU not

However, it is not like that in today's society.

20. *bo bis-tiŋ bo bir mončak-tar-nıŋ buruŋ-gu*
this we-GEN this one Monchak-PL-GEN before-RELCL

sald-ı   irgin
customs-3POSS EVID

This was one of our Monchak's previous customs.

21. *kazir-gi   niykim bo-za   buruŋ-gu   niykim-ge*
now-RELCL society   be-COND before-RELCL society-DAT

oxša-bas
resemble-NEGPRSINDF

As for contemporary society, it is not the same as the previous society.

22. *üytkönü deŋ emes üytkönü käzir bo-za   soyulda-an*
because equal not   because now be-COND civilize-PSTPRT

dapšı   de-en   mın-dıg bir eki kogam eki niykim
developed say-PSTPRT this-EQU one good society good society

Because they are not equal. Because, nowadays, it's such a good civilized, developed good society.

23. *käzir-gi   šag bilen tegindee šag oxša-bas*
now-RELCL time with past   time be.similar.to-NEGPRSINDF

The present time and the past time are not the same.

24. *ol užun käzir-gi   niykim-de buruŋ-gu-dan   biršama*
that for   now-RELCL society-LOC before-RELCL-ABL somewhat

amdı xuburuldu öskörüs de   bar
now   changeable change   also EXIST

Now, there are also some notable changes in the current society as compared to the previous one.

25.   *üytkönü käzir-gi   žalıı   žalıı-lar*
because   now-RELCL young.man young.person-PL

eržet-ken-nen   gedeer turmustan-ır   bol-sa
grow.up-PSTPRT-ABL after   get.married-PRSINDF be-COND

ol ganžaar de-ze   baštay olar tanı-ž-ır
he how   say-COND before   they know-REL-PRSINDF

Because nowadays a young man or young people get married after they have grown up. That is to say that they would know each other beforehand.

26.   *tanı-ž-ıp   žoru-un-nan   gedeer xošula-ž-ır*
know-REC-CONV walk-PSTPRT-ABL after   speak-REC-PRSINDF

ınža-ap   žoru-un
do.that-CONV walk-PSTINDF

After they have gotten acquainted and they would converse (be in love).

27.   *bir biri-si-n   gör-böyün   doy*
one one.of-3POSS-ACC see-NEGCONV wedding

žaza-bas   burun-gu-ša   emes
make-NEGPRSINDF before-RELCL-EQU NEGCOP

They will not get married without seeing each other; it is not like in the past.

28. *üytkönü iyilee-zi   eki   bo-p   kööl-ü-ŋge*
     because   both-3POSS good be-CONV feeling-3POSS-DAT

     žak-sa   baza ol iyilee bir biri-si-n   eki
     please-COND and that both   one one.of-3POSS-ACC good

     gör-se   ol bar-ıp ada-eyi-zi-ŋge   ayd-ıp
     see-COND that go-CONV father-mother-3POSS-DAT tell-CONV

     ol arkılı ada-iye-zi   žöp gör-se   bar-ıp
     it through father-mother-3POSS right see-COND go-CONV

     doy žaza-ar
     wedding make-PRSINDF

     Because if the two of them get along well, please each other's
     heart, and if they both like each other, he will go and tell his
     parents. After that, if their parents think it's fair (agree), they will
     go and get married.

29. *mın-dıg žibe xalıptaš-kan*
     this-EQU thing form-PSTINDF

     This kind of thing has become the norm.

30. *üytgönü käzir bo-za   ol iyi žibe eki   bol-gan-nan*
     because now   be-COND that two thing good be-PSTPRT-ABL

     gedeer bir biri-zi-ŋge   domakta-ž-ıp   bir
     after   one one.of-3POSS-DAT speak-REC-CONV one

biri-si-ŋge   žetkilin bil-ip   bol-gan-nan   gedeer
one.of-3POSS-DAT sufficient know-CONV be- PSTPRT-ABL after

ol iyi bar-ɪp ada-iye-zi-ŋge   ayd-ɪp
that two go-CONV father-mother-3POSS-DAT tell-CONV

ada-eyi-zi   eki bo-p   buruŋ-gu-ša   emes
father-mother-3POSS good be-CONV before-RELCL-EQU NEGCOP

et   žibe al-bas
livestock thing take-NEGPRSINDF

Because as for nowadays, after those two have become well acquainted and gotten to know each other very well by talking to one another, these two will go to tell their parents. Their parents will get along well and will not accept livestock or things(gifts) like before.

31. *ol äwöli ool-dɪŋ ö-ö   žokdug bol-sa   urug*
     that even   boy-GEN family-3POSS poor   be-COND girl

     o-nuŋ ö-ö-ŋgö   bar-mas   žagday bar
     he-GEN family-3POSS-DAT go-NEGPRSPRT situation EXIST

There were cases even like this, that if the boy's family was poor, the girl would not go to his house (marry him.)

32. *ool-duŋ ö-ö-nüŋ   turmuž-u ödö gudu bo-za kedey*
     boy-GEN family-3POSS-GEN life-3POSS very low   be-COND poor

     bo-za   am-dɪg niykim-dik beedil-i   ɪn-dɪg guda
     be-COND now-EQU society-ADJ condition-3POSS that-EQU low

     bol-sa ol urug-nuŋ ada-eyi-zi   orta uru-u-n
     be-COND that girl-GEN father-mother-3POSS there girl-3POSS-ACC

ber-bes
give-NEGPRSINDF

If the boy's family's living condition is low and poor, and if their
current social status is so low, the girl's parents will not give their
daughter there (consent to marry him.)

33.   *birakta käzir-gi   bo niykim-niŋ xuuylu-zu bar*
       however now-RELCL this society-GEN law-3POSS   EXIST

       However, this present day's society has its law.

34.   *urug ool-dar-nıŋ ara-zı-nda   bot-tar-ı*
       girl   boy-PL-GEN interval-3POSS-LOC self-PL-3POSS

       dıb-ıž-ıp   erkin   žaagay doy   žaza-ar
       find-REC-CONV voluntarily nice   wedding make-PRSINDF

       Girls and boys find each other among themselves and get married
       happily on a voluntary basis.

1. 13 House Building

Narrated by Torgun of Akkaba Village in September1995 in Urumchi

1.   *dıba-lar-nıŋ ög-lör-i   tuwralı xoožu*
      Tuva-PL-GEN house-PL-3POSS about   story

      A Story about the Tuvas' Houses.

2.   *bis-tiŋ akkaba-nıŋ ög-lör-i-niŋ   göb-ü   daŋnıŋ*
      we-GEN Akkaba-GEN house-PL-3POSS-GEN many-3POSS always

žay-ın   bol-ur-da   gidis ög-ge   olur-ur
summer-INSTR be-PRSPRT-LOC felt   house-DAT live-PRSINDF

Always when it is summer, most of our households in Akkaba live
in felt homes.

3.   *malčı-lar xoy kadar-ır   inek kadar-ır*
     herder-PL sheep herd-PRSINDF cow herd-PRSINDF

     Herders herd the sheep and herd the cows.

4.   *giži-ler daŋnıŋ gidis ög-ge   olur-ur*
     person-PL always felt   house-DAT live-PRSINDF

     People always live in felt houses (when they herd).

5.   *gidis ög-nüŋ   išd-i-n   ıyaš-tan žaza-ar*
     felt   house-GEN inside-3POSS-ACC wood-ABL make-PRSINDF

     They make the inside of the felt house out of wood.

6.   *baza išd-i-n   sırla-p   ga-ar*
     and   inside-3POSS-ACC paint-CONV put-PRSINDF

     Also they paint it all inside.

7.   *böörüŋke žibe-šibi-zi   bol-ur*
     globular   things.and.such-3POSS be-PRSINDF

     It is something that is round.

8.   *sarakayla-y sarakayla-y šar-ıp   žütüülük žep-penin*
     tighten-CONV tighten-CONV wrap-CONV strong   rope-INSTR

šar-ıp   ga-ar
wrap-CONV put-PRSINDF

They wrap it up real tight, wrapping it with strong ropes.

9.   *duguruk kelbeerlig gıldır ga-ar*
      round   shaped   so.that put-PRSINDF

They put it up so that it is round in shape.

10.   *žamdık ög-lör-ni   gör de   üsd-ü   bööröŋke*
       some   house-PL-ACC look EMPH upside-3POSS spherical

       bagana kelbeerlig ga-ar
       pillar shaped   put-PRSINDF

Just look at some of the houses, they put them up in the shape of a
spherical top.

11.   *tögörök gıldır xaraaža žaza-ar*
       round   so.that roof-ring make-PRSINDF

They make the roof-ring round.

12.   *žamdık biri-zi   žibe-šibi   töbe ga-ar*
       some   one.of-3POSS things.and.such roof put-PRSINDF

They put on some sort of roof.

13.   *gidis-ti xoy-nuŋ düg-ü-n   sawa-aš   teresin-ge*
       felt-ACC sheep-GEN wool-3POSS-ACC strike-CONV grass.mat-DAT

       ga-ap   baz-ar
       put-CONV make-PRSINDF

They make the felt by beating the sheep's wool and putting it on a grass mat.

14.   *teresin-niŋ   üsd-ü-ŋge   ga-aš   izig sug*
grass.mat-GEN surface-3POSS-DAT put-CONV hot   water

žaž-ɪp   baz-ar
pour-CONV press-PRSINDF

They put it on top of the grass mat, pour hot water on it and press it.

15.   *izig sug žaš-kan-nan   soŋgaar dedir   argamžɪ-nɪn*
hot   water pour-PSTPRT-ABL after   backward lasso-INSTR

šar-ɪp   dɪrd-ar
wrap-CONV pull-PRSINDF

After they have poured hot water over it, they tie a lasso-rope around it and pull it back and forth.

16.   *bir saat emese iyi saat kirelig dɪrt-kaš dedir*
one hour   or   two hour about   pull-CONV backward

žug-gaš   gurga-d-ɪr
wash-CONV dry-CAUS-PRSINDF

After pulling it back and forth for around one or two hours, they wash and dry it.

17.   *bir ay-nan   soŋgaar bɪž-ɪr-ɪr   de-p   izig sug*
one month-ABL after   ripen-CAUS-PRSIND say-CONV hot water

gud-up   bɪž-ɪr-ɪr
pour-CONV ripen-CAUS-PRSINDF

After a month, when it's ready, they prepare it by pouring hot water on it.

18.   *soson on-u gurga-d-ir*
      after   it-ACC dry-CAUS-PRSINDF

      Then they dry it.

19.   *kez-ip   böörüŋke bagana kelbeerlɪg on iyi žü-ü-n*
      cut-CONV spherical pillar   shaped   twelve edge-3POSS-ACC

      kez-ip   ga-ar-da   debiyür kelbeerlig bo-p
      cut-CONV put-PRSPRT-LOC fan   shaped   be-CONV

      gal-ɪr
      stay-PRSINDF

      They cut it up, and when they finish cutting twelve feathers in the shape of a spherical top, it takes the shape of a fan.

20.   *oson on-u daara-ar   daara-ar-nan   soŋgaar*
      then   it-ACC sew-PRSINDF sew-PRSPRT-ABL after

      gidis ög   gɪl-ɪp   žaylaw-ga   ün-ör
      felt   house make-CONV summer.pasture-DAT move.out-PRSINDF

      Then they sew it, and after sewing it, they make a felt house and move to the summer pasture.

21.   *kɪstak-tɪŋ išd-i-nde-gi   keybir malčɪ ewes*
      village-GEN inside-3POSS-LOC-RELCL some   herder NEGCOP

      giži-ler ɪyaš ög-gö   olur-ur
      person-PL wood house-DAT live-PRSINDF

Some people in the village who are not herders live in wood houses.

22.   *ıyaš ög-nüŋ   ortu-zu-n   aldı metir gıl-ıp*
        wood house-GEN middle-3POSS-ACC six   meter make-CONV

        ga-ar
        put-PRSINDF

        They make the middle (length) of a wood house six meters long.

23.   *örgün-ü-n   beš metir emeze dört metir gıl-ıp*
        width-3POSS-ACC five meter or   four meter make-CONV

        ga-ar
        put-PRSINDF

        They make its width five meters or four meters.

24.   *üsd-ü-n   xoyug ıyaš emeze sırgabul-dan*
        top-3POSS-ACC rafter   wood or   sirgabul-ABL

        žon-up   ga-ar
        plane-CONV put-PRSINDF

        They make the top by planing the rafter wood or sirgabul[11].

25.   *oo-ŋ üsd-ü-nün   sigen ga-ar*
        it-GEN top-3POSS-INSTR hay   put-PRSINDF

        They put hay along the top of it.

---

[11] *sirgabul*: long tapered pole, part of a felt house frame.

26.   *oson   doburak ga-ar   širikte-er*
       then   dirt   put-PRSINDF smooth.out-PRSINDF

Then they put dirt, and they smooth it out.

27.   *keybır ög-lör   üsd-ü-n   daktayla-p   al-ır*
       some   family-PL top-3POSS-ACC lay.board-CONV take-PRSINDF

Some families lay boards on top.

28.   *üš   dörbölžin-nig gıldır ga-ar*
       three square-ADJ   so.that put-PRTINDF

They make it so it has three rooms.

29.   *dört dörbülžin-nig gıldır ga-aš-tan   daktayla-p*
       four square-ADJ   so.that put-CONV-ABL lay.board-CONV

       al-sa   da bol-ur
       take-COND also be-PRSINDF

After making it so it has four rooms, they may also lay boards.

30.   *ald-ı-n   ga-ar-da   gaz-ıp   al-ır*
       under-3POSS-ACC put-PRSPRT-LOC dig-CONV take-PRSINDF

When they put in the floor, they dig it (they level the ground).

31.   *keybiri-zi daš ga-ap   ga-ar*
       some-3POSS stone put-CONV put-PRSINDF

Some of them put down stone.

32.   *ald-ı-nga   daš ga-ap   gag-sa   bıžıg bol-ur*
       under-3POSS-DAT stone put-CONV put-COND solid be-PRSINDF

If they put down stone on the floor, it will be solid.

33. *keybir beedil-i   gel-bes   giži-ler daš*
     some   condition-3POSS come-NEGPRSPRT person-PL stone

     gag-bas
     put-NEGPRSINDF

     People without means do not put down stone.

34. *dašta-y   al-bas*
     lay.stone-CONV take-NEGPRSINDF

     They are unable to lay stone.

35. *äytew ald-ɪ-n   tegiste-en   šigi bol-gaš-tan*
     anyhow under-3POSS-ACC smooth-PSTPRT like be-CONV-ABL

     üsd-ü-nüŋ   ɪyaš-ɪ-n   ga-ap   ga-ar
     top-3POSS-GEN wood-3POSS-ACC put-CONV put-PRSINDF

     Anyhow, after it appears to be smoothed, they put the wood on top
     of it.

36. *bir ɪyaž-ɪ-n   kerd-ip   žoŋ-gaš   üsd-ü-nün*
     some wood-3POSS-ACC carve-CONV plane-CONV top-3POSS-ABL

     žeŋges ga-ap   eptešdir-ip   ga-ar
     moss   put-CONV do.carefully-CONV put-PRSINDF

     They cut up and plane some logs and carefully put moss on top of
     them.

37. *žeŋges-tiŋ üsd-ü-nün   ɪyaš ga-ar*
     moss-GEN   top-3POSS-ABL wood put-PRSINDF

They put logs on top of the moss.

38. *bir ög-nüŋ   tuwɪrga-zɪ-n   ga-ar-da   on dört ɪyaš*
     one house-GEN wall-3POSS-ACC put-PRSPRT-LOC fourteen wood

     bol-ur
     be-PRSINDF

     When they build the walls of a house, there will be fourteen logs.

39. *eŋ bičii ga-ar-da   dört bölmö-lüg ga-ar*
     SUP small put-PRSPRT-LOC four room-ADJ   put-PRSINDF

     When they put up the smallest (house) they make four rooms.

40. *oo-ŋ žašt-ɪ-nda   bir bölmö gɪldɪr ga-ar*
     it-GEN outside-3POSS-LOC one room   so.that put-PRSINDF

     They also build another room outside (the house).

41. *žašt-ɪ-nda-gɪ   bölmö-ge gɪž-ɪn   et žem*
     outside-3POSS-LOC-RELCL room-DAT winter-INSTR meat foods

     žibe ga-ap   al-ɪr
     thing put-CONV take-PRSINDF

     They put the winter meat and provisions in that outside room.

42. *gɪž-ɪn   ži-ir   žem žibe-zi-n   ga-ar*
     winter-INSTR eat-PRSPRT food thing-3POSS-ACC put-PRSINDF

     They put their provisions which they eat in the winter there.

43. *žay-ɪn   bol-ur-da   išd-i-n*
     summer-INSTR become-PRSPRT-LOC inside-3POSS-ACC

šeberle-p   žem gıl-ıp   iž-er
clean-CONV food make-CONV eat-PRSINDF

When summer comes, they clean up the inside of it (that room), make food and eat it.

44. *žay-ın   gerbiš gıldır meš ga-ap   baza žem*
summer-INSTR brick   so.that oven put-CONV and   food

gıl-ıp   iž-er
make-CONV eat-PRSINDF

In the summer, they make an oven out of bricks, and make food and eat it.

45. *bıž-ır-ıp   al-ır*
be.cooked-CAUS-CONV take-PRSINDF

They cook it.

46. *žibe   ga-ap   al-ır*
something put-CONV take-PRSINDF

They put things on it (the food).

47. *ga-an   ög-lör-i-nıŋ   išd-i-ŋge   keybiri-zi*
put-PSTPRT house-PL-3POSS-GEN inside-3POSS-DAT some-3POSS

xonaša ög   žıd-ar   ög urug-dar-ı-nıŋ   žıd-ar
guest   room lie-PRSPRT room child-PL-3POSS-GEN lie-PRSPRT

ö-ö   gıl-ıp   al-ır
room-3POSS make-CONV take-PRSINDF

Inside of the houses that they built, some of them make a guest room, a bedroom, and a children's bedroom.

48. *keybiri-zi   daktayla-p   al-ır*
     some.of-3POSS lay.boards-CONV take-PRSINDF

     Some of them lay boards.

49. *keybiri-zi   ald-ı-n   semontta-p al-ır*
     some.of-3POSS under-3POSS-ACC cement-CONV take-PRSINDF

     Some of them put down cement floors.

50. *men boda-sa-m   ald-ı-n   semontta-p al-sa*
     I   think-COND-1SG under-3POSS-ACC cement-CONV take-COND

     bıžıg tamaša   žibe šigi bol-ur
     solid wonderful thing like be-PRSINDF

     I would think it would be something solid and perfect if one made a cement floor.

51. *keybiri-zi ak   doburak ga-aš-tan   tapda-p*
     some-3POSS white earth   put-CONV-ABL trample-CONV

     al-ır
     take-PRSINDF

     Some of them, after putting down kaolin (clay), trample it down.

52. *oo-ŋ išd-i-nde   baza žem gıl-ır   žıd-ar*
     it-GEN inside-3POSS-LOC also   food make-PRSPRT lie-PRSPRT

     xonaša ög   bol-ur
     guest   room be-PRSINDF

Inside of it (this room) they also prepare food. It will be a
bedroom or guest room.

53. *keybir amtan-nar bod-u-nuŋ   žagday-ı*
     some   people-PL self-3POSS-GEN condition-3POSS

     gel-be-se   ıyı ög   üš ög-nen   žoru-y
     come-NEG-COND two house three house-INSTR go-CONV

     be-er
     give-PRSINDF

If some people do not have the means, they get by with a two or
three (room) house.

Tales of human life/personal experiences

2. 1 A personal history of an elementary school student

Narrated by Odun of Kanas Village in September1995

1. *me-eŋ ad-ım   odun*
   I-GEN name-1SG.POSS Odun

   My name is Odun.

2. *me-eŋ aga-m   baxšı*
   I-GEN older.brother-1SG.POSS teacher

   My older brother is a teacher.

3. *žeerbi žıl iš   isto-di mäktip-ye*
   twenty year work do-PAST school-DAT

   He worked twenty years at the school.

4. *awa-m   ög-dö   mal   malda-p   dur malčın*
   mother-1SG.POSS home-LOC livestock breed-CONV stay herder

   My mother is at home taking care of the animals. She is a herder.

5. *me-eŋ aga-m   onzur ortalaw oŋšu-p   dur*
   I-GEN older.brother-1SG.POSS Onzur middle   study-CONV stay

   My older brother, Onzur is studying in the middle school.

6.   *ulug aga-m*   *tiwiy-de*   *alday-da*
     big   older.brother-1SG.POSS gymnasium-LOC Altay-LOC

My oldest brother is at the physical training center in Altay.

7.   *bir žıl   bol-du*
     one year be-PAST

It's been a year.

8.   *am žoru-y   žoru-y   nomšu-ur   bol-du*
     now walk-CONV walk-CONV study-PRSPRT be-PAST

Now he will study by taking his time.

9.   *duŋma-m*   *oyunčümök basdawıš mäktip-te*
     younger.brother-1SG.POSS Oyunchümök elementary school-LOC

     nomšu-p   dur
     study-CONV stay

My younger brother Oyunchümök is studying in the elementary
school.

10. *bod-um*   *ortalaw mäktip oŋšu-p*   *dur-men*
     self-1SG.POSS middle   school   study-CONV stay-1SG

I myself am studying in the middle school.

11. *ortalaw birinči žıl-ım*
     middle   first   year-1SG.POSS

It's my first year in the middle school.

2. 2 A personal history of a middle school student

Narrated by Omdun of Kanas Village in September1995

1. *me-eŋ ad-ım   omdun*
    I-GEN   name-1SG.POSS Omdun

    My name is Omdun.

2. *aga-m   žeerbi žıl dogdur bol-gan*
    older.brother-1SG.POSS twenty year doctor   be-PSTINDF

    My older brother has been a doctor for twenty years.

3. *mal   dogdur-u*
    animal doctor-3POSS

    He is a veterinarian.

4. *žeŋge-m   taraačın malčın*
    older.sister-in-law-1SG.POSS farmer   herder

    My older sister-in-law is a farmer, a herder.

5. *ulug egiči-m   aldın ken-de   ište-p   žıd-ır*
    big older.sister-1SG.POSS gold mine-LOC work-CONV lie-PRSINDF

    My eldest sister is working in the gold mine.

6. *äymen aga-m   taraačın*
    Äymen older.brother-1SG.POSS farmer

    My older brother Äymen is a farmer.

7. *mal   malda-p   žoru-ur*
    animal breed.animal-CONV walk-PRSINDF

    He is herding animals.

8. *morzu aga-m   da   taraačın*
    Morzu older.brother-1SG.POSS also farmer

    My older brother Morzu is also a farmer.

9. *mal   malda-p   žoru-ur*
    animal breed.animal-CONV walk-PRSINDF

    He is herding animals.

10. *egiči-m   erge   žügär*
    older.sister-1SG.POSS pamper female

    My older sister is a pampered girl.

11. *nomšu-p   žıd-ır*
    study-CONV lie-PRSINDF

    She is studying.

12. *iyinči bän-de*
    second class-LOC

    (She is) in second grade.

13. *bod-um   dörtünči bän nomšu-p   žıd-ır   men*
    self-1SG.POSS fourth   class study-CONV lie-PRSINDF 1SG

    I myself am studying in the fourth grade.

14.   *on dört žaš-tıg   men*
        ten four year-ADJ 1SG

        I am fourteen years old.

2. 4 A personal history of a surgeon

Narrated by Kadir of Buwirshin county in September1995

1.   *me-eŋ ada-iye-m   burun sıtalin ša-a-nda   beri žer*
        I-GEN   parents-1SG.POSS before Stalin time-3POSS-LOC here land

        aŋdar-gaš-tan bo ara-ga   ge-ep   dur-gan   irgin
        turn-CONV-ABL this place-DAT come-CONV stay-PSTINDF EVID

        Before, my parents came here to this region to live after they had
        been exiled during Stalin's time.

2.   *osun ol gel-gen-nen   gedeer bo ara-ga   bis dur-up*
        then that come-PSTPRT-ABL after   this place-DAT we stay-CONV

        čuwašilik-ke   dur-gan-nan   gedeer bis-tiŋ dee
        Chuwashulik-DAT stay-PSTPRT-ABL after   we-GEN that

        žer-de   negizinen ol xumiy žurd-u-n   töz-ü
        place-LOC basically   that whole people-3POSS-ACC all-3POSS

        delew žurd-u   de-er
        Telew people-POSS say-PRSINDF

        After they had come, we stayed around here, settling in
        Chuwashulik, (and) all those living there called all of our people –
        the Telew people.

3. *ol gel-gen   žer-ibis*
    that come-PSTPRT place-1PL.POSS

    That was the place we came from.

4. *bo ara-ga   gel-geš   bo mončak žurt-tuŋ*
    this place-DAT come-CONV this Monchak people-GEN

    išd-i-ne   gel-geš   žurt-ka   siŋ-ip
    inside-3POSS-DAT come-CONV people-DAT absorb-CONV

    olur-men
    sit-1SG

    I have been assimilated since we came to this place and came to
    live together with these Monchak people.

5. *gadı žor-up   öz-üp   käzir osun bögün men*
    together walk-CONV grow-CONV now   then today I

    töz-ü   dıba-nıŋ ara-zı-nda   xoožu-p   olur
    all-3POSS Tuva-GEN interval-3POSS-LOC speak-CONV sit

    ebes-pin   be
    NEGCOP-1SG Q

    Living and growing up together with them, now today, am I not
    entirely among the Tuvas, speaking (like them)?

6. *bis kara oy-ga göž-üp   gel-gen-nen   beer bir*
    we Kara Oy-DAT move-CONV come-PSTPRT-ABL since one

    mıŋ   tos žüs   aldan iyi-nen beer öz-ü   kara
    thousand nine hundred sixty two-ABL since self-3POSS Kara

oy-ga dur-up osun birinči bän-nen bašta-p
Oy-DAT stay-CONV then first class-ABL start-CONV

nomšu-du-m
study-PAST-1SG

After we moved to Kara Oy, that is after 1962, we settled in Kara Oy, and then I started first grade there.

7. *nomšu-p gel-geš ses-ke žed-ir bütür-üp*
study-CONV come-CONV eight-DAT reach-PRSPRT finish-CONV

nomšu-du-m
study-PAST-1SG

Continuously studying, I finished the eight grades.

8. *bis-tiŋ bo ara-ga dɪba mekteb-ibis sezinči*
we-GEN this interval-DAT Tuva school-1PL.POSS eighth

bän-ge žed-ir gene bar
class-DAT reach-PRSPRT only EXIST

Here, our Tuvan school is only up to eighth grade.

9. *örlö-p gedeer örlö-p nomšu-p argaža oku-p*
rise-CONV after rise-CONV study-CONV further study-CONV

osunda awdan-dɪg birinči orta mekdep-ke gel-geš men
here county-ADJ first middle school-DAT come-CONV I

dedir mool-ča bol-sun dɪba-ča bol-sun
backward Mongol-EQU be-3IMP Tuva-EQU be-3IMP

nomču-za-m   da   dedir   töz-ü-n   kazak-ča
study-COND-1SG EMPH backward all-3POSS-ACC Kazak-EQU

nomšu-du-m
study-PAST-1SG

As I grow up, I continued my studies, I came to the Number 1 middle school in our county to study there regardless that (the instruction) was Mongolian or Tuvan, and I repeated everything in Kazak again.

10. *kazak-ča nomna-p   bol-gan-nan   gedeer šüübür*
kazak-EQU study-CONV be-PSTPRT-ABL after   exam

ber-geš-ten   öörügü mektep-ke öd-üp   al-gaš-tan
give-CONV-ABL high   school-DAT pass-CONV take-CONV-ABL

bar-ıp   ürümži šinžiaŋ yıxue yuan de-p
go-CONV Ürümchi Xinjiang Medical College say-CONV

koy-ar   bis sonda ol   mektep-te aldı žıl
place-PRSINDF 1PL there   that school-LOC six year

nomšu-du-m
study-PAST-1SG

After finishing studying Kazak, and after I had passed the entrance exam, I entered college. I went to the college which we call "Xinjiang Medical University" in Urumchi and I studied six years in that school.

11. *ol mektep-ti bütür-gen-nen   gedeer ge-ep   bo*
that school-ACC finish-PSTPRT-ABL after   come-CONV this

bod-um-nuŋ   žer-im-e   ge-ep
self-1SG.POSS-GEN place-1SG.POSS-DAT come-CONV

böl-ün-üp   gel-gen-nen   geder ımdı-ga
distribute-PASS-CONV come-PSTPRT-ABL after   now-DAT

žed-er   on žeže žıl bol-du išde-p   žıt-kan-nan
reach-PRSPRT ten some year be-PAST work-CONV lie-PSTPRT-ABL

beri
since

I was assigned to (work in) my own place after I had finished that
school. Up to now, it's been some 10 years since I have been
working here.

12. *bagay emes*
     bad   NEGCOP

It's not bad.

13. *äytew   bičii bot žer-ibis-te-gi   gadı*
     anyhow little self place-1PL.POSS-LOC-RELCL together

törü-ün   kazak bo-zun kıdat   ulus-tar-ı
give.birth-PSTPRT Kazak be-3IMP Chinese nationality-PL-3POSS

bol-sun töz-ü-nüŋ   ara-zı-nda   bod-um-ča
be-3IMP all-3POSS-GEN interval-3POSS-LOC self-1SG.POSS-EQU

bičii išde-n-gen   bo-p   dur-men
little work-REFL-PSTPRT be-CONV stay-1SG

Anyhow, I am trying to do my best to work (to serve) among all people who are our relatives, no matter whether they are Kazaks or are Chinese.

14. *eki išde-n-ip   žıd-ır-men   be bagay*
     good work-REFL-CONV lie-PRSINDF-1SG Q bad

     išde-n-ip   žıd-ır-men   be ında-gı   kalık baška
     work-REFL-CONV lie- PRSINDF-1SG Q here-RELCL people other

     da ulus-tar   töz-ü   men-i olar bagala-p
     also nationality-PL all-3POSS I-ACC they evaluate-CONV

     be-er   de-p   sen-ip   dur-men
     give-PRSINDF say-CONV believe-CONV stay-1SG

     I believe that the people here and also the other ethnic nationalities will all evaluate me, whether I am doing a good job or a bad job.

15. *bo on žıl-dan beer negizinen men baštay gel-gen-nen*
     this ten year-ABL since basically I   first   come-PSTPRT-ABL

     beer deri iš-tı   žarala-n-gan-nar-nı   gör-üp
     since skin work-ACC wound-REFL-PSTPRT-PL-ACC see-CONV

     bir žeže žıl öskör-böyün   išde-di-m
     one some year change-NEGCONV work-PAST-1SG

     For the last ten years, since I first came here, I have been basically working on curing skin wounds. I have been curing those who got wounds on their skin. I haven't changed my job for many years.

16. *wayke   de-er-bis   xırurgiya de-er*
     surgical.department say-PRSINDF-1PL hirurgiya say-PRSINDEF

We call it Waike (Surgical Department) or Hirurgiya (Surgery.)

17.   *ɪnda išde-p   žɪd-ɪr-men*
there work-CONV lie-PRSINDF-1SG
I am working there.

18.   *ɪndan   beer käzir äytew bagay emes   bičii*
from.that since now   anyhow bad   NEGCOP little

xörüm bö de-p   olur-bus
better   Q say-CONV sit-1PL

Anyhow, since then, it's not bad now, we are doing a little better.

19.   *bis bo ara-a   ge-ep   olur-gan-nan   beer men*
we this place-DAT come-CONV stay-PSTPRT-ABL since I

baštay gel-gen-nen   beer bo bis-tiŋ
early   come-PSTPRT-ABL since this we-GEN

awdan-ɪbɪs-ta   akkaba-nan ge-ep   bo ara-a
county-1PL.POSS-LOC Akkaba-ABL come-CONV this place-DAT

olur-up ög bo-p   olur-gan išd-i-nen
live-CONV house be-CONV sit-PSTPRT inside-3POSS-ABL

olur-gan giži-ler bol-gan töz-ü   žaŋgɪs gene men
sit-PSTPRT people-PL be-PSTPRT all-3POSS alone   only I

Since we came here to settle and (from)the beginning of my arrival, I am the only person who came from Akkaba and formed a family and resided in our county.

20.   *osun bir žɪl-dan gedeer xara daš de-en*
then one year-ABL after   black stone say-PSTPRT

žer-de-gi   *ıstansa-ga tärbiye de-en*   *bir*
place-LOC-RELCL station-DAT Tärbiye say-PSTPRT one

žalıı-bıs   *žaŋgıs ge-ep*   *išde-n-ip*
young.man-1PL.POSS alone   come-CONV work-REFL-CONV

žad-ır
lie-PRSINDF

Then after a year, one of our young men named Tärbiye came here
alone and has been working in a (electric power) station in a place
called Black Stone.

21. *osun iyi örögö bol-du-bus*
     then   two family be-PAST-1PL

     Then we became two families.

22. *am bo enir žıl-dan beer öz soluŋgı de-en*   *bis-tiŋ*
     now this last year-ABL since self Solunggi say-PSTPRT we-GEN

     bir aga-bıs   *ge-ep*   *wenžaw*
     one old.brother-1PL.POSS come-CONV culture.and.education

     žü-ge   ište-n-ip   *käzir üš örögö bol-du-bus*
     bureau-DAT work-REFL-CONV now   three family be-PAST-1PL

     Now we have become three families, since last year one of our
     own older brothers named Solunggi came to work in the Wenjiao
     Ju (Bureau of Culture and Education.)

23. *o-oŋ bod-u   burun-gı-nan   axırında-p   bičii eki*
     it-GEN self-3POSS before-RELCL-ABL slow.down-CONV little good

de-er bis
say-PRSINDF-1PL

We would say all this is slowly getting a little better than before.

2. 5 A personal history of a retired school principal

Narrated by Kongir of Akkaba Village in September1995

1. *bis-tiŋ bo akkaba-da žurt-tu   mončak de-er*
    we-GEN this Akkaba-LOC people-ACC Monchak say-PRSINDF

    They call the people in this Akkaba of ours Monchaks.

2. *olar erte šag-da   bo orus-tuŋ   säbet žaysaŋ köl-ü*
    they early time-LOC this Russian-GEN soviet Zaysang lake-3POSS

    xommalga de-p   žer-i-nen   gel-gen   irgin
    Hommalga say-CONV place-3POSS-ABL come-PSTINSF EVID

    It seems that in earlier times they came from a place called
    Hommalga (near) this Soviet Zaysang lake of the Russians.

3. *ol mıŋ   tos žüs   on žedinči žıl-dar-ı   könö šar*
    it thousand nine hundred ten seventh year-PL-3POSS old   tsar

    patča-zı oylad-ıp bo žer-ge äke-ep   ga-an
    king-3POSS chase-CONV this place-DAT bring-CONV leave-PSTINDF

    In 1917, the old Tsarist emperor chased them leaving them in this
    place.

4. *oson borta gel-geli   buruŋ-gu   ulug ulus-tar-nıŋ*
    later here   come-CONV before-RELCL old   people-PL-GEN

ayd-ɪr-ɪ-nda   *bes žüs   žeže žɪl-dan artɪk*
say-PRSPRT-3POSS-LOC five hundred many year-ABL more

bol-gan
be-PSTINDF

According to the old folks, it has been more than five hundred years or so since they came here.

5. *borta gel-gen-men   mɪŋ   tos žüs   dörtön*
    here come-PSTINDF-1SG thousand nine hundred forty

    sezinči žɪl gel-gen-men   bo
    eighth   year come-PSTINDF-1SG this

    I came here, I came here in 1948, it was.

6. *ol gel-gen   žɪl-dan bašta-p   mektep*
    that come-PSTPRT year-ABL start-CONV school

    gak-tɪr-d-ɪp   nom ööröt-dü-m   bolar-ga
    build-CAUS-CAUS -CONV lesson teach-PAST-1.SG these-DAT

    Starting from that year that I came, I had them (the Tuva) build a school and I have taught them.

7. *dörtön tozɪnči žɪl-dan bašta-p   mektep-te iš gɪl-ɪp*
    forty   ninth   year-ABL start-CONV school-LOC job do-CONV

    mugalɪm bol-du-m   šiawžaŋ bol-du-m   bo
    teacher   be-PAST-1SG principal be- PAST-1SG this

    I have been a teacher employed at the school starting in1949, and I have been principal, it was.

8.   *amdı demalıs-ka   ün-üp   žet-tı-m   men*
        now   retirement-DAT go.out-CONV reach-PAST-1SG I

Now I am retired.

9.   *käzir bo žurt buruŋ-gu-zı-nan   ebeešte-en*
        now   this people before-REFCL-3POSS-ABL decline-PSTPRT

        bol-ba-za   göböy-gön   žer-i   žok
        be-NEG-COND increase-PSTPRT place-3POSS NEGEXIST

Now, this hometown has declined from what it was, or anyway
there's no way it went up, no way.

10.   *dörtön tozınčı žıl-gı   dört žüs   sezen tın-nan käzir*
        forty   ninth   year-RELCL four hundred eighty life-ABL now

        barı   üš žüs   tozan tın gal-dı   ebeešte-di
        altogether three hundred ninety life remain-PAST decline-PAST

Of 480 people in 1949, now (only) 390 people remain altogether.
It has declined.

11.   *bo-oŋ göb-ü   aarıg sırgak*
        this-GEN many-3POSS sick   ill

Most of them are sick and ill.

12.   *käzir bičii eki bo-p   olur-gan-ı   bo*
        now   little good be-CONV stay-PSTPRT-3POSS this

Now, they've been getting a little better.

13.   *bir žer-de   žıg-ıl-ıp   nom ertem mektep-te*
        one place-LOC gather-PASS-CONV book learning school-LOC

ortalaw-ga žed-ir   nomž-up   dur
middle-DAT reach-PRSPRT study-CONV stay

They are gathering together and are studying in an educational school which has reached middle school level.

14. *bod-u-nuŋ   dıl-ı   dıba dıl   bırak dıba*
self-3POSS-GEN language-3POSS Tuvan language but   Tuvan

dıl-dıŋ   bod-u   iš-ke   as-pas
language-GEN self-3POSS work-DAT pass-NEGPRSINDF

Their own language is Tuvan, but Tuvan by itself will not work.

15. *bis-tiŋ nomna-d-ır   žibe-bis   žıŋ mool*
we-GEN learn-CAUS-PRSPRT thing-1PL.POSS true Mongol

dıl-ı   baza ol dıl-dı   ööröd-ür   kerek
language-3POSS and that language-ACC teach-PRSPRT necessary

The thing (that) we teach is pure Mongolian, and we have to teach that language.

16. *dıba-nıŋ ool-dar-ı-ŋga   bolšuug-ı   kün*
Tuva-GEN child-PL-3POSS-DAT way.of.life-3POSS day

öt-küz-üp   olur-gan bo
pass-CAUS-CONV sit-PSTPRT this

This is the way of life for Tuvan children.

17. *mal-dıg   bay-ı   da bar žo-o   da bar*
livestock-ADJ rich-3POSS also EXIST NEGEXIST-3POSS also EXIST

There are (those) both rich and poor in livestock.

18. *gɪžɪ töz-ü deŋ emes*
     person all-3POSS equal NEGCOP
     Everyone is not equal.

19. *ekɪ-zɪ de bar bagay-ɪ da bar*
     good-3POSS also EXIST bad-3POSS also EXIST

     There is both good and bad.

20. *bo akkaba-nɪŋ žurd-u-nuŋ žalpɪ beedil-i*
     this Akkaba-GEN people-3POSS-GEN general condition-3POSS

     baška žok
     other NEGEXIST

     This is the general situation of these people of Akkaba. There is
     nothing else (to say).

2. 6 A personal history of a college student

Narrated by Torgun of Akkaba Village in September1995 in Urumchi

1. *me-eŋ ad-ɪm torgun*
    I-GEN name-1SG.POSS Torgun

    My name is Turgun.

2. *bo žɪl on žedi žaš-tɪg men*
    this year seventeen year-ADJ 1SG

    I am seventeen years old this year.

3. *akkaba-nɪŋ išd-i-nde bis-ti mončak de-p*
    Akkaba-GEN inside-3POSS-LOC we-ACC Monchak say-CONV

ayd-ɪr
say-PRSINDF

They call us Monchak in Akkaba.

4. *baška giži-ler mončak de-p   ayd-ɪr*
    other   person-PL Monchak say-CONV say-PRSINDF

    Others call us Monchak.

5. *bis bod-ubus   išd-ibis-te   dɪba-bɪs*
    we self-1PL.POSS inside-1PL.POSS-LOC Tuva-1PL

    We call ourselves Tuva among ourselves.

6. *men taraŋkay de-en   giži-niŋ   uru-u-men*
    I   Tarangkay say-PSTPRT person-GEN daughter-3POSS-1SG

    I am the daughter of Tarangkay.

7. *bis-tiŋ ög-de   žedi giži bar*
    we-GEN house-LOC seven person EXIST

    There are seven people in our family.

8. *men dördünči-zi bol-ur-men*
    I   fourth-3POSS be-PRSINDF-1SG

    I am the fourth in the family.

9. *aba-m   burun bis bičii dur-ar-da   žok*
    mother-1SG.POSS early   we small stay-PRSPRT-LOC NEGEXIST

    bo-p   gal-ɪpdur
    be-CONV stay-PNARR

My mother passed away when we were very small.

10.   *me-eŋ ulug iyi aga-m   bar*
      I-GEN big two older.brother-1SG.POSS EXIST

I have two big older brothers.

11.   *eŋ ulug egiči-m   ad-ı   külžüŋ*
      SUP big elder.sister-1SG.POSS name-3POSS Külzhüng

My eldest sister's name is Külzhüng.

12.   *iyinči aga-m-nıŋ   ad-ı   tärbiye*
      second older.brother-1SG.POSS-GEN name-3POSS Tärbiye

My (second) elder brother's name is Tärbiye.

13.   *üžünči aga-m-nıŋ   ad-ı   altınča*
      third older.brother-1SG.POSS-GEN name-3POSS Altincha.

My (third) elder brother's name is Altıncha.

14.   *xoŋ   osunda-men torgun*
      after.all here-1SG   Torgun.

Hey, and here I am, Torgun.

15.   *mee-ŋ čoŋgar buyun buyunbat ulanbayır čıŋgıs*
      I-GEN Chonggar Buyun Buyunbat Ulanbayir Chinggis

      de-en   duŋma-lar-ım   bar
      say-PSTPRT younger.brother-PL-1SG.POSS EXIST

I have younger brothers named Chonggar, Buyun, Buyunbat, Ulanbayır and Chinggis.

16. *mee-ŋ aga-m*   *sezen aldınčı žıl bo mektep-ten*
     I-GEN elder.brother-1SG.POSS eighty sixth   year this school-ABL

     bütür-gen
     graduate-PSTINDF

     My elder brother graduated from this school in 1986.

17. *iyinči aga-m*   *sezenči žıl ge-ep*
     second elder.brother-1SG.POSS eightieth year come-CONV

     bütür-gen
     finish-PSTINDF

     My second brother came here in 1980 and graduated.

18. *egiči-m*   *tozančı žıl gel-gen*
     elder.sister-1SG.POSS ninetieth year come-PSTINDF

     My elder sister came here in 1990.

19. *bod-um*   *tozan üžünči žıl gel-gen-men*
     self-1SG.POSS ninety third   year come-PSTPRT-1SG

     I myself came here in 1993.

20. *gel-gen*   *soŋgaar men mool dıl   domaktan-ıy*
     come-PSTPRT after   I   Mongol language speak-CONV

     al-bas-pın   *de-p*   *dur-ar-da*   *dıba*
     take-NEGPRSINDF-1SG say-CONV stay-PRSPRT-LOC Tuva

     ündüsüden de-p   *ayt-tı*
     nationality say-CONV say-PAST

After I came, they said I was from the Tuva nation, since I could not speak Mongolian.

21.   *ard-ı-nan   mool-dıŋ   išd-i-ŋge   žoru-y*
back-3POSS-ABL Mongol-GEN inside-3POSS-DAT walk-CONV

žoru-y   eki   domaktan-ır bol-du-m
walk-CONV good   speak-PRSPRT be-PAST-1SG

Later, being among the Mongols constantly, I was able to speak good Mongolian.

22.   *bis-ti eŋ baštay ge-ep   dur-ar-da   kazak*
we-ACC SUP first   come-CONV stay-PRSPRT-LOC Kazak

de-p   ayd-ır
say-CONV say-PRSINDF

When we first came here, they would call us Kazaks.

23.   *baška okuwšı-lar bis-ti   alday-nıŋ žibi-ler-i   kazak*
other   student-PL   we-ACC Altay-GEN thing-PL-3POSS Kazak

de-p   ayd-ır
say-CONV say-PRSINDF

Other students would say that those who came from Altay are Kazaks.

24.   *bırak ta   ayd-ır-da   bis-ter kazak de-er-de   iye*
but   EMPH say-PRSPRT-LOC we-PL   Kazak say-PRSPRT-LOC yes

de-y   sal-ır-bıs
say-CONV put-PRSINDF-1PL

However, when they say we are Kazaks, we simply acknowledge it and say "Yes, (we are Kazaks.)"

25. *bɩrak ta   bis-ter bälen-tügön de-p*
but   EMPH we-PL so.and.so   say-CONV

žibele-bes-pis
argue-NEGPRSINDF-1PL

And we would not argue about it.

26. *bolar uk-pas   bis-tiŋ dɩl-ɩbɩs-tɩ*
they   understand-NEGPRSINDF we-GEN language-1PL.POSS-ACC

osunda
here

Here, they do not understand our language.

27. *bis-ter baxšɩ-lar nomšu-ur-da   keybir nom-nar-nɩ*
we-PL   teacher-PL read-PRSPRT-LOC some   lesson-PL-ACC

šala-mužuk bil-ip   dur-ar-bɩs
insufficient   know-CONV stand-PRSINDF-1PL

We do not understand some of the lessons completely when the teachers are reading.

28. *ard-ɩ-nan   bir iyi üš   ay-nan   soŋgaar öörön-e*
after-3POSS-ABL one two three month-ABL after   learn-CONV

bar-dɩ-bɩs
go-PAST-1PL

Later, after one, two, three months (pass) we began to learn.

29. *bis-ter žeže   mončak bol-sa   da   bis-ter mool-dıŋ*
     we-PL how.much Monchak be-COND EMPH we-PL Mongol-GEN

     išd-i-ŋge   gir-ip   öörön-üp dadıg žor-up
     inside-3POSS-DAT enter-CONV learn-CONV hard   walk-CONV

     dur-ar-da   baška okuwšı-lar-nan kem
     stand-PRSPRT-LOC other   student-PL-ABL worse

     gal-bayın   žor-ur-bus
     remain-NEGCONV walk-PRSINDF-1PL

     No matter how many Monchaks we are, we are not inferior to
     other students when we are trying to study very hard among the
     Mongols.

30. *keybir baxšı-lar bil-ir*
     some   teacher-PL know-PRSINDF

     Some teachers know this.

31. *keybir baxšı-lar bil-bes*
     some   teacher-PL know-NEGPRSINDF

     Some teachers do not know this.

32. *bil-er   baxšı-lar elek gıl-gan   žibe žige*
     know-PRSPRT teacher-PL fun   make-PSTINDF thing correct

     domaktan-gar de-p
     speak-2PL.IMP say-CONV

     Those teachers who know have made fun of (us) saying: "Hey
     folks, speak correctly."

2. 7 A true story in life

Narrated by Erik of Kaba county in September1995

1. *bis-tiŋ ög   bo xanas žer-i-ŋge   gadaŋgır soŋgu*
    we-GEN family this Kanas place-3POSS-DAT Gadanggir northern

    üzük ača bulak de-en   žer-ler-ge   burun-nan
    Üzük   Acha brook say-PSTPRT place-PL-DAT before-ABL

    gıšta-p   žerle-p   gel-e   žıt-kan
    spend.the.winter-CONV reside-CONV come-CONV lie-PSTINDF

    Our family had been living and spending the winters in places
    called Gadanggir, Northern Üzük, Acha Brook in Kanas in the
    past.

2. *bo žook-ta bir   žıl-dar-ı   bir iyi-i-nen   žer*
    this near-LOC some year-PL-3POSS one aspect-3POSS-ABL soil

    gaaŋ bo-p   boraan-žaškın bol-bayın   bir
    aridity be-CONV snow.storm   be-NEGCONV one

    iyi-i-nen   žut   üsd-ü-ŋge   žaštıyık-tan
    aspect-3POSS-ABL calamity above-3POSS-DAT outside-ABL

    žaa   žibe ün-üp   dur irgin
    enemy thing come-CONV stay EVID

    Recently, some years (ago), on the one side (hand), the soil
    (weather) has been dry and there was no snow storm
    (precipitation), and on the other hand, there was a calamity
    (killing weather) plus an outside enemy invasion.

3.   *bod-dar-ɪ-nɪŋ   olur-gan   kɪšta-a-nda*
self-PL-3POSS-GEN live-PSTPRT village-3POSS-LOC

žer-i-nen   sigen žibe xaᶃ-a   al-bayɪn
place-3POSS-ABL grass   thing mow-CONV able-NEGCONV

akkaba-nɪŋ beti   iyi-i-nde-gi   dörölži
Akkaba-GEN this.side slope-3POSS-LOC-RELCL ridge

de-en   bir žer-ge   ge-ep   sigen xa-ap
say-PSTPRT one place-DAT come-CONV grass   mow-CONV

gɪšta-ar   bo-p   sigen öy-ü-nde   sigen
spend.winter-PRSPRT be-CONV grass   season-3POSS-LOC grass

žibe-si-n   žɪg-gaš   güz-ün   onɪnčɪ ay-da
thing-3POSS-ACC pile.up-CONV autumn-INSTR tenth   month-LOC

ge-ep   ol žer-de   gɪšta-an-nan
come-CONV that place-LOC spend.winter-PSTPRT-ABL

soŋgaar bir gažaa-xamaa ga-ar   bo-p   iyi alɪškɪ
after   one barn-thing   build-PRSPRT be-CONV two brothers

gɪštaw   ga-ap   žɪd-ɪr   iyik
winter.encampment build-CONV lie-PRTINDF EVID

They were unable to cut grass on their land in the village where
they were living, so they came to a place named Ridge on the
slope of this side of the Akkaba, where they (decided to) cut grass
and spent the winter, and piled up (stocked up) grass and so during
the grass cutting time (grass-season); they came in the autumn, in
October to that place, and after having spent the winter there, they

apparently intended to build a barn and so, the two (blood) brothers intended to build a winter encampment.

4. *bir gün ög-nüŋ   ee-zi   ög   ga-ap   ɪyaš žibe*
    one day house-GEN owner-3POSS house build-CONV wood thing

    žon-up   xɪy-ɪp žɪd-ar-da   üš   boo
    plane-CONV cut-CONV lie-PRSPRT-LOC three rifle

    az-ɪn-gan   židig   garak-tɪg šerig ge-ep   bo
    hang-REFL-PSTPRT piercing eye-ADJ   soldier come-CONV this

    ara-ga   giži gel-di   be de-p   dur
    place-DAT person come-PAST Q say-CONV stay

    One day, when the owner of the house was building a house, planing and cutting wood, three sharp-eyed soldiers came with rifles hanging from their necks (shoulders) and asked: "Did anyone come here?"

5. *iyi žibe dur-gaš-tan   žok giži   gel-be-en*
    two thing stay-CONV-ABL no   person come-NEG-PSTINDF

    de-er-de   üš   orus   šerig gɪštag-nɪŋ
    say-PRSINDF-LOC three Russian soldier winter.camp-GEN

    murnuu-nda baalɪg-dɪ   až-ɪr
    south-LOC   mountain.pass-ACC cross-PRSPRT

    šab-ɪp   žoru-y   bar-dɪ irgin
    gallop-CONV walk-CONV go-PAST EVID

    As both (were) standing there and said: "No, no one has come," the three Russian soldiers crossed the mountain pass on the front side of the winter encampment, and were apparently galloping away.

6. *o-oŋ erten-i nde   iyi alıškı ugaan-ı-nda   žibe*
    it-GEN next.day-3POSS-LOC two brothers mind-3POSS-LOC thing

    žok   šagıš-ta iž-i-n   gı-ıp   dur-ar-da
    NEGEXIST time-LOC work-3POSS-ACC do-CONV stay-PRSPRT-LOC

    göböy ulug boo as-tın-gan   orus   šerig-ler-i
    many   big   rifle hang-PASS-PSTPRT Russian soldier-PL-3POSS

    ge-ep   dur
    come-CONV stay

    The next day, when the two brothers had nothing on their mind and were doing their jobs, many Russian soldiers came with their large rifles hanging from their necks (shoulders).

7. *išd-i-nde   bir ulug šen-nig baštı-ı   bar   ırgin*
    inside-3POSS-LOC one big   rank-ADJ leader-3POSS EXIST EVID

    There was a high ranked leader (general) among them (apparently).

8. *gel-e   la sös žok   bo ara-ga   giži gel-di*
    come-CONV EMPH word NEGEXIST this place-DAT person come-PAST

    be sener giži su-up   al-dı-gar   de-p   iyi
    Q you.PL person hide-CONV take-PAST-2PL say-CONV two

    žibe-ni dud-up   xol-u-n   bagla-p a-p
    thing-ACC capture-CONV hand-3POSS-ACC tie-CONV take-CONV

kıšta-a-nıŋ   *murnuu ıyı-ı-nda-gı*   *gılın arga*
village-3POSS-GEN south   side-3POSS-LOC-RELCL dense forest

ara-zı-ndan   *gudu xay de-p* *žoru-up*   *dur irgin*
interval-3POSS-ABL down drive-CONV walk-CONV stay EVID

As soon as they arrived, without saying any (other) words, they
asked: "Did anyone come here? You are hiding someone," they
grabbed the two (poor) things, tied their hands, and were
driving/taking them downwards (through) the middle of the dense
forest on the south side of the village.

9.   *iyi žibe arga žok*   *göböy bo šerig-ler-i-nıŋ*
     two thing way NEGEXIST many   this soldier-PL-3POSS-GEN

     žebe-zi-ŋge   *šıda-bayın*   *žoru de-en*
     thing-3POSS-DAT endure-NEGCONV walk say-PSTPRT

     žü-ü-nge   *gudu*   *sös žok*   *žor-up*
     direction-3POSS-DAT downwards word NEGEXIST walk-CONV

     dur irgin
     stay EVID

The two of them had no choice but to endure whatever these many
soldiers said and walk downwards the direction that they were told
to go. (The two of them walked in the direction they were told to
go, having no way but to bear the things of these many soldiers.)

10. *o- oŋ bilen arga išd-ı-ŋge*   *apar-ıp*   *baza*
     it-GEN with   forest inside-3POSS-DAT take-CONV and

     gak-kaš-tan   *bir žeže surax-tar* *sura-p* *dur irgin*
     beat-CONV-ABL one some question-PL ask-CONV stay EVID

So, having taken them to the middle of the forest and beaten them, (the soldiers) asked them some questions.

11.   *siler   bo žer-ge   žüge gel-di-ger*
       you.PL this place-DAT why   come-PAST-2PL

       "Why did you all come here?"

12.   *siler-niŋ   bo dur-gan   žer-ler-ge   baška giži-ler*
       you. PL-GEN this stay-PSTPRT place-PL-DAT other person-PL

       gel-di   be orus   šerig-ler-i   gel-di   be boo
       come-PAST Q Russian soldier-PL-3POSS come-PAST Q rifle

       as-tın-ın   giži-ler gör-dü-ler be de-p   dur ırgın
       hang-REFL-PSTPRT person-PL see-PAST-2PL Q say-CONV stay EVID

       They asked: "Did anyone else come to these places where you're staying? Did Russian soldiers come here? Did you see people with rifles?"

13.   *iyi-lee-zi   olar-ga bis giži gör-be-di-k   bo*
       two-COLL-3POSS they-DAT we person see-NEG-PAST-1PL this

       ara-ga   iškim gel-be-di   bis žer-ibis-te
       place-DAT nobody come-NEG-PAST we place-1PL.POSS-LOC

       aŋna-p   gɪšta-abɪs-ta-gɪ   sigen
       hunt-CONV winter.camp-1PL.POSS-LOC-RELCL grass

       ün-gön   soŋgaar ɪ-ŋga sigen ga-p
       sprout-PSTPRT after   it-DAT grass mow-CONV

       gɪšta-ar   bo-p   ög   ga-ap
       spend.winter-PRSPRT become-CONV house build-CONV

žɪd-ɪr-bɪs   de-er   irgin
lie-PRSINDF-1PL say-PRSINDF EVID

The two of them told them (the soldiers): "We didn't see anyone.
No one came here. We are hunting in our own place, and came
here to cut the grass after it had been grown in our winter
encampment and we are building a house in order to spend winter
here."

14.   birak olar iyi žibe-niŋ söz-ü-ŋgö   kön-bö-y
       but   they two thing-GEN word-3POSS-DAT believe-NEG-CONV

olar-nɪ ad-ar   de-p   dur-ar-da
they-ACC shoot-PRSINDF say-CONV stay-PRSINDF-LOC

ard-ɪ-nan   baza bir žeže orus   šerig-ler-i
behind-3POSS-ABL and one some Russian soldier-PL-3POSS

ge-ep   dur irgin
come-CONV stay EVID

But they did not believe what these two (poor) things were saying,
and when they were about to shoot them, some (other) Russian
soldiers came after them.

15.   orus   šerig-ler-i-niŋ   išd-i-nde   žedeen bir
       Russian soldier-PL-3POSS-GEN inside-3POSS-LOC huge   one

šen-i   bar biri-zi-n   me-eŋ aža-m
rank-3POSS EXIST one.of-3POSS-ACC I-GEN father-1SG.POSS

burun tanɪ-za   gerek
before know-COND necessary

It turned out that my father had been acquainted in the past with one among the Russian soldiers who held high rank.

16.   *tanı-ž-ıp*   *o-nun*   *aralaž-ıp*   *žoru-ur*
know-REC-CONV he-INSTR associate.with-CONV walk-PRSINDF

irgin
EVID

They had known each other and had associated with one another.

17.   *o-oŋ* *bilen ol at-tan*   *düž-ö*   *ga-ap*   *olar-nıŋ*
it-GEN with he horse-ABL descend-CONV remain-CONV they-GEN

žügö tut-un-gan-ı-n   *man-žay-ı-n*
why capture-REFL-PSTPRT-3POSS-ACC situation-3POSS-ACC

sura-p   *dur irgin*
ask-CONV stay EVID

Then he got off the horse immediately and asked about the essence (situation) and why they had been captured (arrested).

18.   *olar ol orus-ka*   *bod-dar-ı-nıŋ*   *žügö ge-ep*
they that Russian-DAT self-PL-3POSS-GEN why come-CONV

ınga   *sigen ga-ap*   *žıt-kan*   *man-žay-ı-n*
to.there grass mow-CONV lie-PSTPRT situation-3POSS-ACC

ayd-ıp   *be-er*   *irgin*
tell-CONV give-PRSINDF EVID

They told that Russian why they had come here to cut grass.

19. *o-oŋ   bilen orus   dıl-ı-nan*   *ol orus*
     it-GEN with   Russian language-3POSS-INSTR that Russian

     gıdı-ı-nda-gı   *orus-tar-ga   ayd-ır-da*   *olar*
     side-3POSS-LOC-RELCL Russian-PL-DAT tell-PRSPRT-LOC they

     da bälendey   pozitsiya bil-dir-be-en
     also any.particular position   know-CAUS-NEG-PSTINDF

     ııtta-bayın   dur-up   dur irgin
     say-NEGCONV stay-CONV stay EVID

     Then, when that Russian told those Russians next to him in
     Russian (the details), they (other Russians) did not make any
     comment and did not say anything, kept mum.

20. *o-oŋ   bilen me-eŋ aža-m*   *burun žeže de-en*
     it-GEN with   I-GEN father-1SG.POSS before several say-PSTPRT

     bilen gıdı-ı-nda-gı   *tanıš   oruz-u-ŋga*
     with side-3POSS-LOC-RELCL acquainted Russian-3POSS-DAT

     aga-zı   iyi-ler-zi   teyle-p   ganžalsada
     brother-3POSS two-PL-3POSS beseech-CONV no.matter.what

     bis-tiŋ tın-ıbıs-tı   gıy-a   gör-gür   bis bo
     we-GEN life-1PL.POSS-ACC spare-CONV see-2SG.IMP we this

     ara-ga   mınžap tın azıra-n-ır   užun gel-di-k
     place-DAT this.way life rear-REFL-PRSPRT for   come-PAST-1PL

     de-er   irgin
     say-PRSINDF EVID

Then, even though my father had previously told the acquainted Russian next to him several times, the two brothers had to beseech (him) saying: "Please spare our lives, no matter what! We just came here in order to struggle for existence (make a living in this way)."

21. *bis siler-diŋ   eškanday   ɪn-dɪg   mɪn-dɪg*
     we   you.all-GEN any.kind   that-EQU this-EQU

     žibe-ler-iŋiz-ben   katɪž-ɪbɪs   žok
     thing-PL-2PL.POSS-INSTR connections-1PL.POSS NEGEXIST

     de-p   dur irgin
     say-CONV stay EVID

     They said: "We do not have any connections with your business whatsoever."

22. *o-oŋ bilen ol tanɪ-ɪr   oruz-ɪ*
     it-GEN with   he know-PRSPRT Russian-3POSS

     gɪdɪ-ɪ-ŋda-gɪ   orus-tar-ga   ayd-ɪp
     side-3POSS-DAT-RELCL Russian-PL-DAT say-CONV

     bolar-dɪŋ žagday-ɪ-n   dedir
     these-GEN situation-3POSS-ACC again

     dedir ug-un-dur-up   olar-nɪŋ bot ara
     again understand-REFL-CAUS-CONV   they-GEN   self among

     išd-i-nde   žaala-ž-ɪp   žoru-ur-nan   xabar-sɪz
     inside-POSS-LOC conquer-REC-CONV   walk-PRSPRT-ABL news-PRIV

     irgin-i-n   baylanɪs   žo-o-n
     EVID-3POSS-ACC connections NEGEXIST-3POSS-ACC

ayd-ɪr-da   olar-nɪ sal-dɪr-ɪr-ga
say-PRSPRT-LOC they-ACC put-CAUS-PRSPRT-DAT

gozul-up   dur irgin
agree-CONV stay EVID

Then, when that acquainted Russian told it to those Russians next
to him and explained to them again and again their situation and
said that they apparently (two brothers) didn't have any
information about the fights between them (Russians) and had
nothing to do with it, they agreed to release them (two brothers).

23.   *birak orus-tar olar-ga mɪn-dɪg talap ga-ap   dur irgin*
      but   Russian-PL they-DAT this-EQU request put-CONV stay EVID

But the Russian stated the following requirements to them.

24.   *sener gožugar-nan des-pes-sener*
      you.PL small.yurt-ABL run.away-NEGPRSINDF-2PL.IMP

      gožugar-ga   olur-ur-sener
      small.yurt-DAT stay-PRSINDF-2PL.IMP

"You can't run away from your small yurt. You have to stay in the
small yurt."

25.   *ol giži-ler münkün bo maŋay-da   žažɪr-ɪn-ɪp*
      that person-PL maybe   this surrounding.area-LOC hide-RFL-CONV

      žat-kan bo-za žanada ge-ep   magat   žok
      lie-PSTPRT be-COND again come-CONV prediction NEGEXIST

It is possible that those people are hiding in this area and they may
come back again, it's hard to say.

26.   *bis žaštın   güzöd-ür-büs*
       we outside guard-PRSINDF-1PL

   We will be guarding outside.

27.   *eger ıŋay   beer dez-er   bol-sa-gar*
       if   away.from this.way run.away-PRSPRT be-COND-2PL

   siler-ni   ad-ar-bıs   de-p   dur irgin
   you.PL-ACC shoot-PRSINDF-1PL say-CONV stay EVID

   They said: "We will shoot you if you run away from this point
   (here.)"

28.   *o-oŋ bilen iyi žibe gož-u-ŋga   gel-se   iyi*
       it-GEN with   two thing tent-3POSS-DAT come-COND two

   ad-ı   žok
   horse-3POSS NEGEXIST

   Then the two brothers came to their tent and found that their two
   horses were missing.

29.   *birak baška boo žepsek šüüt   žebe-ler-i-ŋge*
       but   other rifle weapons chores thing-PL-3POSS-DAT

   deeš-pe-en   irgin
   touch-NEG-PSTINDF EVID

   But they apparently had not touched other things such as rifles,
   weapons and work things/tools.

30.   *baška žibe-zi-n   töz-ü-n   ab-ba-p   dur irgin*
       other thing-3POSS-ACC all-3POSS-ACC take-NEG-CONV stay EVID

They had not taken any of the other things at all.

31.   *o-oŋ   bilen erten-i-nde   o des-ken   orus*
       it-GEN with   next.day-3POSS-LOC that run.away-PSTPRT Russian

       da gel-beyin   dur
       also come-NEGCONV stay

Then, the next day, the runaway Russians didn't come either.

32.   *bet-te-gi   olar-nıŋ bot-tar-ın   dut-kan*
       hillside-LOC-RELCL they-GEN self-PL-3POSS-ACC capture-PSTPRT

       orus-tar   da gel-be-en   dür irgin
       Russian-PL also come-NEG-PSTINDF stay EVID

Those Russians on the hillside who had captured them (the brothers) didn't come either.

33.   *o-oŋ   bilen gıšta-a-n   ga-gaš   iyi žibe*
       it-GEN with   winter.camp-3POSS-ACC leave-CONV two thing

       dalaš -dulaštan aal-ı-ŋga   dez-ip   ge-ep   dur
       hurriedly   village-3POSS-DAT run-CONV come-CONV stay

       irgin
       EVID

Then, the two (poor) things left the winter encampment behind them and came running to their village in a flurry.

34.   *e mında endi bis-tiŋ bod-um-nuŋ   aba-m   endi*
       oh here   then we-GEN self-1SG.POSS-GEN mother-1SG.POSS then

bo   xoožu-nu burun-nan bis-ke talay ret ayd-ɪp
this story-ACC   before-ABL we-DAT many time tell-CONV

ber-gen
give-PSTINDF

Well, here, then my own mother had previously told us this story many times.

35. *mɪnda-gɪ aža-bɪz-dɪŋ   žaa ayt-kan   sös-tör-ü*
here-RECL father-1PL.POSS-GEN just say-PSTPRT word-PL-3POSS

iškɪp   gayda žoru-za-ŋ   da   giži-nen   göp
anyhow where walk-COND-2SG EMPH person-INSTR many

tanɪ-š-sa-ŋ   išgɪp öl-gön-de   de   bol-sa
know-REC-COND-2SG anyhow   die-PSTPRT-LOC EMPH be-COND

ol seŋ-e   bir ekilik   gɪl-ɪr
it you-DAT one good.deed make-PRSINDF

What our father had said above was that, no matter, wherever you go, it would do you good if you made a lot of friends even if you were dying.

36. *bo saam bis-tiŋ tɪn-ɪbɪs-tɪ   a-p   ga-an*
this time   we-GEN life-1PL.POSS-ACC take-CONV remain-PSTPRT

ol tanɪ-ɪr   orus   bol-du
that know-PRSPRT Russian be-PAST

This time it was that Russian whom I knew who saved our lives.

37. *ol užun mun-nun mɪnaar urpak-tar-ga   ayd-ɪp*
that for   this-ABL since   descendent-PL-DAT tell-CONV

ga-ar   kerek   de-en   mɪndɪg   söz-ü
put-PRSPRT necessary say-PSTINDF this-EQU word-3POSS

bar   irgin
EXIST EVID

He (father) had such (last) words saying: "Therefore, from now on, it is necessary to tell (pass on) this to our children."

2.7 Searching for a wife

Narrated by Bolat of Akkaba Village in September1995

1. *on-u al-gaš   žor-up   olur-up xanas-ka bar-gaš*
    it-ACC take-CONV go-CONV sit-CONV Kanas-DAT go-CONV

    bis-tiŋ xuda-bɪs   bol-ur   giži-niŋ
    we-GEN in-laws-1PL.POSS be-PRSPRT person-GEN

    urug-lar-ɪ-nɪŋ   žada-a-ŋga   bar-dɪ-m
    girl-PL-3POSS-GEN dorm-3POSS-DAT go-PAST-1SG

    After I took it (the letter), I set off and went towards Kanas and I went to the dormitory of the girls whose father is one of our in-laws.

2. *mektep-te okuwšɪ-lar žɪd-ɪr   irgin*
    school-LOC student-PL lie-PRSPRT EVID

    Students were staying at the school.

3. *orta at-tɪ   ber-geš   gudul-ɪp   gel-geš*
    there horse-ACC give-CONV get.rid.of-CONV come-CONV

ulug-lar-nıŋ ara-zı-ŋga   bar-ıp
big-PL-GEN   place-3POSS-DAT go-CONV

dur-gan-ım-da   aragı iš oy aragı iš
stay-PSTPRT-1SG.POSS-LOC alcohol drink hey alcohol drink

de-di
say-PAST

They said "Drink vodka, hey drink vodka!" when I was
going/joining among the adults after I had given my horse (to the
children to take care of it) and had gotten rid of it.

4. *žok men aragı iš-pes-pin   de-di-m*
    no I   alcohol drink-NEGPRES-1SG say-PAST-1SG

I said: "No, I don't drink vodka."

5. *aragı iš-pe-ze-ŋ   ganžap urug-lar-ga gıy*
    alcohol drink-NEG-COND-2SG how   girl-PL-DAT hail
    de-er-sen
    say-PRSINDF-2SG

"How could you go talk to the girls if you don't drink vodka?"

6. *aragı iš-pe-ze-ŋ   urug-lar-ga sös ayd-a*
    alcohol drink- NEG-COND-2SG girl-PL-DAT   word tell-CONV

    al-ır-sen   be
    able-PRSINDF-2SG Q

"Can you talk to the girls if you don't drink vodka?"

7. *aragı iš-pe-ze-ŋ   sös domaktan-ıy*
    alcohol drink-NEG-COND-2SG word speak-CONV

al-bas   de-p   gım ayt-tı
able-NEGPRSINDF say-CONV who tell-PAST

"Who said that you can't talk to the girls if you don't drink vodka?"

8.   oson pižiu iš   de-p   dört bödölge pižiu äkel-dir-di
     then beer drink say-CONV four bottle   beer bring-CAUS-PAST

Then they asked me to drink some beer and had someone bring four bottles of beer.

9.   ol pižiu-nı iž-ip   bol-gan-nan   gedeer bir urug
     that beer-ACC drink-CONV be-PSTPRT-ABL after   one girl

     žügür-üp gel-geš dur-a   gal-gaš   üš dört urug
     run-CONV come-CONV stay-CONV remain-CONV three four girl

     al gatkır-dı
     well laugh.loudly-PAST

After we finished drinking the beer, one girl came running and stood there, then three or four girls burst into laughter.

10. bolar men-i žügä elek gıl-ıp   dur žüge
     these I-ACC why fun make-CONV stay why

     gatkır-ıž-ıp   dur
     laugh.loudly-REC-CONV stay

Why they are making fun of me? Why they are laughing together?

11. gım gıda-zı-n   göstür-üp dur de-p
     who butt-3POSS-ACC show-CONV stay say-CONV

ınžal-sa-m   da   gatkır-ıž-dı
say.so-COND-1SG.POSS EMPH laugh.loudly-REC -PAST

They were still laughing loudly to each other even though I said:
"Nobody is showing his butt."

12. *dee men-ge sasın biči-p   ber-ip   bo-nu*
     that I-DAT   letter write-CONV give-CONV this-ACC

     apar-ıp   ber de-en   ol
     deliver-CONV give say-PSTPRT he

     He wrote a letter for me and he asked me to deliver it (to her).

13. *bis gonžug dööy-büs*
     we very   resemble-1PL

     We resemble each other very much.

14. *men-ni ol de-p   xoožıla-š-kan   urug žügür-d-ip*
     I-ACC   him say-CONV court-REC-PSTPRT girl   run-CAUS-CONV

     žed-ip   ge-p   dur men tildeš-eyin
     reach-CONV come-CONV stay I   confide.in.one.another-1SG.IMP

     be de-p
     Q say-CONV

     The girl who is dating him, thought I was him so she came
     running up in order to confide in (me).

15. *bo ara-da   ıyad-ıp   gatkır-ıp olur irgin*
     this place-LOC be.embarrassed-CONV laugh-CONV sit   EVID

So, apparently, she was laughing here because she was embarrassed.

16. *ol ara-ga   olur-up xooǯıla-ž-ıp   äŋgimele-z-ip*
    that place-DAT sit-CONV speak-REC-CONV tell-REC-CONV

    göböy urug-lar gel-di
    many girl-PL   come-PAST

    Many girls came to that place in order to converse and chat together.

17. *am bičii ugaan boda-p   al-ba-za-m*
    now little wisdom think-CONV take-NEG-COND-1SG

    Now I think it's time for me to think a little bit wisely.

18. *göböy urug-lar-nıŋ ara-zı-ŋga   oy žiŋxua   gayda*
    many girl-PL-GEN   interval-3POSS-DAT hey Zhinghua where

    de-er-de   käzir gel-ir   de-p   bir döžök-te
    say-PRSPRT-LOC now   come-PRSINDF say-CONV one bed-LOC

    žaŋgıs urug gal-dı
    alone girl remain-PAST

    When I went among the many girls and said: "Hey! Where is Zhinghua?", one girl who remained alone sitting on the bed said: "She will come now."

19. *oo-ŋ   gıdı-ı-ŋga   žıd-ıp   al-gaš   sen*
    she-GEN side-3POSS-DAT lie.down-CONV take-CONV you

    žiŋxua-nı   bil-er-sen   be de-er-im-de
    Zhinghua-ACC know-PRSINDF-2SG Q say-PRSPRT-1SG.POSS-LOC

žok di-di
no   say-PAST

When I lay down next to her and asked her if she knew Zhinghua, she said: "No."

20. *xol-u-n   dolga-ar-ɪm-da   tanɪ-ɪr-men*
hand-3POSS-ACC twist-PRSPRT-1SG.POSS-LOC know-PRSINDF-1SG

žä   tanɪ-ɪr-men   käzir gel-ir   dur-gan
okay know-PRSINDF-1SG now come-PRSPRT stay-PSTINDF

di-di
say-PAST

When I twisted her hands, she said: "I know her. Okay, I know her. She is supposed to come now (is about to come now)."

21. *edert-d-ip   ekel-er-men   de-p   amdɪ-gɪ urug*
lead-CAUS-CONV bring-PRSINDF-1SG say-CONV that-RELCL girl

žoru-y   bar-dɪ
walk-CONV go-PAST

That girl left saying: "I will bring her."

22. *osun men oyna-p   oyna-p   žan-ɪp   gel-di-m*
then I   play-CONV play-CONV return-CONV come-PAST-1SG

Then I returned after playing and playing around for a while.

23. *oson dagɪn xaba-ga bir urug bar   de-p   ešti-di-m*
then again Kaba-DAT one girl EXIST say-CONV hear-PAST-1SG

Then again, I heard that there is a girl in Kaba.

24. *ol ɪn-dɪg   eki žaaš   ɪndɪg žaagay di-di*
    she that-EQU good well.behaved such beautiful say-PAST

    They said that she is so good and well-behaved, and so beautiful.

25. *e oo bo žiŋxua-ga   bar-ayɪn de-p   at-ka*
    yes okay this Zhinghua-DAT go-1SG.IMP say-CONV horse-DAT

    mun-a   sal-ɪp   göžö-nü örlö-p   bar-a
    mount-CONV put-CONV street-ACC ascend-CONV go-CONV

    žɪt-sa-m   möŋküy kargɪš-dɪ
    lie-COND-1SG Möngküy meet-PAST

    "Yes, Good!" So I decided that I should go to visit this Zhinghua.
    I got on the horse and as I was ascending (going up) the street I
    met with Möngküy.

26. *oo gaya ba-ar-sen*
    hey where go-PRSINDF-2SG

    "Hey, where are you going?"

27. *xala-a   ba-ar-men*
    city-DAT go-PRSINDF-1SG

    "I am going to the city."

28. *o ɪnžan men de ba-ar-men*
    hey then I also go-PRSINDF-1SG

    "Hey, then I will go too."

29.   *erteŋgi gün gedeer möŋküy-ge   bar-sa-m   oy men*
next   day   after   Möngküy-DAT go-COND-1SG oh I

bar-a   al-bas   bol-du-m   žaa žıl-da
go-CONV able-NEGPRSPRT be-PAST-1SG new year-LOC

ba-ar   bol-ba-za-m   de-di
go-PRSPRT be-NEG-COND-1SG say-PAST

The next day when I went back to Möngküy, he said: "I couldn't
go. I might be able to go during the New Year."

30.   *oson men žagaa biči-p   ber-eyin   sen apar-ıp*
then I   letter write-CONV give-1SG.IMP you deliver-CONV

ber-ši   de-p   eptig   bičii saazın-ga žagaa
give-EMPH say-CONV convenient small paper-DAT letter

biči-p   ber-di   biči ool-dar-nıŋ
write-CONV give-PAST small child-PL-GEN

dekter-i-nen   or-gaš
notebook-3POSS-ABL tear.up-CONV

He said: "Then I will write a letter for you (to deliver). Could you
please deliver it?" After that he tore a page out of a small
children's notebook and he carefully wrote a letter on that small
piece of paper.

31.   *men bayagıdı xanas-ka   ba-ar-da   žibe-ge*
I   long.ago Kanas-DAT go-PRSPRT-LOC thing-DAT

bar-dı-m   da žaa žıl-ga žibe al-dı-m
go-PAST-1SG EMPH new year-DAT thing take-PAST-1SG

When I went to Kanas a long time ago, I went to the place (shop) and bought things for New Year.

32.　*žor-up*　*žor-sa-m*　　*bo mampıy de-p*　　*bir galžı*
　　go-CONV run-COND-1SG this Mampıy say-CONV one lunatic

　　bar　*ol kargıš-tı*
　　EXSIT he meet-PAST

　　While I was walking around, I ran into that lunatic guy named Mampiy.

33.　*o*　*gaylap žor-sen de-er-de*　　*adaš men*
　　hey where　run-2SG say-PRSPRT-LOC friend I

　　akkaba-nan gel-di-m　　　*di-di-m*
　　Akkaba-ABL come-PAST-1SG say-PAST-1SG

　　When he asked me: "Hey, what are you doing here?" I said: "My friend, I came from Akkaba."

34.　*ad-ıŋ*　　*gım de-er-de*　　*bolat bol- ur*
　　name-GEN who say-PRSPRT-LOC Bolat   be-PRSINDF

　　di-di-m
　　say-PAST-1SG

　　When he asked, what is your name, I told him it was Bolat.

35.　*tanı-ž-ıp*　　*soŋ bis-ter de*　*akkaba-ga*
　　know-REC-CONV after we-PL also Akkaba-DAT

　　ba-ar-bıs　　*di-di*　*ol*
　　go-PRSINDF-1PL say-PAST he

After getting acquainted, he said: "We will go to Akkaba some day as well."

36. *xanas-ka   ge-ep   gal-dɪ-m   sen amdɪ*
     Kanas-DAT come-CONV remain-PAST-1SG you   now

     oyna-t-pas-sen   be
     play-CAUS-NEGPRSINDF-2SG Q

     "I have come to Kanas (I am here in Kanas). Why don't you show me around now?"

37. *amdɪ gɪm-nan   xoožɪla-ž-ɪr-sen*
     now   who-INSTR speak-REC-PRSINDF-2SG

     "Now whom are you going to converse with?"

38. *kanas-ka   bod-um-ša   urug-lar murug-lar žibe izde-p*
     Kanas-DAT self-1SG-EQU girl-PL   RDP-PL   thing search-CONV

     gel-di- m
     come-PAST-1SG

     As for me, I came to Kanas to look for girls and so.

39. *mampɪy-ga kargɪž-ɪp   gal-gaš   žor-up*
     Mampiy-DAT meet-CONV remain-CONV walk-CONV

     gežee   oyun bol-du
     evening party be-PAST

     After hanging around with Mampiy, we went a party in the evening.

40. *oyun-ga   bar-dı-bıs*
     party-DAT go-PAST-1PL

     We went to the party.

41. *oyun-da göböy urug-lar dur irgin*
     party-LOC many   girl-PL   stay EVID

     There sure were many girls at the party.

42. *göböy urug-lar-nıŋ išd-i-nen   bir urug-nu*
     may   girl-PL-GEN   inside-3POSS-ABL one girl-ACC

     gıdı-ım-a   ekkel-p   ber-di
     side-1SG.POSS-DAT bring-CONV give-PAST

     (They) brought one girl among (from) the many girls next to me.

43. *se-eŋ   ad-ıŋ   gım*
     you-GEN name-2SG.POSS who

     "What is your name?"

44. *ayt-pas*
     say-NEGPRSINDF

     (She) does not tell.

45. *sura-za-m   sös   ayt-pas*
     ask-COND-1SG word say-NEGPRSINDF

     (She) does not say a word when I ask her.

46. *o mampıy bo žibe-ŋ   ünübey be*
     hey Mampiy this thing-2SG.POSS dumb   Q

"Hey, Mampiy, is this thing (girlfriend) of yours dumb?"

47.   *ünübey bol-sa   me-eŋ dıl-ım   bar*
       dumb   be-COND I-GEN tongue-1SG.POSS EXIST

"If she is dumb, I have a tongue (I am not dumb.)"

48.   *demgi ayt-kan-ıbıs   bar*
       specific say-PSTPRT-1PL.POSS EXIST

We have made a certain agreement.

49.   *güštüg-büs dı-di   üš   dört urug*
       strong-1PL   say-PAST three four girl

Three or four girls said: "We are strong."

50.   *ög-nüŋ   ard-ı-ŋga   bar-ıp bir bödölge aragı*
       house-GEN back-3POSS-DAT go-CONV one bottle   alcohol

       a-p   a-p   ındı-gı-ga   iž-ir-t
       take-CONV take-CONV that.one-RELCL-DAT drink-CAUS-CAUS

"Just take a bottle of vodka and go behind the house, have her drink it"

51.   *am žiŋxua   gayda de-di-m*
       now Zhinghua where say-PAST-1SG

I said: "Now, where is Zhinghua?"

52.   *ol ög-de   žoru-ur   bol-du*
       she home-LOC walk-PRSPRT be-PAST

She would be at home.

53. *demgi urug dɪp-kan   bol-dɪ ba bir eki dile-yin*
    same   girl find-PSTPRT be-PAST Q one good look.for-1SG.IMP

    žiŋxua   de-en   urug-nu
    Zhinghua say-PSTPRT girl-ACC

    Let me have a careful look to see if that girl has found the girl
    named Zhinghua.

54. *žiŋxua   de-en   urug-ni ekkel-p   ber-dɪ*
    Zhinghua say-PSTPRT girl-ACC bring-CONV give-PAST

    (They) brought the girl named Zhinghua.

55. *e de-p   bar-ɪp dud-up   al-dɪ-m*
    ok say-CONV go-CONV grab-CONV take-PAST-1SG

    I said: "Okay!" and went over and grabbed (her.)

56. *iyilee-ger xoožɪla-ž-gar de-p   žoru-y   bar-dɪ*
    both-2PL   chat-REC-2PL say-CONV walk-CONV go-PAST

    (She) left saying: "The two of you go ahead to talk to each other!"

57. *iyilee-en   gal-dɪ-bɪs*
    both-1PL   remain-PAST-1PL

    The two of us stayed.

58. *al dee-ni ayd-ɪr-men   mo-nu ayd-ɪr-men*
    well that-ACC say-PRSINDF-1SG this-ACC say-PRSINDF-1SG

    Well, I talk about this and talk about that.

59. *dee xaba-ɲan dura   se-eŋ   ad-ıŋ-nı*
     that Kaba-ABL straight you-GEN name-2SG.POSS-ACC

     dıŋna-aš-tan   izde-p   gel-di-m
     hear-CONV-ABL search-CONV come-PAST-1SG

     I came all the way straight from Kaba after hearing your name (to look for you).

60. *ol gandıg žaŋgıs giži   giži bol-bas   žaŋgıs*
     it how   single person person be-NEGPRSINDF single

     gezek   ot bol-bas
     charred.log fire be-NEGPRSINDF

     A single person cannot constitute a person and a single charred log cannot constitute (make) a fire. (A single person is no person, a single log cannot form a fire)

61. *se-ŋge deŋ giži izde-p   gel-di-m*
     you-DAT equal person search-CONV come-PAST-1SG

     I have came to look for a person (girl) like you.

62. *se-eŋ   ad-ıŋ-nı   dıŋna-aš-tan gel-di-m*
     you-GEN name-2SG.POSS-ACC hear-CONV-ABL come-PAST-1SG

     I came after I heard your name.

63. *sen-i   arnawlı izde-p   gel-di-m   xaba-nan*
     you-ACC intended search-CONV come-PAST-1SG Kaba-ABL

     I came from Kaba just to look for you.

64. *ɪ-ŋga   gandɪg de-er-sen*
     that-DAT how   say-PRSINDF-2SG

     What do you say (think) about it?

65. *urug-da ɪɪt   žok*
     girl-LOC sound NEGEXIST

     There is no sound from the girl. (The girl was silent.)

66. *žer   dɪrba-p   dur*
     earth plow-CONV stay

     (She) is scraping the dirt (with her foot).

67. *oy o-gar   dež-il-ip   gal-ɪr*
     hey it-2SG.POSS make.hole.in-PASS-CONV remain-PRSINDF

     Hey, that (shoe) of yours will get a hole.

68. *ɪnžal-ba-gar*
     do.thus-NEG-2SG.IMP

     (Please) don't do that.

69. *žer depse-p dur-up   al-dɪ*
     earth kick-CONV stay-CONV take-PAST

     She stood there (and) kept kicking the dirt.

70. *žer depse-p dur-sa-gar   bätiŋge-ŋ-niŋ*
     earth kick-CONV stay-COND-2SG shoe-2SG.POSS-GEN

     baž-ɪ   dež-il-ip   gal-ɪr
     head-3POSS make.holes.in-PASS-CONV remain-PRSINDF

If you keep kicking the ground, the toes of your shoes will get holes.

71.   *baž-ɪ-n   uušta-p dur-up   al-dɪ*
head-3POSS-ACC rub-CONV stay-CONV take-PAST

She stood there, rubbing her head.

72.   *ɪyɪ üš sagat žalɪn-dɪ-m*
two three hour   beg-PAST-1SG

I begged her for two or three hours.

73.   *adak   soo bol-du-bus*
at.the.end agree be-PAST-1PL

Finally we reached an agreement.

74.   *šɪn ba*
true Q

(It's) true?

75.   *šɪn*
true

(It's) true.

76.   *ekkel xol-uŋ-nu   de-p   xol tud-uš-tu-bus*
bring   hand-2POSS-ACC say-CONV hand hold-REC-PAST-1PL

(I) said: "Give me your hand!" and we grasped each other's hands.

77.   *kal-gan   aragɪ-nɪ   iž-ip   xoožɪla-ž-ɪp*
remain-PSTPRT alcohol-ACC drink-CONV converse-REC-CONV

ırla-ž-dı-bıs   iyi-le-en
sing-REC-PAST-1PL two-COLL-1PL

The two of us drank the leftover vodka, and we talked and sang together.

78. *dewde -mında-nı xoožıla-p baž-ıbıs-tın*
this.and.that-ACC   talk-CONV head-1PL.POSS-ABL

öt-kön-nü   xoožıla-p epdig   xoožıla-p bir talay
pass-PSTPRT-ACC talk-CONV carefully talk-CONV one quite.a.few

tanı-ž-ıp gal-dı-bıs
know-REC-CONV remain-PAST-1PL

We got to know each other quite well after we had thoroughly talked about this and that, about what had been passing through our head (in life).

79. *bo aldınčı ay-da   akkök   kud-up   xoožıla-ž-ıp*
this sixth   month-LOC white-blue pour-CONV speak-REC-CONV

ulug amtan-nar bar-ıp   kudalaž-ıp   gelir žıl
senior people-PL go-CONV become.in-laws-CONV next year

doy   žaza-dı-bıs
wedding make-PAST-1PL

This June, we decided to pour the white-blue to throw a party and the elders went there and we proposed our engagement and the next year we got married.

80. *o-dan soŋgaar da   bar-ıp dur-ar-bız*
it-ABL after   EMPH go-CONV stay-PRSINDF-1PL

Even after that (the wedding), we are still going there (visit them).

81.   *xanas-tɪŋ köl-ü-ŋge   bar-ɪp   uzun gužur-ga   bar-ɪp*
Kanas-GEN lake-3POSS-DAT go-CONV long Guzhur-DAT go-CONV

žay-ɪn   ba-ar-da   šimi aragɪ iž-er-bis
summer-INSTR go-PRSPRT-LOC milky drink drink-PRSINDF-1PL

We go to Lake Kanas and to the long Guzhur and we drink milky
vodka (milk-spirit) when we go there during the summer.

82.   *bo urug šimi aragɪ bol-ba-za   ažɪg aragɪ*
this girl   milky drink be-NEG-COND bitter drink

iš-pes
drink-NEGPRSINDF

This girl only drinks milky alcohol (milk-spirits), not bitter vodka.

83.   *men-nen šog-už-ar*
I-INSTR   strike-REC-PRSINDF

(She) fights with me.

84.   *monžak aragɪ iš-pes   irgin ele   gonžug*
Monchak drink drink-NEGPRSINDF EVID EMPH very

pa-pa
wow wow

"Wow, wow, that's great that Monchak doesn't drink!"

85.   *bo urug aragɪ iš-pes   emes   pe ɪnžaarda*
this girl   alcohol drink-NEGPRSINDF NEGCOP Q   therefore

men-nen sog-už-ar
I-INSTR   strike-REC-PRSINDF

Don't you know that this girl doesn't drink alcohol so she fights with me. (said sarcastically)

86.   *ınža-y   ınža-y   bot-tar-ı-nan   gadı   aragı*
thus.do-CONV thus.do-CONV self-PL-3POSS-INSTR together alcohol

iž-er   bol-du-m
drink-PRSPRT be-PAST-1SG

Gradually by doing so, I began to drink together with them (here he talks about his wife because she taught him how to drink.)

87.   *e   amdı eki*
hey now   good

Hey, now it's good.

88.   *žoor sanatoriya-ga bar-gay ı-ŋga bar-ıp*
uphill sanatorium-DAT go-CONV it-DAT go-CONV

xona-ar-bıs
spend.night-PRSINDF-1PL

We go to the hillside sanatorium and spend the night there.

89.   *köl-ge   eštir-ir-bis*
lake-DAT swim-PRSINDF-1PL

We swim in the lake.

90.   *ı-ŋga bar-ıp   pižiu iž-er-bis*
it-DAT go-CONV beer   drink-PRSINDF-1PL

We go there and drink beer.

91.   *ɪ-ŋga bar-gay oyna-ar-bɪs   žä bol-du*
       it-DAT go-CONV play-PRSINDF-1PL okay be-PAST

       We go there and play. Ok, that's it.

92.   *köl-ge   bar-ɪp   oyna-p   oyna-p   ge-er-bis*
       lake-DAT go-CONV play-CONV play-CONV come-PRSINDF-1PL

       We go to the lake and play around there then return.

93.   *biyle-r-bis   mozika-nɪn*
       dance-PRSINDF-1PL music-INSTR

       We dance with music.

94.   *loyɪnži   al-ɪr-bɪs*
       tape.recorder take-PRSINDF-1PL

       We bring a tape recorder.

95.   *taŋsa ɪn-dɪg   ɪn-dɪg   žibe-ge biyle-er-bis*
       dance that-EQU that-EQU thing-DAT dance-PRSINDF-1PL

       We do a sort of ballroom dance.

96.   *ulug ulug gɪžɪ-ler   bar-dɪ*
       senior senior person-PL go-PAST

       The elders went there.

97.   *bir egiči-m   bar*
       one elder.sister-1SG.POSS EXIST

I have an older sister.

98.   *oyna-ar*   *de-p*   *ol bar-dı*
        play-PRSINDF say-CONV she go-PAST

        She went there in order to play.

99.   *bir žeŋge-m*   *bar*
        one older.sister-in-law-1SG.POSS EXIST

        I have an older sister-in-law.

100.   *ol da bar-dı*
        she also go-PAST

        She also went.

101.   *nak ola-p*   *büd-ör*
        exact do.that-CONV end-PRSINDF

        It ends exactly like this.

102.   *kuda-nıŋ bod-u-nuŋ*   *ekkel de-en*   *žebe-zi-n*
        in.law-GEN self-3POSS-GEN bring   say-PRSPRT thing-3POSS-ACC

        loyınži   *sagat pälte*   *poburuk*   *de-en*   *šigi*
        tape.recorder watch overcoat   woolen.cloth say-PSTPRT like

        žibe-zi-n   *apar-ıp*   *be-er-bis*
        thing-3POSS-ACC deliver-CONV give-PRSINDF-1PL

        We bring along things like a tape recorder, watch, overcoat, and
        woolen cloth, things that our in-laws said to bring.

Folk tales

3. 1 "Old Lady Dektene"

Narrated by Bolat of Akkaba Village in September1995

1. *erte burun šag-da bir kara xalžan at-tɪg   dege*
   early before time-LOC one black blaze   horse-ADJ he.goat

   xalžan at-tɪg   dektene xoočun de-p   bir xoočun
   blaze   horse-ADJ Dektene old.lady say-CONV one old.lady

   bol-updur
   be-PNARR

   A long time ago, there was an old lady named Old Lady Dektene who h ad a h orse w ith a b lack b laze, a nd a h orse w ith a g oat (-shaped) blaze.

2. *dektene xoočun-nuŋ dege-si-n   sag-sa   sidi-i*
   Dektene old.lady-GEN he.goat-3POSS-ACC milk-COND urine-3POSS

   süt bol-ur   mɪya-a   aaršɪ   üs   bol-ur
   milk be-PRSINDF dung-3POSS curd.cheese butter be-PRSINDF

   When Old Lady Dektene milks her goat (-blazed horse), its urine becomes milk, and its feces becomes cheese and butter.

3. *on-u   kündölü ži-p   žoru-ur*
   it-ACC e veryday eat-CONV walk-PRSINDF

   She eats this everyday.

4. *bir žɪlgɪžɪ aškɪyak dege   xalžan at-tɪg   dektene*
   one horseman old.man he-goat blaze   horse-ADJ Dektene

xoočun-ga   ge-ep   dege xalžan at-tɪg   xoočun-nuŋ
old.lady-DAT come-CONV goat   blaze   horse-ADJ old.lady-GEN

üz-ü-n   ži-ir
butter-3POSS-ACC eat-PRSINDF

An old horse-herder comes to Old Lady Dektene who has the horse with a goat blaze and eats the butter of the old lady who has the horse with a goat blaze.

5. *üz-ü   ɪn-dɪg   taptɪg*
    butter-3POSS that-EQU   sweet

    (Her) butter is so tasty.

6. *aaršɪ-sɪ-n   ži-ir*
    cheese-3POSS-ACC eat-PRSINDF

    (He) eats (her) cheese.

7. *aaršɪ-zɪ   ɪn-dɪg   taptɪg*
    cheese-3POSS that-EQU   tasty

    (Her) cheese is so tasty.

8. *üy bo-nu   gaylap al-dɪr-dɪ-gar   gaday de-p*
    hey this-ACC where   take-CAUS-PAST-2PL auntie say-CONV

    sura-ar   ɪrgɪn
    ask-PRSINDF EVID

    "Hey, auntie! Where did you get this?" he asks her.

9.   *oy äkem   bo me-eŋ dege-m-niŋ   sidi-i   süt*
oh my.dear this I-GEN he.goat-1SG.POSS-GEN urine-3POSS milk

bol-ur   mɪya-a   aaršɪ bol-ur
be-PRSINDF dung-3POSS cheese be-PRSINDF

"Oh, my dear, the urine of this goat of mine becomes milk, and its feces becomes cheese."

10.   *oo de-p   gur-u-ŋga   oraa-p al-gaš xara*
oh say-CONV sash-3SG.POSS-DAT wrap-CONV take-CONV black

xat-tɪg xaan-ga apar-ɪp   be-er   irgin
berry-ADJ khan-DAT deliver-CONV give-PRSINDF EVID

Saying "Oh!", he wraps it up in his sash, takes it and brings it to the Black Berry Khan.

11.   *xara xat-tɪg   xaan dörtön šeri-i-n   ederd-ip*
black berry-ADJ khan forty   soldier-3POSS-ACC lead-CONV

gel-ir
come-PRSINDF

The Black Berry Khan comes leading his forty soldiers.

12.   *bödöne mun-up gel-geš-ten   xoošun-nu gɪy de-p*
quail   ride-CONV come-CONV-ABL old lady-ACC call say-CONV

ɪɪtta-ar   irgin
emit.sound-PRSINDF EVID

After he mounts his quail and comes, the Khan emits a cry: "Call the old lady at once!"

13.   *žılgıžı   aškıyak ge-ep   gıy de   de-er   irgin*
horseman old.man come-CONV call say-IMP say-PRSINDF EVID

The old horseman comes and says : "Call her (the old lady)!"

14.   *žüü bol-du ogl-um   de-er-de   xaan siler-ni*
what be-PAST son-1SG.POSS say-PRSPRT-LOC khan you.POL-ACC

gıy de-p   žıd-ır   de-er
call-CONV lie-PRSINDF say-PRSINDEF

When she says "What is it, my son?", he says "The Khan is calling you."

15.   *ol žügö gıy de-er*
he why call-PRSINDF

"Why he is calling (me)?"

16.   *ol me-eŋ dege-m-ni   gıy de-p dur ba de-eš-ten*
he I-GEN he.goat-1SG.POSS-ACC call-CONV stay Q say-CONV-ABL

gızıl tıt-tıŋ   žardı-zı-nan   seleme žaza-ar
red   larch.tree-GEN sliver-3POSS-ABL sword   make-PRSINDF

Afterwards she thinks, "Probably he is calling my goat (blazed horse)," she creates a sword from the needles of a red larch tree.

17.   *dörtön šeri-i-n   tögöle-p   ortu-zu-ŋga*
forty   soldier-3POSS-ACC surround-CONV middle-3POSS-DAT

dur-ar-da   dege xalžan ad-ı-nın
stand-PRSPRT-LOC he.goat blaze horse-3POSS-INSTR

bar-gaš-tan   dörtön šeri-i-n   gɪr-a
go-CONV-ABL forty   soldier-3POSS-ACC slaughter-CONV

gak-kaš   tük žok   ölür-üp ga-an   irgin
vanquish-CONV any NEGEXIST kill-CONV beat-PSTINDF EVID

When she stands in the middle of his forty soldiers surrounding her, she goes (among them) on the horse with the goat blaze, and cuts down his forty soldiers and kills them until none remain.

18. *xara xat-tɪg   xaan-nɪ gag-ar-da   xara xat-tɪg*
     black berry-ADJ khan-ACC hit-PRSPRT-LOC black berry-ADJ

     xaan-nɪŋ tayžɪ-zɪ   dez-er   irgin
     Khan-GEN crown.prince-3POSS flee-PRSINDF EVID

     When she knocks down the Black Berry Khan, the crown prince of the Black Berry Khan runs away.

19. *dez-e   olur-up dez-e   olur-up xara xat-tɪg*
     run-CONV sit-CONV run-CONV sit-CONV black berry-ADJ

     xaan-nɪŋ tayžɪ-zɪ-nɪŋ   edi-i   düš-köš-ten
     Khan-GEN crown.prince-3POSS-GEN boot-3POSS fall-CONV-ABL

     kek   bo-p   už-a   ba-ar   irgin
     cuckoo be-CONV fly-CONV go-PRSINDF EVID

     He runs and he runs, and because the boots of the crown prince of the Black Berry Khan fall off, he becomes a cuckoo and flies away.

20. *kek-tiŋ   daman-ɪ gɪzɪl bol-up gal-gan   irgin*
     cuckoo-GEN sole-3POSS red   be-CONV remain-PSTINDF EVID

The soles of the cuckoo became red and remained.

21. *oo-ŋ   gatın-ı-nıŋ   ala   torga   bo-p   už-a*
     he-GEN wife-3POSS-GEN colored woodpecker be-CONV fly-CONV

     ba-ar   ırgin tıt   sokta-p
     go-PRSINDF EVID larch.tree pound–CONV

     His (the crown prince's) wife becomes a multicolored woodpecker
     and flies away, pounding the larch tree.

22. *xara xat-tıg   xaan-nıŋ bod-u   dez-ip   olur-up*
     black berry-ADJ Khan-GEN self-3POSS run-CONV sit-CONV

     dez-ip   olur-up sug-lug žer-ge   gel-ir-de
     run-CONV sit-CONV water-ADJ place-DAT come-PRSPRT-LOC

     gara bodaŋ   bol-gaš-tan gara žer-ni   gaz-ıp   bodaŋ
     black wild.boar be-CONV-ABL black land-ACC dig-CONV wild.boar

     bo-p   žoru-y   ba-ar   ırgin
     be-CONV walk-CONV go-PRSINDF EVID

     Black Berry Khan runs and runs, and when he comes to a place
     with water he becomes a black boar, and digs at the black earth
     (ground) and goes along as a boar.

23. *dege xalžan at-tıg   dektene xoočun-nuŋ murnu-u-ŋga*
     goat blaze horse-ADJ Dektene old lady-GEN front-3POSS-DAT

     bir meyge xaya-nıŋ üsd-ü-ŋge   olur-up al-gaš-tan
     one meyge cliff-GEN top-3POSS-DAT sit-CONV take-CONV-ABL

žıyt žıyt de-p   ed-er   irgin
chirp chirp say-CONV utter.a.sound-PRSINDF EVID

In front of Old Lady Dektene who has a horse with a goat blaze, a meyge[12] perches down on a cliff, and begins chirping.

24.   *žed-er-iŋ-ge   žed-ip   al-gaš-tan   men-i*
      reach-PRSPRT-2SG.POSS-DAT reach-CONV take-CONV-ABL I-ACC

      elek gıl-ır-ga   žet-ti-ŋ   be de-eš-ten   tıt
      fun make-PRSPRT-DAT reach-PAST-2SG Q say-CONV-ABL larch.tree

      žardı seleme-zi-nin   meyge-ni ga-ar-da
      sliver sword-3POSS-INSTR meyge-ACC hit-PRSPRT-LOC

      meyge-m-niŋ   kuduru-u-n üz-güš-ten   dege
      meyge-1SG.POSS-GEN tail-3POSS-ACC tear-CONV-ABL he.goat

      xalžan ad-ı-n   žar-a   gag-gaš bod-u-nuŋ
      blaze   horse-3POSS-ACC split-CONV hit-CONV self-3POSS-GEN

      žaba-a-n   žar-a   gag-gaš ol žer-ge   ge-ep
      colt-3POSS-ACC split-CONV hit-CONV that place-DAT come-CONV

      dektene xoočun öl-üpdür
      Dektene old.lady die-PNARR

So she says "You've already reached as far as you want to reach, and now we've come to the point of making fun of me?" When she knocks down the *meyge* with her sword made of larch tree slivers, she tears off the tail of my *meyge*. After she has split in two the horse with the goat blaze and after she has split in two her own (quail's) colt, Old Lady Dektene comes to that place and dies.

---

[12] *meyge*: a kind of bird.

25. *osunun meyge-niŋ kuduru-u šolak bo-p gal-gan*
after.this meyge-GEN tail-3POSS short be-CONV remain-PSTINDF

irgin
EVID

And so the tail of the *meyge* became short.

26. *meyge-niŋ kuduru-u šolak bo-p xara xat-tɪg xaan-nɪŋ*
meyge-GEN tail-3POSS short be-CONV black berry-ADJ khan-GEN

bod-u bodaŋ bo-p tayžɪ-zɪ kek
self-3POSS wild.boar be-CONV crown.prince-3POSS cuckoo

bo-p daman-ɪ gɪzɪl bo-p irgin
be-CONV sole-3POSS red be-CONV EVID

The tail of the *meyge* became short, the body of the Black Berry Khan became a wild boar, the crown prince became a cuckoo, and its soles became red.

27. *gatɪn-ɪ torga bol-up ɪyaš sokta-p už-a*
wife-3POSS woodpecker be-CONV wood hit-CONV fly-CONV

ba-ar dur
go-PRSINDF EMPH

His wife became a woodpecker, and flies around pounding on trees.

3. 2 A blue gizzard sparrow with a multicolored waist

Narrated by Balzhin of Akkaba Village in September1987 in Urumchi

1.   *bir gök bödöge-lig beldir ala   kuškaš bo-p   dur*
      one blue gizzard-ADJ waist   multicolor sparrow be-CONV EMPH

      There was a sparrow with a blue gizzard and multicolored waist.

2.   *bir kün xaak-tɪŋ   baž-ɪ-ŋga   ge-ep*
      one day shrubbery-GEN head-3POSS-DAT come-CONV

      xon-ar-da   bödöge-zi   žar-ɪl-ɪp
      perch-PRSPRT-LOC gizzard-3POSS split-PASS-CONV

      gal-ɪr   irgin
      remain PRSINDF EVID

       One day its gizzard was punctured when it perched on the top of a
      shrub.

3.   *oson doŋgur öškü-gö ge-ep   me-eŋ*
      then   hornless goat-DAT come-CONV I-GEN

      bödöge-m-ni   žɪlga-p ber-in   de-er
      gizzard-1SG.POSS-ACC lick-CONV give-2POL.IMP say-PRSINDF

      irgin
      EVID

      Then i t c ame t o a h ornless g oat a nd s aid: "Lick m y gizzard f or
      me."

4.   *se-eŋ   bödöge-ŋ-ni   žılga-ba-y   ak   dur-gay*
     you-GEN gizzard-2SG.POSS-ACC lick-NEG-CONV EMPH stay-CONV

     ak   bod-um-nuŋ   iyis anay-ım-nıŋ   šarana-zı-n
     EMPH self-1SG.POSS-GEN twin kid-1SG.POSS-GEN placenta-3POSS-ACC

     žılga-y   al-bayın   dur-men de-er   irgin
     lick-CONV able-NEGCONV stay-1SG say-PRSINDF EVID

     (The goat) said: "Don't mention licking your gizzard, I was not
     even able to lick my twin kids' placenta bile."

5.   *osunda börü-gö gel-geš   bo öškü-nüŋ iyi anay-ı-n*
     then   wolf-DAT come-CONV this goat-GEN two kid-3POSS-ACC

     že de-er   irgin
     eat say-PRSINDF EVID

     Then it came to a wolf and said: "Eat the goat's two kids!"

6.   *oson börü öškü-ŋ-nüŋ   anay-ı-n   že-bey   ek*
     then   wolf goat-2POSS-GEN kid-3POSS-ACC eat-NEGCONV EMPH

     dur-gay ak   kudak-ta düš-kön   kazı-m-nı
     stay-CONV EMPH well-LOC fall-PSTPRT kazi-1SG.POSS-ACC

     že-y   al-bayın   dur-men de-er   irgin
     eat-CONV able-NEGCONV saty-1SG say-PRSINDF EVID

     Then the wolf said: "Don't mention eating your goat's kids, I was
     not even able to eat my *kazi*[13] that had fallen into the well."

     ---

     [13] *kazi* is the fat under a horse's ribs.

7.   *osunda ool-dar-ga gel-geš   ool-dar ool-dar bo börü-nü*
       then   child-PL-DAT come-CONV child-PL child-PL this wolf-ACC

       žar-gak   de-er   ırgın
       stab-2PL.IMP say-PRSINDF EVID

       Then it came to children and said: "Kids, kids, slaughter this
       wolf!"

8.   *se-eŋ börü-ŋ-nü   žar-bay   ak dur-ba-y*
       you-GEN wolf-2SG.POSS-ACC stab-NEGCONV EMPH stay-NEG-CONV

       ak   bod-ubuz-duŋ   šagaa-da   ad-ar
       EMPH self-1PL.POSS-GEN spring.festival-LOC shoot-PRSPRT

       ža-bıs-tı   žaza-p   al-bayın   dur-bus
       bow-1PL.POSS-ACC make-CONV able-NEGCONV stay-1PL

       de-er   ırgın
       say-PRSINDF EVID

       (They) said: "Don't mention killing off your wolf, we haven't
       even been able to make the bows that we will shoot with during
       the spring festival."

9.   *aškıyak aškıyak bo ool-dar-dı xak de-er-de*
       old.man old.man this child-PL-ACC hit   say-PRSINDF-LOC

       se-eŋ ool-dar-ıŋ-nı   xak-pay   ak
       you-GEN child-PL-2SG.POSS-ACC hit-NEGCONV EMPH

       dur-bay   ak bod-um-nuŋ   gazı-m-nı
       stay-NEGCONV EMPH self-1SG.POSS-GEN kazi-1SG.POSS-ACC

ködür-üp žada-p   *dur-men de-er*   *irgin*
carry-CONV be.unable-CONV stay-1SG say-PRSINDF EVID

When it (came to an old man and) said: "Old man, old man, beat the kids." (he) said: "Don't mention beating your kids, I am not even able to carry my own *kazi*."

10.   *güskö güskö bo aškıyak-tıŋ gazı-zı-n*   *sor*
    mouse mouse this old.man-GEN kazi-3POSS-ACC suck

    de-er   *irgin*
    say-PRSINDF EVID

It (came to a mouse and) said: "Mouse, mouse, suck the old man's *kazi*."

11.   *aškıyak-tıŋ gazı-zı*   *dur-bay*   *ak*
    old.man-GEN kazi-3POSS stay-NEGCONV EMPH

    bod-um-nuŋ   *gıš-kı*   *ži-ir*   *žem-im-ni*
    self-1SG.POSS-GEN winter-RELCL eat-PRSPRT food-1SG.POSS-ACC

    dažı-p   *žada-p*   *dur-men de-er*   *irgin*
    convey-CONV be.unable-CONV stay-1SG say-PRSINDF EVID

(The mouse) said: "Don't mention sucking the old man's *kazi*, I am even unable to convey my own food for the winter."

12.   *urug-lar urug-lar bo güskö-nüŋ gıš-kı*   *ži-ir*
    girl-PL   girl-PL   this mouse-GEN winter-RELCL eat-PRSPRT

    žem-i-n   *dažı-p*   *ber-ger*   *de-er-de*
    food-3POSS-ACC convey-CONV give-2PL.IMP say-PRSINDF-LOC

güskö-nüŋ žem-i   dur-bay   ak   bod-ubus-tuŋ
mouse-GEN food-3POSS stay-NEGCONV EMPH self-1PL.POSS-GEN

šagaa-da   ged-er   tabɪžak-ɪbɪz-dɪ
spring.festival-LOC wear-PRSPRT garment-1PLPOSS-ACC

žaza-p   žada-p   dur-buz de-er   irgin
make-CONV be.unable-CONV stand-1PL say-PRSINDF EVID

When it said: "Girls, girls, carry the winter food of the mouse",
the girls said: "Don't mention about (carrying) the food for the
mouse, we are not even able to make our own garments to wear
during the spring festival."

13. *xoošun-nar xoošun-nar bo urug-lar-nɪ bar-ɪp   xak*
old.lady-PL old.lady-PL   this girl-PL-ACC go-CONV hit

de-er-de   se-eŋ   urug-lar-ɪŋ   dur-ba-y   ak
say-PRSPRT-LOC you-GEN girl-PL-2SG.POSS stay-NEG-CONV EMPH

bod-um-nuŋ dü-üm-nü   sawa-b žada-p
self-1SG-GEN wool-1SG.POSS-ACC card-CONV be.unable-CONV

dur-men de-er   irgin
stay-1SG say-PRSINDF EVID

When it said: "Old ladies, old ladies, go beat up these girls.", the
old ladies said: "Don't mention (beating up) your girls, we are not
even able to card our own wool."

14. *gazɪrgɪ gazɪrgɪ bo xoošɪn-nar-nɪŋ ak dü-ü-n*
whirlwind whirlwind this old.lady-PL-GEN white wool-3POSS-ACC

dür-üp   ɪyaš-tɪŋ baž-ɪ-ŋga   šaš de-er-de
roll.up-CONV tree-GEN head-3POSS-DAT scatter say-PRSINDF-LOC

xoošun-nar-nıŋ dü-ü-n   *ıyaš-dıŋ baž-ı-nga*
old.lady-PL-GEN wool-3POSS-ACC tree-GEN head-3POSS-DAT

oraa-y   *šaž-ar*   *irgin*
wrap-CONV scatter-PRSINDF EVID

When it said: "Whirlwind, whirlwind, blow away these old ladies' white wool and scatter it in the tree!" (the whirlwind) wraps up (the white wool) and scatters it.

15.   *oson xoočun bar-gaš-tan uru-u-n*   *gag-ar*   *irgin*
then old.lady go-CONV-ABL girl-3POSS-ACC hit-PRSINDF EVID

Then the old lady goes there and beats her girls.

16.   *urug-lar bar-gaš-tan*   *güskö-nüŋ žem-i-n*
girl-PL   go-CONV-ABL mouse-GEN food-3POSS-ACC

dažı-ır   *irgin*
carry-PRSINDF EVID

The girls go there and carry (away) the mouse food.

17.   *güskö bar-ıp aškıyak-tıŋ gazı-zı-n*   *sor-ar*   *irgin*
mouse go-CONV old.man-GEN *kazi*-3POSS-ACC suck-PRSINDF EVID

The mouse goes there and sucks the old man's *kazi*.

18.   *aškıyak bar-gaš-tan ool-dar-nı gag-ar*   *irgin*
old.man go-CONV-ABL child-PL-ACC hit-PRSINDF EVID

The old man goes there and beats the boys.

19.   *ool-dar bar-gaš-tan   börü-nü ölür-ür   irgin*
       child-PL go-CONV-ABL wolf-ACC kill-PRSINDF EVID

       The boys go and kill the wolf.

20.   *börü bar-gaš-tan   doŋgur öškü-nüŋ iyi anay-ɪ-nɪŋ*
       wolf go-CONV-ABL hornless goat-GEN two kid-3POSS-GEN

       biri-si-n   ži-ir   irgin
       one.of-3POSS-ACC eat-PRSINDF EVID

       The wolf goes and eats one of the hornless goat's two kids.

21.   *doŋgur öškü bar-gaš-tan   gök bödögö-lüg*
       hornless goat go-CONV-ABL blue gizzard-ADJ

       kuškaš-tɪŋ bödöge-zi-n   žɪlga-ar   irgin
       sparrow-GEN gizzard-3POSS-ACC lick-PRSINDF EVID

       The hornless goat goes and licks the gizzard of the sparrow with
       the blue gizzard.

3. 3 Old man and old lady

Narrated by Erkit of Kaba county in September1995

1.   *erte erte burun ežen xaan zaman-ɪ-nan   da   burun*
      early early before Ezhen Khan time-3POSS-ABL EMPH before

      dɪr
      EMPH

      Once upon a time, it was even before the time of Ezhen Khan.

2.   *ertede   bo giži büd-üp   tur-gan-nan   soŋgaar*
in.olden.days this man form-CONV stay-PSTPRT-ABL after

In olden days after humans came into being.

3.   *bir daɣ   išd-i-nde   een   zer-de   iyi aškıyak*
one mountain inside-3POSS-LOC untended place-LOC two old.man

xoočun bo-p   dur di-dir
old.lady be-CONV stay say-EMPH

It is said that there were an old man and an old lady living in an
untended (deserted) place on a mountain.

4.   *ol aškıyak xoočun žudaŋ irgin*
that old.man old.lady poor   EVID

The old man and old lady were poor.

5.   *žudaŋ bol-gaš-tan   kündölögü emidirel žibe-zi-niŋ*
poor   be-CONV-ABL daily   life   thing-3POSS-GEN

ereydep   žaza-p   gımıyla-p dur-ar   irgin
barely.enough make-CONV live-CONV stay-PRSINDF EVID

Being poor, they eked out a bare living in their daily life.

6.   *o-oŋ bilen bir žöböree-nen ga-an   žaŋgıs žadır-ı*
it-GEN with   one bark-INSTR build-PSTPRT only   tent-3POSS

bar   irgin
EXIST EVID

They only had one tent, a single tent made of bark.

7.   *ald-ɪ-nga*   *döžön-gön-ü*   *žaŋgɪs la*
       underneath-3POSS-DAT pad-PSTPRT-3POSS only   EMPH

       gež-i   öškü gež-i   bar   irgin
       skin-3POSS goat   skin-3POSS EXIST EVID

       The pad they had underneath was a single piece of raw hide, a
       goat skin.

8.   *bir bagay ton-nar-ɪ*   *bol-sa   gerek*
       one bad   fur.line.coat-PL-3POSS be-COND necessary

       It so happened that they had a poorly-lined fur coat.

9.   *o-oŋ bilen bo aškıyak xoočun žeže   žɪl-dan beer*
       it-GEN with   this old.man old.lady several year-ABL since

       görgüzü-ü   urug da kin-i-nen   urug -tarɪg
       showing-3POSS child also navel-3POSS-ABL child.and.such

       bol-bayın   žoru-ur   irgin
       be-NEGCONV walk-PRSINDF EVID

       So for several years, the old man and old lady did not have
       children, did not have children of their own.

10.   *ol užun bo ganžaar bod-u   aškıyak xoočun urug-tarɪg*
       that for   this how   self-3POSS old.man old.lady child.and.such

       bol-ba-dɪ   o-nu ganžaar de-p   dur-ur   irgin
       be-NEG-PAST it-ACC how   say-CONV stay- PRSINDF EVID

       Therefore, the old man and old lady were wondering (why) they
       did not have children of their own and what they could do about it.

11.   *soŋ bis-tiŋ   ard-ıbıs-tan   erder-ir   ürösün*
       after we-GEN back-1PL.POSS-ABL follow-PRSPRT seed

       bol-ba-za   soŋ bis-tiŋ ürösün-übüs üsdü-ür
       be-NEG-COND later we-GEN seed-1PL.POSS be.broken.off-PRSPRT

       bol-du de-p   ıgla-p   sıkta-p   gara-a-nıŋ
       be-PAST say-CONV cry-CONV weep-CONV eye-3POSS-GEN

       žaž-ı   töz-ü   gurga-aš-ka   žedir ıgla-p   dur
       tear-3POSS all-3POSS dry-CONV-DAT till   cry-CONV stay

       Later (they thought that) if we do not have any descendent who
       follows behind us, we will be the last of our line, and they were
       crying and crying till (all) the tears in their eyes dried up.

12.   *bir kün ınža-p   tur-ar-da   am aškıyak*
       one day do.so-CONV stay-PRSINDF-LOC now old.man

       üŋgö-göš-dön aŋna-yın   de-p   ad-ı-n
       get.up-CONV-ABL hunt-1SG.IMP say-CONV horse-3POSS-ACC

       mun-gaš žor-up   ge-ep   žıd-ar-da   bir
       ride-CONV walk-CONV come-CONV lie-PRSPRT-LOC one

       ezim-nig žer-niŋ   gıdı-ı-nda   žöbüree-lig ıyaš-tıŋ
       wood-ADJ place-GEN side-3POSS-LOC bark-ADJ   tree-GEN

       ara-zı-nan   bir gerel   ün-üp
       middle-3POSS-ABL one radiance emerge-CONV

       dur-ar   irgin
       stay-PRSINDF EVID

One day, as usual, the old man got up and wanted to go hunting, and while he was riding along on his horse, a radiance (light) emerged from among the bark-covered trees at one side of the forest.

13.   *ırak-tan gö-ör-dü*   *žažıra-p*   *gerel* *ün-üp*
    afar-ABL see-PRSPRT-LOC strew-CONV radiance emerge-CONV

    dur-gan
    stay-PSTINDF

Looking from afar, one could see the radiance emanating and spreading in all directions.

14.   *bo gerel*   *žebe-niŋ gıdı-ı-ŋga*   *bar-sa*   *bir bižii urug*
    this radiance thing-GEN side-3POSS-DAT go-COND one small girl

    irgin
    EVID

As he came close to the radiance thing- it was a small girl.

15.   *bir on beš on aldı-ga gel-gen*   *bol-sa*   *gerek*
    one ten five ten six-DAT come-PSTPRT be-COND necessary

It looked like she was about fifteen or sixteen years old.

16.   *tın žok*   *žıd-ır*   *irgin*
    life NEG.EXIST lie-PRSINDF EVID

(She) was lying lifeless (dead).

17.   *on-ı ekkel-geš-ten aškıyak bo žübe bol-gan*   *bo*
    it-ACC bring-CONV-ABL old.man this what be-PSTINDF this

The old man said, "What happened?" as he was bringing her (down from the tree).

18. *giži bol-ur   de-eš-ten   ottu-u-nuŋ   od-u*
person be-PRSINDF say-CONV-ABL flint-3POSS-GEN fire-3POSS

   de-p   žibe-zi   bol-ur   diba-nıŋ burun amdı-gı
say-CONV thing-3POSS be-PRSINDF Tuva-GEN before now-RELCL

   sereŋge žibe žok   ža-ar   žibe žok
match   thing NEGEXIST kindle-PRSPRT thing NEGEXIST

   onsoonda ottu-u-n   ša-ap   kıpsı-r   irgin
then   flint-3POSS-ACC strike.fire-CONV light-PRSINDF EVID

   emes   pe
NEGCOP Q

Because he thought she might survive, he had a thing called steel-flint-fire. In the past, the Tuva did not have things like today's matches and lighters. Then he struck the flint and lighted it, wasn't it right.

19. *o uttu-nuŋ išd-i-ŋge   suk-kan   žanžı-ı-nıŋ*
that bag-GEN   inside-3POSS-DAT put-PSTPRT quiver-3POSS-GEN

   gıdı-ı-nda   bir aŋ-nıŋ   öd-ü-nön   žaza-an
side-3POSS-LOC one wild.game-GEN gall-3POSS-ABL make-PSTPRT

   em-i   bar irgin
drug-3POSS EXIST EVID

He had medicine made from the gall of wild game that he (usually) kept in that bag next to the quiver.

20.   *ga-ap   žoru-un*
       put-CONV walk-PSTINDF

He was keeping (it there.)

21.   *o amdɪ-gɪ   žibe-zi-n   al-gaš-tan   urug-nuŋ tɪn*
       that now-RELCL thing-3POSS-ACC take-CONV-ABL girl-GEN life

       žok   žɪt-kan   urug-nuŋ aas-ɪ-ŋga   iyi damdɪ
       NEGEXIST lie-PSTPRT girl-GEN mouth-3POSS-DAT two drop

       damzɪ-ɪr   irgin
       drip-PRSINDF EVID

He took (out) that very stuff of his and dropped two drops in the
mouth of the girl, the girl who was lying there without life
(lifeless).

22.   *osonda amdɪ-gɪ   urug bičii kezek-ten soŋgaar šimže-p*
       then   now-RELCL girl little time-ABL after   move-CONV

       tɪn gir-er
       life enter-PRSINDF

Then, after a little while, that girl moved and came back to life.

23.   *tɪn gir-geš-ten   ol domaktan-ɪr*
       life enter-CONV-ABL she speak-PRSINDF

After she revived she spoke.

24.   *gör-se amdɪ iyi gara-a   gör-bös   irgin*
       see-COND now two eye-3POSS see-NEGPRSINDF EVID

As he looked at (her), (he found out that) her two eyes were blind.

25. *o-oŋ   bilen amdɪ-gɪ   aškɪyak uškar-ɪp*
it-GEN with now-RELCL old.man carry.in.front.of.the.horse-CONV

a-p   murnuu-ga ö-ö-ŋge   a-p
take-CONV front-DAT   home-3POSS-DAT take-CONV

gel-er   irgin
come-PRSINDF EVID

So, that old man carried her in front of him and brought her home.

26. *žä xoočun bögün men arga išd-i-nen   mɪn-dɪg*
well old.lady today I   forest inside-3POSS-ABL this-EUQ

mɪn-dɪg bɪr urug ta-p   al-dɪ-m
this-EUQ one girl   find-CONV take-PAST-1SG

"Ok, old lady, today I found such and such girl in the forest."

27. *bo da bɪr kurmusdu-nuŋ alday-nɪŋ me-ŋge ber-gen*
this also one heaven-GEN   Altay-GEN I-DAT   give-PSTINDF

biz-ke ber-gen   buyan-ɪ   kep-dig
we-DAT give-PSTINDF fortune-3POSS form-ADJ

This looks like a fortune that was given to me, to us, by the Heavenly Altay (God.)

28. *mo-nu azɪra-gay   de-p*
this-ACC adopt-1PL.IMP say-CONV

He said: "Let's adopt this (her.)"

29.   *gežee   bol-gan-nan   soŋgaar amdɪ-gɪ   urug-nu ge-ep*
      evening be-PSTPRT-ABL after   now-RELCL girl-ACC come-CONV

      žɪt-kɪr-ɪp   gag-sa   düne   amdɪ bo urug-nuŋ butkun
      lie-CAUS-CONV put-COND at.night now   this girl-GEN whole

      magamud-u-nan gerel   örlö-n-ör
      body-3POSS-ABL radiance emit-REFL-PRSINDF

      After it had become evening and as they came to put that girl to
      sleep, a radiance emanated from the whole body of this girl now at
      night.

30.   *ol gerel   kün-de örlö-n-ör   irgin*
      that radiance day-LOC emit-REFL-PRSINDF EVID

      That radiance emanates every day.

31.   *ol gerel-de amdɪ-gɪ   xoočun-nuŋ gara-a*
      that light-LOC now-RELCL old.lady-GEN eye-3POSS

      gör-bös   bo-za   da   gerel-de düne   siir-nen
      see-NEGPRSPRT be-COND EMPH light-LOC at.night sinew-ABL

      žaza-an   udazɪn žibe-zi-nen   ton
      make-PSTPRT string   thing-3POSS-INSTR fur-lined.coat

      žibe-zi-n   daara-p etik-kep   daara-p
      thing-3POSS-ACC sew-CONV all.kinds.of.clothing sew-CONV

      xoočun kün-de emdirel öt-küz-ör   irgin
      old.lady day-LOC life   pass-CAUS-PRSINDF EVID

In that light, at night, that old lady would sew lambskin garments and all kinds of clothing with bowstring made of sinew even though her eyes couldn't see anything. The old lady spends her everyday life (like this.)

32. *kündüs gara-a   gör-bö-ze   de   düne   ol   gerel-den*
daytime eye-3POSS see-NEG-COND EMPH at.night that light-ABL

ınža-ap   daara-p   dur
do.thus-CONV sew-CONV stay

Even though she cannot see during the day, she is sewing thus at night by that light

33. *o-oŋ   bilen bir žeže   žıl öd-üp   urug-nu azıra-p*
it-GEN with one several year past-CONV girl-ACC raise-CONV

žad-ar-da   bir aŋžı žalıı   gel-er   aŋna-p
lie-PRSPRT-LOC one hunter young.man come-PRSINDF hunt-CONV

When several years had passed, one young man, a hunter came hunting, while they were raising the girl.

34. *o-oŋ   at-kan   o-o   žer-de   gal-bas*
he-GEN shoot-PSTPRT arrow-3POSS earth-LOC remain-NEGPRSINDF

ın-dıg žalıı   irgin
that-EQU young.man EVID

He was such a young man that his arrows would never drop on the ground when he shoots.

35. *o-oŋ   bilen bo žalıı   gel-geš-ten   urug-ga*
it-GEN with this young.man come-CONV-ABL girl-ACC

kööl   düž-üp   gal-ır   irgin
feeling fall-CONV stay-PRSINDF EVID

Then, when this young man came, he fell in love with this girl.

36.   *o-oŋ bilen kööl düž-üp   gal-gan-ı-n   aškıyak*
it-GEN with feeling fall-CONV stay-PSTPRT-3POSS-ACC old.man

xoočun bil-geš-ten   ol iyi ög   kuda bo-p
old.lady know-CONV-ABL that two family in-laws become-CONV

amdı-gı   urug-nu amdı-gı žalıı-ga   be-er
now-RELCL girl-ACC now-RELCL young.man-DAT give-PRSPRT

bol-gaš-tan   iyilee-zi-ni   öglen-dir-ip
be-CONV-ABL two.of.them-3POSS-ACC be.married-CAUS-CONV

a-p   dur di-dir
take-CONV stay say-EMPH

Then, after the old man and the old lady found out that he had fallen in love with her, the two families became in-laws, and after (they) had given (married) that girl to that young man, they had the two of them get married, so they say.

37.   *iyilee-zi-n   oolgu-up a-p   dur*
both-3POSS-ACC adopt-CONV take-CONV stay

öglön-dür-göš-tön
be.married-CAUS-CONV-ABL

They adopted the two of them after their marriage.

38.   *o-oŋ bilen o žalıı   da gežee irgin*
it-GEN with that young.man also diligent EVID

After all, the young man was also diligent.

39. *aŋ   žibe-ni   göböy ad-ar   irgin*
    wild.game thing-ACC many   shoot-PRSINDF EVID

He hunts a lot of wild game and so.

40. *aŋ-nıŋ   geš žibe-zi-nen   et žibe   daara-ar   irgin*
    game-GEN skin thing-3POSS-ABL belongings sew-PRSINDF EVID

They sew useful belongings out of the wild game skins and so.

41. *o-oŋ bilen töz-ü   ton   zibe daara-p ged-ip*
    it-GEN with all-3POSS fur.coat thing sew-CONV wear-CON

    edik biž-ip   daara-p ged-ip   de-en   šigi
    boot cut.out-CONV sew-CONV put.on-CONV say-PSTPRT like

    xoočun urug töz-ü   ın-dıg   isker   irgin
    old.lady girl all-3POSS that-EQU dexterous EVID

Then, all of them sewed fur line coats and wore them, they cut out
boots, sewed them, and put them on. Both the old lady and the girl
were so dexterous.

42. *töz-ü   žibe žaza-ar*
    all-3POSS thing make-PRSINDF

They make everything.

43. *emdirel-i-n öt-küz-üp   mal   žibe azıra-p   aray*
    life-3POSS-ACC pass-CAUS-CONV livestock thing raise-CONV slowly

    aray emdirel-i seere-p   kün-nön kün-gö seere-en
    slowly life-3POSS better-CONV day-ABL day-DAT improve-PSTINDF

They spend their lives raising livestock and their life slowly improved and their living conditions became better and better day-by-day.

44.　*buruŋ-gu　ıyaš žöbüree žadır-lıg ö-ö-n*
　　before-RELCL wood bark　　tent-ADJ　house-3POSS-ACC

　　töz-ü-n　　ga-aš-tan　　　eki žaagay ıyaš-tar-nan
　　all-3POSS-ACC abandon-CONV-ABL good pretty　wood-PL-ABL

　　ög-lör　ga-ap　　dur di-dir
　　house-PL build-CONV stay say-EMPH

They abandoned all of their previous wood bark tent houses and built pretty and good houses out of new wood.

45.　*emidirel-i kün-nön kün-gö eki bol-gaš-dan　urug saattıg*
　　life-3POSS day-ABL　day-DAT good be-CONV-ABL girl　pregnant

　　bo-p　　　urug-tarıg-lıg bo-p　　　ınžaŋgaštan bolar
　　become-CONV children-ADJ　become-CONV therefore　　they

　　šaa žadıra-p　　žaagay emidirel-di öt-küz-üp-tür
　　time flourish-CONV better　life-ACC　　pass-CAUS-PNARR

　　di-dir
　　say-PRT

After their lives had become better from day to day, the girl became pregnant and they had children and, therefore, their lives flourished and they spent good lives (lived a good life), so they say.

46.　*bo sonda žurt išd-i-nde　　o da bol-sa deedis*
　　this then　people inside-3POSS-LOC that also be-COND heaven

xurmustu burgan-nıŋ ber-gen   *žayan-ı-n*   *mın-dıg*
Kurmustu Buddha-GEN give-PSTPRT fortune-3POSS-ACC this-EQU

irgin de-er   *bir sös ülögür žibe-ler gal-gan*
EVID say-PRSINDF one word tale   thing-PL remain-PSTINDF

irgin di-dir
EVID say-PRT

After that, a saying or tale remained among the people saying thus
it was (good) fortune bestowed from Heaven, Kurmustu[3] and
Buddha if it is (like) this, so they say.

3. 4 Shanagash Hunters

Narrated by Chilinggi of Kaba county in September1995

1.   *bis-tiŋ alday dıba-lar-ı-nda*   *šanagaš de-p*   *bir söök*
     we-GEN Altya Tuva-PL-3POSS-LOC Shanagash say-CONV one bone

     bol-gan
     be-PSTINDF

     There had been a bone clan[4] named Shanagash among our Altay
     Tuvans.

2.   *šanagaš žurd-u*   *burun-nan tenek de-p*
     Shanagash people-3POSS before-ABL fool   say-CONV

     ayd-ıl-ıp   *žoru-gun*   *žurt-tan*   *biri-zi*
     tell-PASS-CONV walk-PSTPRT people-ABL one.of-3POSS

---

[3] Kurmustu: the chief of the thirty-three gods.
[4] Among many peoples in Central Eurasia, the word for bone also means clan, hence the
translation "bone clan." (e.g. Kazak, Mongols, Tibetans, etc.)

The Shanagash people are one of the peoples said to be fools since long ago.

3. *bir šag erte-de iyi šanagaš adaš bo-p*
    one time early-LOC two Shanagash friend become-CONV

    aŋ-ga   ün-üp   dur-gun   irgin
    wild.game-DAT go.out-CONV stay-PSTINDF EVID

    One time in the past (once upon a time), two Shanagash became friends and went out hunting.

4. *žer-ge aŋna-p žoru-uš iyi žibe bir žeže kün*
    place-DAT hunt-CONV walk-CONV two thing one several day

    aŋna-za   da   aŋ žibe kar-gıš-payın   dur
    hunt-COND EMPH game thing encounter-CONV-NEGCONV stay

    irgin
    EVID

    As they hunted at places, the two fellows did not encounter any (wild) game even though they were hunting there for several days.

5. *o-oŋ bilen künösün žibe-zi-n   doos-tu-p   bir*
    it-GEN with food.supply thing-3POSS-ACC finish-CAUS-CONV one

    kün gežee gož-u-nga   šay xayın-dır-ıp   iž-ip
    day evening tent-3POSS-DAT tea boil-CAUS-CONV drink-CONV

    dur-gaš iyilee-zi iyi at-tı   goš-tıŋ gıdı-ı-nga
    stay-CONV both-3POSS two horse-ACC tent-GEN side-3POSS-DAT

    ezer-lig at-tı   sal-ıp   gag-sa   gerek
    saddle-ADJ horse-ACC place-CONV put-COND necessary

When, they had finished up the food supplies (they ran out of food supply) and one evening as they were boiling (making) tea and were drinking it, (it) so happened that (they) had left their two horses with the saddles near (next to) their tent.

6.   *o-oŋ bilen kün čala xaraŋgıla-p ba-ar žıd-ar-da*
       it-GEN with   day half get.dark-CONV go-PRSPRT lie-PRSPRT-LOC

     ot-tuŋ žırıg-ı-nan biri-zi gör-gün bolgayax
     fire-GEN light-3POSS-ABL one.of-3POSS see-PSTPRT supposedly

As it became half dark, supposedly one of them saw (something) through the firelight.

7.   *bir xara ala   xaŋgırla-an xoŋgura-an bir žibe-niŋ*
      one black multicolored ring-PSTPRT jingle-PSTPRT one thing-GEN

     žor-ur-u-n   gör-gün
     walk-PRSPRT-3POSS-ACC see-PSTINDF

He saw a black multicolored thing walking (around), with ringing and jingling sounds.

8.   *o-oŋ bilen ol gıdı-ı-nda-gı   ež-i-ŋge*
      it-GEN with   he side-3POSS-LOC-RELCL friend-3POSS-DAT

     ayd-ır   ırgın
     say-PRSINDF EVID

Then he told it to his friend beside him.

9.   *ezer-lig žonak-tıg   bol-ur   ba*
     saddle-ADJ saddle.flap-ADJ be-PRSINDF Q

Would there be (a creature) that has a saddle and a saddle flap?

10.   *xaŋgɪrlɪg xuŋgurlug bol-ur   ba*
       ringing   jingling   be-PRSINDF Q

       Would there be (a creature) that makes ringing and jingling sounds?

11.   *ala-lɪg   xula-lɪg   bol-ur   ba*
       multicolored- ADJ light.bay- ADJ be-PRSINDF Q

       Would there be (a creature) that is multicolored and light bay?

12.   *gɪdɪ-ɪ-nda-gɪ   ež-i   bol-ur   la*
       side-3POSS-LOC-RELCL friend-3POSS be-PRSINDF EMPH

       de-en   ɪrgɪn
       say-PSTINDF EVID

       His friend next to him said: "Yes, there is."

13.   *o-oŋ bilen gɪdɪ-ɪ-nda-gɪ   ež-i   dälde-p*
       it-GEN with side-3POSS-LOC-RELCL friend-3POSS take.aim-CONV

       ad-ar   bo-p   dur ɪrgɪn
       shoot-PRSPRT be-CONV stay EVID

       Then, his friend next to him was about to take aim and shoot.

14.   *šuluun boo-nu al de-p   dur*
       quick   rifle-ACC take say-CONV stay

       He said: "Quick, pick up the rifle!"

15.   *o-oŋ bilen gɪdɪ-ɪ-nda-gɪ   dur-gan   ež-i*
       it-GEN with side-3POSS-LOC-RELCL stay-PSTPRT friend-3POSS

boo-zu-n   al-a   sal-a   mees-te-gi
rifle-3POSS-ACC take-CONV lay-CONV sunny.side-LOC-RELCL

dur-gan   xara baran-nɪ   xara bɪdɪra-zɪ-nan
stay-PSTPRT black silhouette-ACC black shotgun-3POSS-INSTR

ün-dür-üp   dur
go.out-CAUS-CONV stay

Then, his friend beside him grasped his rifle immediately and fired at the black silhouette on the sunny side of the hill with his black shotgun.

16.   *o-oŋ bilen iyi žebi žügür-üp bar-sa   xara ala*
it-GEN with two thing run-CONV go-COND black dappled

ezer-lig   at   irgin di-dir
saddle-ADJ horse EVID say-EMPH

So, as the two friends ran out, the black dappled thing was the horse with the black saddle, so it is told.

3. 5 Shaman healers

Narrated by Chilinggi of Kaba Village in September1995

1.   *žä bo eter erte bo zaman-nɪŋ zaman-ɪ-nda   bo dɪba*
well this early early this time-GEN   time-3POSS-LOC this Tuva

žer-i-nde   xam baxšɪ žibe-ler bol-gan   irgin
place-3POSS-LOC shaman healer thing-PL be-PSTINDF EVID

Well, a long, long time ago, in the time of times, there were shamans, healers and such people in this Tuvan land.

2.   *o-oŋ   bilen bo erte šag-da   bo aarɪg-doorug amtan*
it-GEN with   this early time-LOC this illness.disease people

išd-i-nde   göböy bo-p   dur
inside-3POSS-LOC many   be-CONV stay

Then, in this early time, there were many diseases and illnesses among the people.

3.   *o-oŋ bilen bo xam   baxšɪ-lar ge-ep*
it-GEN with   this shaman healer-PL come-CONV

xamna-ar   irgin gürümnö-ör   irgin
shamanize-PRSINDF EVID exorcize-PSTINDF EVID

Then, these shamans and healers would come shamanize and exorcize (it).

4.   *giži-ler   keybire-zi ekir-ip   žɪd-ar   irgin*
people-PL some-3POSS be.cured-CONV lie- PRSINDF EVID

Some people were cured.

5.   *žamdɪg biri-zi   ekir-bey   öl-üp   žɪd-ar*
some   one.of-3POSS be.cured-NEGCONV die-CONV lie- PRSINDF

irgin
EVID

Some were not cured and died.

6.   *ol šag-da   bo emži-domžu   bo dogdur de-p*
that time-LOC this physicians.and.such this doctor   say-CONV

zibe bol-bas
thing be-NEGPRSINDF

At that time, there were no such people as physicians and doctors.

7. *o-oŋ bilen ol žurt-tuŋ   iš-i-nde-gi   keybir bičii göp*
    it-GEN with this people-GEN inside-3POSS-LOC some   little many

    gör-gön   amtan-nar bo xam-baxšɪ keybire-si-n
    see-PSTPRT people-PL   this shaman healer some-3POSS-ACC

    ekir-t-ip   žɪd-ɪr   bo keybire-si žüge
    be.cured-CAUS-CONV lie-PRSINDF this some-3POSS why

    ekir-bes   de-er
    cure-NEGPRSINDF say-PRSINDF

    Then, those among the people who had seen a little bit more (had
    experienced more various vicissitudes of life) questioned why the
    shamans and healers only cured some of them and not the others.

8. *olar-ga güdük gümänen-er   ɪrgin*
    they-DAT doubt suspect-PRSINDF EVID

    They doubted and suspected them (shamans and healers).

9. *o-oŋ bilen bir xam   baxšɪ o-oŋ išd-i-nde   bir*
    it-GEN with   one shaman healer it-GEN inside-3POSS-LOC one

    gürümži bol-sa   gerek
    exorcist   be-COND necessary

    However, it turned out that there was a shaman healer among
    them who was very skilled in exorcisms.

10.   *bir kün biri-niŋ   ool-u   aarı-p   ga-ap   dur*
one day one.of-GEN son-3POSS be.sick-CONV remain-CONV stay

One day, someone's son got sick.

11.   *o-ŋga xaaš de-en   bo-za gerek*
he-DAT cold   touch-PSTPRT be-COND necessary

It looks like he caught a cold.

12.   *ol ö-ö-ŋgö   bar-ıp ol xon-ar   irgin*
that house-3POSS-DAT go-CONV he spend.night- PRSINDF EVID

He went to that house and spent the night there.

13.   *emne-p   domna-p de-en   šigi o-nu   gürümnö-p*
cure-CONV treat-CONV say-PSTPRT like he-ACC exorcize-CONV

dom   šübö-zü-n   žibele-p xamna-p
incantation thing-3POSS-ACC do-CONV shamanize-CONV

gürümnö-p   ınža-ar   irgin
exorcize-CONV do.that-PRSINDF EVID

(The Shaman) tried to cure and treat him by exorcizing and doing incantations and shamanizing and exorcizing.

14.   *žazal žibe-zi-n   žaza-ar   irgin*
zhazal thing-3POSS-ACC make-PSTINDF EVID

He made his *zhazal*[16] stuff.

15.   *gežee xon-ar-da   ol ög ee-zi   bir*
evening spend.night-PRSPRT-LOC that house owner-3POSS one

---

[16] *zhazal*: things that are made of dough to represent genies and devils or Satan.

žem   žibe žaza-p   et   žibe dül-üp   ınžal-gan
meal thing make-CONV meat thing stew-CONV do.that- PSTINDF

irgin
EVID

While he was spending the night (there,) the owner of that house
made a meal, stewing meat and such.

16.   *geže   xon-up   dur*
      evening spend.night-CONV stay

He spent the night there.

17.   *xon-up   bol-gaš bo amtan-nar-ga men*
      spend.night-CONV be-CONV this people-PL-DAT I

      bod-um   sen-dir-eyin   de-p   xam-baxšı
      self-1SG.POSS believe-CAUS-1SG.IMP say-CONV shaman.healer

      görümžı daŋ bilen dur-up   al-gaš   olar-ga bir
      exorcist dawn with get.up-CONV take-CONV they-DAT one

      xooču ayd-ır   irgin ög   ee-zi-ŋge
      story tell-PRSINDF EVID house owner-3POSS-DAT

After spending the night there, the shaman healer exorcist got up
at dawn and thought, "I should convince these people myself;"
and he told a story to the house owner.

18.   *žä se-eŋ ogl-uŋ-nu   aar-dı-p   dur-gan*
      ok you-GEN son-2SG.POSS-ACC fall.sick-CAUS-CONV stay-PSTPRT

      bir baška žibe emes   irgin
      one other thing NEGCOP EVID

"Okay, there is nothing else that is causing your son to be sick."

19.   *dün mɪ-ŋga iyi šulmus gel-di   de-er   irgin*
       night this-DAT two devil   come-PAST say-PRSINDG EVID

He said: "Last night two devils came here."

20.   *ol iyi šulmus amtan udu-un   soŋ ežik-ti až-ɪp*
       that two devil   people sleep-PSTPRT after door-ACC open-CONV

       gir-di
       enter-PAST

Those two devils opened the door and entered after the people had
gone to sleep.

21.   *gir-geš-ten   gel-geš-ten   düün   gežee sener*
       enter-CONV-ABL   come-CONV-ABL yesterday evening you.PL

       meŋ-ge dül-üp   ber-gen   et-ten   gal-gan
       I-DAT   stew-CONV give-PSTPRT meat-ABL remain-PSTPRT

       mün-nüŋ üsd-ü-nde-gi   xorgun-ga oyna-dɪ
       broth-GEN top-3POSS-LOC-RELCL fat-DAT   play-PAST

       de-p   ayd-ɪr   irgin
       say-CONV say-PRSINDF EVID

He told (them): "After they had come and entered, they played on
the fat that was on the surface of the broth that was left over from
yesterday evening's meat that you stewed for me."

22.   *o-oŋ bilen ol xorgan-ga oyna-p   dur-gaš-tan*
       it-GEN with   that fat-DAT   play-CONV stay-CONV-ABL

biri-zi-niŋ   *daman-ı*   *xorgun-ga gir-e*   *bar-dı*
one.of-3POSS-GEN sole-3POSS fat-DAT   enter-CONV go-PAST

de-er   *irgin*
say-PRSINDG EVID

He said: "Then, when they were playing on the fat, one them sank his feet into the broth."

23.   *xorgun-ga gir-geš*   *o-oŋ išd-i-nde*   *o-oŋ bir*
fat-DAT   enter-CONV it-GEN inside-3POSS-LOC it-GEN one

bopu-u   *düž-üp*   *gal-dı*   *de-p*   *dur*
bootee-3POSS fall-CONV remain-PAST say-CONV stay

He said: "When (his feet) sank into the fat, one of his bootees came off in the (fat)."

24.   *mege bol-sa*   *gör-gür*   *de-eš-ten*   *bar-ıp*   *paš-ta-gı*
false   be-COND see-2PL.IMP say-CONV-ABL go-CONV pot-LOC-RELCL

xorgun-nu aš-kaš   *bod-u*   *düün-dö-gü*   *su-up*
fat-ACC   open-CONV self-3POSS night-LOC-RELCL insert-CONV

go-on   *bižii bir amtan-nıŋ*   *gidis-ten žaza-an*   *bir*
put-PSTPRT small one person-CONV felt-ABL make-PSTPRT one

bopu-u-n   *uštu-p*   *ekkel-ir*   *irgin*
bootee-3POSS-ACC dredge.up-CONV bring-PRSINDF EVID

After telling (this): "If (you think) it's a lie, then see," he went and moved aside the fat in the pot, and dredged up a little person's bootee that was made of felt which he himself had put there during the night, and brought it out.

25. *bo amtan šın ba äle   de-er-de   šın de-p*
     this people true Q EMPH say-PRSPRT-LOC true say-CONV

     ınža-ar   ırgın
     thus.do- PRSINDF EVID

     When this person said, "Is it really true?", the Shaman said: "It is
     true."

26. *o-oŋ bilen ıyi šulmus de-p   ayd-ıp   gel-geš-ten*
     it-GEN with two devil   say-CONV tell-CONV come-CONV-ABL

     dee aar-ıp   žıt-kan   ool-duŋ bir xaay-ı-ŋga
     that become.sick-CONV lie-PSTPRT boy-GEN one nose-3POSS-DAT

     teresin   sug-du
     needle.grass insert-PAST

     Then, after he had told about the two devils, he said: "They came
     to that sick boy and inserted a needle grass into one of his nostrils.

27. *teresin   sug-ar-da   ol bıškır-ıp ıt-tı*
     needle.grass insert-PRSPRT-LOC he sneeze-CONV blow-PAST

     de-er   ırgın
     say-PRSINDF EVID

     He sneezed and blew the needle grass out when they were trying
     to insert it."

28. *o-oŋ baza bir xaay-ı-ŋga   teresin   su-up*
     it-GEN and one nose-3POSS-DAT needle.grass insert-CONV

     žıd-ar-da   men o-nu ür-üp
     lie-PRSPRT-LOC I   it-ACC blow-CONV

dere-en-im-de　　　　　　*iyi šulmus žašta-y*　　　*bar-dı*
send-PSTPRT-1SG.POSS-LOC two devil　　spatter-CONV go-PAST

When they were inserting the needle grass into the other nostril, I blew on them and the two devils spattered away.

29.　*ol žan-a*　　　*bar-dı*
　　it return-CONV go-PAST

　　They ran away (immediately).

30.　*ün-ö*　　　*bar-gaš-tan žoru-y*　　*bar-gaš-tan iyi šulmus*
　　go.out-CONV go-CONV-ABL walk-CONV go-CONV-ABL two devil

　　bir-i-ŋge　　*bir-i*　　*ayd-ıp*　　*žıd-ır*　　　*di-dir*
　　one-3POSS-DAT one-3POSS say-CONV lie-PRSINDF say-EMPH

　　As they went out and ran away, one of the two devils told the other one, so he said.

31.　*ol ög-nüŋ*　　*ee-zi-niŋ*　　　*ad-ı*　　　*bayterek*
　　that house-GEN owner-3POSS-GEN name-3POSS Bayterek

　　bol-sa　　*gerek*
　　be-COND necessary

　　It looks like the name of the house owner was Bayterek.

32.　*bayterek-tiŋ ö-ö-nde*　　　*bopu-um*　　　*gal-dı*
　　Bayterek-GEN house-3POSS-LOC bootee-1SG.POSS remain-PAST

　　sıŋsalıx bir šulmus ayd-ıp　　*žıd-ır*　　　*di-dir*
　　Singsalix one Satan　　say-CONV lie-PRSINDF say-EMPH

He (the shaman) said that one devil was telling the other one:
"Singsalix, one of my bootees remained at Bayterek's house."

33. *ol bir šulmus-tuŋ ad-ı   sıŋsalıx irgin de-p*
     that one devil-GEN   name-3POSS Singsalix EVID say-CONV

     ayt-tı   di-dir
     tell-PAST say-EMPH

     He (the shaman) said: "One devil's name was Singsalix
     apparently."

34. *de-p   biri-zi-ge   biri-zi   žed-i   al-dı*
     say-CONV one.of-3POSS-DAT one.of-3POSS reach-CONV take-PAST

     de-p   sen-dir-gen   irgin
     say-CONV believe-CAUS-PSTINDF EVID

     He convinced them by saying that one (devil) caught up with the
     other one after that.

35. *ol bo burun-gu   erte-de-gi   xam-baxšı*
     that this before-RELCL early-LOC-RELCL shaman.healer

     görümži-ler-niŋ amtan-nı sen-dir-ir   užun
     exorcist-PL-GEN   people-ACC believe-CAUS-PRSPRT for

     iste-en   bir türlü ayla-lar-ı-nıŋ   biri-zi
     do-PSTPRT one various dirty.trick-PL-3POSS-GEN one.of-3POSS

     de-p   amtan mın-dıg žurt išd-i-nde   burun-nan
     say-CONV person this-EQU people inside-3POSS-LOC before-ABL

     mın-dıg tool sös bar žibe
     this-EQU story word EXIST thing

This is such a legend among the people about one of the dirty tricks o f t hose s hamans and h ealers i n t he e arly t imes (used) i n order to make people believe them.

3. 6 A Fortuneteller

Narrated by Erkit of Kaba county in September1995

1. *burun bis-tiŋ   bo xom xanas xaba dɪba-lar-ɪ-nda   bir*
    before we-GEN this Kom Kanas Kaba Tuva-PL-3POSS-LOC one

    at-tɪg   žarɪn   gö-ör   žarɪnži   giži
    name-ADJ shoulder.blade see-PRSPRT fortune.teller person

    bo-p   dur irgin di-dir
    be-CONV stay EVID say-EMPH

    They say that there was a famous fortune teller[6] among the Tuvas of Kom, Kanas, and Kaba who told fortunes by looking at a shoulder blade.

2. *o-oŋ bilen bo žook šag-da bir žaa bo-p   žaa-nɪŋ*
    it-GEN with this near time-LOC one enemy be-CONV enemy-GEN

    giži-ler-i   bod-u-nuŋ   dur-gan   žer-i-n
    person-PL-3POSS self-3POSS-GEN stay-PSTPRT place-3POSS-ACC

    žaala-p   ba-ar   žɪt-kan   soŋgaar ol žer-de
    conquer-CONV go-PRSPRT lie-PSTPRT after   that place-LOC

    dur-gan   zurt-tar soŋgaar šegin-ip   soŋgu dag
    stay-PSTPRT people-PL backward retreat-CONV north mountain

---

[6] *zhawirinzhi*: a fortuneteller who tells fortune by looking at a sheep's shoulder blade; this is called scapulimancy.

gudu ün-sö   gerek
down move-COND necessary

Then, during recent times there was an enemy attack and after the
people of the enemy were about to conquer the land where they
themselves (i.e. Tuva) were staying, it so happened that the people
who lived there moved back down the northern mountain.

3.   *o-oŋ bilen žurt-tuŋ   baštık-tar-ı   žurt-tuŋ*
it-GEN with   people-GEN leader-PL-3POSS people-GEN

ard-ı-ŋga   xaraal   ga-ap   bot-tar-ı
behind-3POSS-DAT watchman set.up-CONV self-PL-3POSS

buruŋgaar göž-üp   bır žer-ge   bar-ıp   xon-up
forwards   move-CONV one place-CONV go-CONV spend.night-CONV

žıt-sa   gerek
lie-COND necessary

It so happened that the leaders of the people had set up guards
behind the people, while they themselves moved forward and
went to a place to spend the night.

4.   *o-oŋ bilen ard-ı-nda   xaraal-da gal-gan   giži*
it-GEN with   back-3POSS-LOC guard-LOC   remain-PSTPRT person

soŋ-u-nda-gı   sürgünžü-ler-niŋ gel-e
end-3POSS-LOC-RELCL pursuer-PL-GEN   come-CONV

žıt-kan-ı-n   gör-üp dedir žurd-u-nuŋ
lie-PSTPRT-3POSS-ACC see-CONV reverse people-3POSS-GEN

bar-gan žer-i-ŋge   žed-e   al-bayın   dur
go-PSTPRT place-3POSS-DAT reach-CONV able-NEGCONV stay

Then, those who were set up as guard behind them saw the
pursuers coming behind them but they were not able to reach the
place on the opposite side where their people had gone.

5.   *o-oŋ bilen soŋ-ɪ-nda   sürgünžü-ler-nen žurt-tar*
      it-GEN with behind-3POSS-LOC pursuer-PL-ABL   people-PL

      xabar bol-bayɪn žaa-nan des-ken   žurt gežee
      news be-NEGCONV enemy-ABL flee-PSTPRT people evening

      bar-ɪp bir žer-ge xon-a   gal-ɪp
      go-CONV one place-DAT spend.night-CONV remain-CONV

      xon-up   žɪt-kan žer-i-ŋge   bir mal
      spend.night-CONV lie-PSTPRT place-3POSS-DAT one animal

      soy-up   et xaynɪ-dɪr-ɪp ži-p   olur-up
      slaughter-CONV meat boil-CAUS-CONV eat-CONV sit-CONV

      dur dün gežee
      stay night evening

Then, the people who fled the enemy did not have any news about
the pursuers behind them, and when they came to a place in the
evening, they spent the night there, and they slaughtered one
animal at the place where they were spending the night, cooked
the meat and were eating at night.

6.   *o-oŋ bilen olur-gan göp-tüŋ išd-i-nde*
      it-GEN with sit-PSTPRT many-GEN inside-3POSS-LOC

      žarɪn   gö-ör   žarɪnžɪ   žarɪn-nɪ
      shoulder.blade see-PRSPRT fortune.teller shoulder.blade-ACC

kız-ıp   dur-gan   ot-ka   ot-tıŋ   žırı-ı-ŋga
burn-CONV stay-PSTPRT fire-DAT fire-GEN light-3POSS-DAT

gör-göš ot žırı-ı-nda   olur-gan amtan-nar-ga
see-CONV fire light-3POSS-LOC sit-PSTPRT person-PL-DAT

ayd-ır   irgin
say-PRSINDF EVID

So the fortune teller (scapulimancer), who was sitting among the
many people, looked at the shoulder blade in the light of the
reddened fire and he told the people who were sitting by the light
of the fire (about it).

7.   *žarın-nı   gör-gön žüü ol žıd-a*
     shoulder.blade-ACC see-PSTPRT what that lie.down-CONV

     gal-ıp   at-kan   žüü ol
     remain-CONV shoot-PSTPRT what that

     What was it that he saw (in) the shoulder blade? Who was it that
     lay down and got shot?

8.   *šuluun des-kileger de-p   žarınžı   ınža-p*
     quick   escape-2PL.IMP say-CONV fortune.teller do.that-CONV

     ayt-kan   gez-de art-ta   gel-gen   sürgünšü-lör
     say-PSTPRT time-LOC behind-LOC come-PSTPRT pursuer-PL

     ol žer-de   xon-up   žıt-kan   zurt-tu
     that place-LOC spend.night-CONV lie-PSTPRT people-ACC

     gorža-p   a-b   al-sa   gerek
     surround-CONV take-CONV take-CONV necessary

When the fortune teller said thus: "Quick, escape!" it so happened that the pursuers who had come after them had already surrounded those people who were spending the night at that place.

9. *o-oŋ bilen olur-gan žurt-tar da žük žük-kö xalɪ-p*
    it-GEN with   sit-PSTPRT people-PL also side side-DAT jump-CONV

    dur irgin
    stay EVID

    Then, (those) people who were sitting there indeed jumped away to all directions.

10. *art-tan   gel-gen   sürgünžü-lör gorža-p*
    back-ABL come-PSTPRT pursuer-PL   surround-CONV

    al-gan
    take-PSTINDF

    The pursuers who had come from behind surrounded them.

11. *olar da boo ad-ɪp   ol ara-dan des-ken*
    they also gun shoot-CONV that place-ABL escape-PSTPRT

    žurt-tan bir žeže-zi   ok-ka   už-up
    people-ABL one some-3POSS bullet-DAT get.shot-CONV

    gal-gan-nar-ɪ   et mal-ɪ-n   ga-aš
    remain-PSTPRT-PL-3POSS thing animal-3POSS-ACC put-CONV

    dünö dez-ip   ün-üp   dur irgin
    at.night escape-CONV come.out-CONV stay EVID

They also fired guns and some of the people who were fleeing from there were shot with bullets, and the rest of them left their belongings and livestock and escaped at night.

12. *o-oŋ   bilen bo dɪba išd-i-nde-gi   ol*
     it-GEN with   this Tuva inside-3POSS-LOC-RELCL that

     žarɪnžɪ-nɪŋ   ol dem   šigi äŋgime-si kazɪr-ge
     fortune.teller-GEN that yonder like story-3POSS now-DAT

     žeder žurt išd-i-nde   ayd-ɪl-ɪp   žor
     up.to   people inside -3POSS-LOC say-PASS-CONV walk

Thus, stories like this one, about that fortune teller among these Tuvas, are being told among the people even up till now.

Songs and Blessing

4. 1 The Fatherland - Kom and Kanas

Sang by Belik of Akkaba Village in September1995

1. *möŋgün žežek kektaman mees-tiŋ*
   silver   flower snowdrop sunny.side.of.mountain-GEN

   öŋ-ü-n   dɪrtta-dɪr-ɪy   moŋ
   color-3POSS-ACC attract-CAUS -CONV Q

   Is it not the silver colored flowers of the snowdrop that attract the color of the sunny side of the mountain?

2. *möŋgü bürün ed-er   kek   amtan-nɪŋ*
   eternal sound make.sound-PRSPRT cuckoo people-GEN

   kööl-ü-n   dɪrtta-dɪr-ɪy   moŋ
   feeling-3POSS-ACC attract-CAUS -CONV Q

   Is it not the everlasting song of the cuckoo that entertains (attract) the people's heart?

3. *ay yay ay yay alday-ɪm   oy yoy oy yoy ös-kön*
   hey hey   Altay-1SG.POSS oh oh   grow-PSTPRT

   žer ažay žurd-um   xom xanas
   place father land-1SG.POSS Kom Kanas

   Hey, hey, my Altay, Oh, oh, the place where I grew up, my fatherland Kom and Kanas.

4. *aldɪn-nan öŋ-nüg   almas-tan   bɪžɪg*
   gold-ABL   color-ADJ diamond-ABL firm

(You are) more beautiful than gold and harder than diamond.

5.   *žüzün bürün žüz žežek amtan-nıŋ žürö-ö-n*
colored leaves face flower people-GEN heart-3POSS-ACC

   dırtta-dır-ıy   moŋ
   attract-CAUS-CONV Q

   Is it not the face (beauty) of the colorful flower that rocks (moves)
   the people's hearts?

6.   *žüzün bürün ed-er   kek   arga-nıŋ*
colored sound make.sound-PRSPRT cuckoo forest-GEN

   öŋ-ün   dırtta-dır-ıy   moŋ
   color-3POSS-ACC beautify-CAUS-CONV Q

   Is it not he colorful song of the cuckoo that beautifies the colors of
   the forest?

7.   *ay yay ay yay alday-ım   oy yoy oy yoy ös-kön*
hey hey   Altay-1SG.POSS oh oh   grow-PSTPRT

   žer ažay žurd-um   xom xanas
   place father land-1SG.POSS Kom Kanas

   Hey, hey, my Altay, oh, oh, the place where I grew up, my
   fatherland Kom and Kanas.

8.   *aldın-nan öŋ-nüg almas-tan   bıžıg*
gold-ABL   color-ADJ diamond-ABL firm

   (You are) more beautiful than gold and harder than diamond.

9.   *ažay   žurt-um   xom xanas*
      father land-1SG.POSS Kom Kanas

      My fatherland Kom and Kanas.

10.   *aldɪn-nan öŋ-nüg   almas-tan   bɪžɪg*
      gold-ABL color-ADJ diamond-ABL firm

      (You are) more beautiful than gold and harder than diamond.

4. 2 Konggiray

Sang by Bermit of Akkaba Village in September1987

1.   *dörtön žet-ken   žɪlgɪ-m-nɪŋ   dörölžü-zü gayda*
      forty   reach- PSTPRT horse-1SG.POSS-GEN herd-3POSS where

      o xoŋgɪray
      oh konggiray

      Where is the herd of my horses that have reached forty? Hey Konggiray.

2.   *dört gožuun žurd-um-nuŋ   törö-zü   gayda*
      four banner people-1SG.POSS-GEN leader-3POSS where

      o xoŋgɪray
      oh konggiray

      Where is the leader of my Four Banner people? Hey Konggiray.

3.   *bežen žet-ken   žɪlgɪ-m-nɪŋ   belžiir-i   gayda*
      fifty   reach-PSTPRT horse-1SG.POSS-GEN pasture-3POSS where

o xoŋgıray
ho konggiray

Where is the pasture-land of my horses that have reached fifty?
Hey Konggiray.

4.   *beš gožuun žurd-um-nuŋ   biy-i   gayda*
five banner   people-1SG.POSS-GEN *biy*-3POSS where

o xoŋgıray
ho konggiray

Where is the *biy*[18] of my Five Banners people? Hey Konggiray.

5.   *aldan žet-ken   žılgı-m-nıŋ   ala-zı*
sixty   reach-PSTPRT horse-1SG.POSS-GEN piebald-3POSS

gayda o xoŋgıray
where   ho konggiray

Where are my piebald horses that have reached sixty? Hey
Konggiray.

6.   *aldı gošuun žurd-um-nuŋ   albatı-zı   gayda*
six   banner   people-1SG.POSS-GEN citizen-3POSS where

o xoŋgıray
ho konggiray

Where are the citizens of my Six Banner people? Hey Honggiray.

7.   *žeden žet-ken   žılgı-m-nıŋ   želiž-ı   gayda*
seventy reach-PSTPRT horse-1SG.POSS-GEN trot-3POSS where

---

[18] A *Biy* is a tribal, clan or village elder who judged cases in customary law.

o xoŋgɪray
ho konggiray

Where is the trot of my horses that have reached seventy? Hey Konggiray.

8.   *žedi gožuun žurd-um-nuŋ   beesi-zi   gayda*
seven banner   people-1SG.POSS-GEN *beesi*- 3POSS where

o   xoŋgɪray
ho konggiray

"Where is the *beesi*[19] of my Seven Banner people? Hey Hongiray.

4. 3 Soyan Clan

Sang by Belik of Akkaba Village in September1995 in Urumchi

1.   *kɪzɪl tɪt-tɪŋ   saad-ɪ-ŋga   gɪmžɪ-m-dɪ*
red pine tree-GEN   tree.sap-3POSS-DAT whip-1SG.POSS-ACC

žed-er-e   al-ba-dɪ-m
reach-CAUS-CONV able-NEG-PAST-1SG

I was unable to reach with my whip to the tree sap[20] of the red pine tree.

2.   *kɪzɪl doru   gulgu-ga ay söz-üm-dü*
red   reddish.brown friend-DAT hey word-1SG.POSS-ACC

žed-ir-e   al-ba-dɪ-m
reach-CAUS-CONV able-NEG-PAST-1SG

---

[19] *Beesi* is a prince of the fourth rank in Manchu times.
[20] *saat* is tree sap used as chewing gums.

I was unable to reach with my words to the reddish brown friend.

3.   *ag-ar   ak-pas   xara sug ad-ɪm*
flow-PRSPRT flow-NEGPRSPRT black water horse-1SG.POSS

duyu-u-n   doža-t-ti
hoof-3POSS-ACC freeze-CAUS-PAST

The flowing, not flowing (hardly flowing) black water froze my horse's hooves.

4.   *al-ɪr   al-bas   amɪrak   sagɪž-ɪm-nɪ*
take-PRSPRT take-NEGPRSPRT sweetheart feeling-1SG.POSS-ACC

žüge žobat-ti
why console-PAST

Sweetheart, why did you console my feelings when you didn't know whether you would take me or not.

5.   *tarbagan-nɪŋ tarčɪ-zɪ   daš*
marmot-GEN   three.year.old.one-3POSS stone

ald-ɪ-nda   de-ž-ir   ey
underneath-3POSS-LOC say-REC-PRSINDF hey

They say to each other that the three-year old female marmot is under the stone.

6.   *tanɪ-š-kan-nɪŋ   biri-zi   taŋdɪ-lar-ga*
know-REC PSTPRT-GEN one.of-3POSS Tangdi-PL-DAT

de-ž-ir   ey
say-REC-PRSINDF hey

They say to each other that one of the acquaintances is in the Tangdi nation (country).

7. *soŋgar   kak-kan   salgın-ga   soguna baž-ı*
    to.the.north blow-PSTPRT gentle.breeze-DAT onion   head-3POSS

    sergeleŋ
    buoyant

    The head of the onion is very buoyant in the gentle breeze that blows north.

8. *soyan söök-tig ool-dar men-i gör-ör-de   sergeleŋ*
    Soyan clan-ADJ boy-PL I-ACC see-PRSPRT-LOC cheerful

    The young men from the Soyan tribe are very cheerful when they see me.

9. *žažıl-dar-nı gör-nen eš   žalıı   bol-sa de-nen eš*
    green-PL-ACC see-IMP friend young.man be-COND say-IMP friend

    (Please) watch the green, friend, and tell (me) if there is a young man, friend.

10. *oya   žık-tı gör-nen eš   žol-dar bol-sa de-nen*
    low-lying area-ACC see-IMP   friend road-PL be-COND say-IMP

    eš
    friend

    Look at the low-lying area, friend, and tell (me) if there are roads, friend.

4. 4 Altay Zhagay

Sang by Balzhin of Akkaba Village in September1987 in Urumchi

1. *xolu-ž-up   ak-kan   e   xom xanas sug*
    join-REC-ONV flow-PSTPRT hey Kom Kanas water

    Hey, water of the Kom and Kanas that are flowing together.

2. *xoyla-ž-ıp   ös-kön   e   urug-lar ey*
    embrace-REC-CONV grow-PSTPRT hey girl-PL   hey

    Hey, girls who have been growing up embracing one another.

3. *sunžu-p   ak-kan   sunda   arıg sug*
    be.strained-CONV flow-PSTPRT extensive clean water

    The extensive clear water is flowing which is strained.

4. *sumunla-ž-ıp   ös-kön   urug-lar ey eš*
    live.in.a.sumun-REC-CONV grow-PSTPRT teenager-PL hey friend

    Hey, friends, girls who have been growing up together living in
    the same *sumun* (district).

5. *kattırž-ıp   ak-kan   xaba xanas ey*
    stand.side.by.side-CONV flow-PSTPRT Kaba Kanas   hey

    Hey, Kanas and Kaba that are flowing side by side.

6. *kattır-ıž-ıp   ös-kön   urug-lar ey*
    laugh-REC-CONV grow-PSTPRT teenage-PL hey

    Hey, teenagers who have been growing up together laughing.

7.   *alday žaagay   bol-gaš-tan   aldı kem-ge   žed-er   be*
     Altay beautiful   be-CONV-ABL six   river-DAT reach-PRSINDF Q

     Even though Altay is beautiful, can it compare with the six rivers?

8.   *amtan žaagay bol-gaš-tan   ada ıye-ge   žed-er   be*
     people rich   be-CONV-ABL father-mother-DAT reach-PRSINDF Q

     Even if people are beautiful, can you compare them favorably
     with your parents?

9.   *žer-ler žaagay bol-gaš-tan   žedi kem-ge   žed-er   be*
     place-PL rich   be-CONV-ABL seven river-DAT reach-PRSINDF Q

     Even though the land is rich, can you compare it favorably with
     the seven rivers?

10. *at-tar   žügürük bol-gaš-tan   argımak-ka   žed-er   be*
     horse-PL swift   be-CONV-ABL fine.horse-DAT reach-PRSINDF Q

     Even if the horses are swift, can you compare them favorably with
     the fine horses?

11. *žalıı-lar   žaagay   bol-gaš-tan amırak eš-ke*
     young.man-PL handsome   be-CONV-ABL beloved   friend-DAT

     žed-er   be
     compare.with-PRSINDF Q

     Even though the young men are handsome, can you compare them
     favorably with the beloved friend?

4.5 Erdene "Elegant"

Sang by Belik of Akkaba Village in September1995 in Urumchi

1. *žer-nen   üŋ-gön   sıgen-dey žüzün öŋgö tanıg-lıg   ey*
   earth-ABL grow-PSTPRT grass-EQU *zhüzün önggö* known-ADJ hey

   Hey, the *zhüzün önggö* [21] is recognizable just as the grass that is growing from the earth.

2. *žergelež-ip   žor-ur-da   ay žeen   üren*
   walk.side.by.side-CONV walk-PRSPRT-LOC hey nephew fellow

   tanıg-lıg
   known-ADJ

   The nephew and niece distinguish themselves from others when they walk together side by side.

3. *xom-nan üŋ-gön   sıgen-dey xoor aspan tanıg-lıg*
   Kom-ABL grow-PSTPRT grass-EQU *koor aspan*   known-ADJ

   The *koor aspan* [22] is as recognizable as the flowers that are growing in Kom.

4. *gožarlaž-ıp   žor-ur-da   gožuun žurd-um*
   form.a.pair-CONV walk-PRSINDF-LOC banner   people-1SG.POSS

   tanıg-lıg
   known-ADJ

   My banner people are recognizable when they are walking in pairs.

---

[21] *Zhüzün önggö*: a flower name.
[22] *koor aspan*: a flower name

5.　*ɪrak žook-tɪ žookšula-t-kan   at-tar   körgüy erdine*
far near-ACC approach-CAUS-PSTPRT horse-PL beauty elegant

The beauty of the horse is elegant when it brings far the near and
makes a long distance short.

6.　*xaduŋman-nɪ tanɪ-š-tɪr-gan   urug-lar körgü erdine*
relative-ACC   know-REC-CAUS-PSTPRT girl-PL beauty precious

The girls who caused the relatives to become acquainted are
treasure.

4. 6 Amirak "Sweetheart"

Sang by Bolat of Akkaba Village in September1995

1.　*sɪralɪg-nɪŋ   išd-i-nen   sɪrla-y   žel-gen*
pine.tree.grove-GEN inside-3POSS-ABL gallop-CONV amble-PSTPRT

sɪɪnak
fawn

The ambling fawn that gallops from within the pine tree grove.

2.　*sɪmɪran-ɪp gula-am-ga   sɪr-ɪ-n   ayt-kan*
whisper-CONV ear-1SG.POSS-DAT secrete-3POSS-ACC tell-PSTPRT

amɪrak
sweetheart

The sweetheart who told the secret by whispering in my ear.

3.　*gadaŋgɪr-nɪŋ ey išd-i-nen   arala-y*
Gadanggir-GEN hey inside-3POSS-ABL wander.round-CONV

žel-gen   sıınak
amble-PSTPRT fawn

The ambling fawn that roams from within the Gadanggir.

4.   *gadı   eder-ip   žoru-ur-da   adaš*
together go.together-CONV walk-PRSPRT-LOC friend

bol-gan   amırak
become-PSTPRT sweetheart

My sweetheart who became a friend while (we were) walking together.

5.   *dolgaytı-nıŋ tal-dar-ı-n   dolga-p   šoorla-p*
Dolgayti-GEN willow-PL-3POSS-ACC twist-CONV make.flute-CONV

oyna-agay
play-1PL.IMP

Let's twist the willows from the Dolgayti and make a flute and play it.

6.   *on on beš-tiŋ išd-i-nde   oyna-p   oyna-p*
ten ten five-GEN inside-3POSS-LOC play-CONV play-CONV

al-agay
take-1PL.IMP

Let's play and play while we still are at the age of ten to fifteen.

7.   *žer eŋgey-niŋ tal-dar-ı-n   šarbax žaza-p*
earth face-GEN   willow-PL-3POSS-ACC basket make-CONV

oyna-agay
play-1PL.IMP

Let's play by making baskets using the willows of the face of the earth.

8.   *žeerbi beš-tiŋ   ara-zɪ-nda   oyna-p   oyna-p*
     twenty five-GEN middle-3POSS-LOC play-CONV play-CONV

     al-agay
     take-1PL.IMP

     Let's play and play while we are still at the age of twenty-five.

4. 7 "Blessing"

Narrated by Solunggu of Akkaba Village in September1995

1.   *xaba xanas xam bolbaday beer   gayga*
     Kaba Kanas Kam bolbaday this.way look

     Kaba, Kanas, Kam Bolbaday, look this way.

2.   *gožuun žurd-um   xom sundaarık sen gal-ba*
     banner people-1SG.POSS Kom Sundaarik you remain-NEG

     Don't be left behind my banner people, Kom and Sundaarik.

3.   *ebeeš-men de-p   kıyad-ıŋ-nı   mugat-pa*
     few-1SG   say-CONV aspiration-2POSS-ACC sadden-NEG

     Don't defeat your aspiration because you are few in numbers (a minority).

4.   *garbal-sa-ŋ*   *da   xar žurt-tan   gal-ıš-pa*
      seek.support-COND-2SG EMPH other people-ABL remain-REC-NEG

      Don't be left behind the other people even though you have to
      seek a way out (of the critical situation.)

5.   *ža iyi žurt-tuŋ   mörü-ü   xayım bol-sun*
      well two people-GEN opportunity-3POSS tie   be-3IMP

      xaduŋma
      fellow.countryman

      Well, may the opportunity of both people be equal, compatriot.

6.   *iyi žurt-tuŋ   nüür-ü-ŋge   salım bol-sun*
      two people-GEN consceince-3POSS-DAT fortune be-3IMP

      xaduŋma
      compatriot

      May the reputation of two people be fortunate, compatriot.

7.   *erge   dut-kan   törö-nüŋ   keere-zi*
      authority hold-PSTPRT ruling.nobility-GEN affection-3POSS

      gel-sin   xaduŋma
      come-3IMP compatriot

      May the affection of the ruling authority (government) come,
      compatriot.

8.   *eki er-ge   žurt žagır-ır   ülüg ber-sin xaduŋma*
      good man-DAT people govern-PRSPRT turn give-3IMP compatriot

May the people (nation) give the good men a turn (opportunity) to
govern, compatriot.

9.   *öörün tik-ken   sarıg bag örgün bol-sun xaduŋma*
     happily sew-PSTPRT leather strap skillful be-3IMP compatriot

     May the happily sewed leather[23] strap[24] be skillful, compatriot.

10. *öz-üp   žet-ken   er žalıı-zı   töröön*
     grow-CONV reach-PSTPRT man young.man-3POSS relative

     bol-sun xaduŋma
     be-3IMP compatriot

     May the young man reach maturity and become a relative,
     compatriot.

11. *ögbe deedis-tiŋ züldö-zü-nen   öršeel bol-sun xaduŋma*
     ancestor nobility-GEN soul-3POSS-ABL mercy be-3IMP compatriot

     May the soul of the noble ancestor show mercy, compatriot.

12. *öör bo-p katıš-pas   žüger urug-lar-ga*
     friends be-CONV participate-NEGPRSPRT female child-PL-DAT

     tıyım   bo-zun xaduŋma
     prohibition be-3IMP compatriot

     May there be a prohibition for the girls who don't want to
     participate on very intimate terms (who don't want to be friends
     with us), compatriot.

---

[23] *sarig*: a leather prepared from goat-skin or sheep-skin, shagreen, rough leather, cf. M.
sar's.
[24] *sarig bag* is a leather ball used for shooting with a bow when playing the game.

13.   *at-kan   ža-lar azıl   bo-p   sın-bas*
       shoot-PSTPRT bow-PL precious be-CONV break-NEGPRSPRT

       bo-zun   xaduŋma
       be-3IMP compatriot

       May the bows we shoot with be precious but never be broken,
       compatriot.

14.   *aa ayt-kan   gıškı kek   šigi ed-ip   gabıyaa*
       oh say-PSTPRT word cuckoo like utter.sound-CONV harmonious

       bo-zun   xaduŋma
       be-3IMP compatriot

       Oh, may the words that have been spoken be harmonious,
       sounding like the cuckoo, compatriot.

15.   *aas   dıl   ayııl   žora-nıŋ   aaz-ı*
       mouth tongue misfortune danger-GEN mouth-3POSS

       ka-al-sın   xaduŋma
       knock-PASS-3IMP compatriot

       May the mouths of those who quarrel and fight be shut, brother.

16.   *ada iye-nıŋ   algıš žoreel-i-nıŋ   geži-i*
       father mother-GEN gratitude wish-3POSS-GEN blessing-3POSS

       gel-sin   xaduŋma
       come-3IMP compatriot

       May our parents' blessings of gratitude and good luck wishes be
       fulfilled, compatriot.

17.   *ee-zi*   *dur-gaš-tan*   *gadı* *mööre-en*   *inek-ten*
owner-3POSS stay-CONV-ABL wrong moo-PSTPRT cow-ABL

žayla-zın
beware-3IMP

May they beware of (those) cows that moo wrongly? while their
owners are still there.

18.   *ežel*   *törö-zü-nüŋ*   *kııra-zı*   *žok*
generous ruling.nobility-3POSS-GEN compassion-3POSS NEGEXIST

eedere-en   *žurt-tan* *žayla-zın*
become.foolish-PSTPRT nation-ABL beware-3IMP

May they avoid becoming those foolish people who don't have
compassion towards (their) generous nation.

19.   *ee-zi*   *dur-gaš-tan*   *gadı* *ulu-un*   *ıt-tan*
owner-3POSS stay-CONV-ABL wrong howl-PSTPRT dog-ABL

žayla-zın
beware-3IMP

May they beware of (those) dogs that howl wrongly while their
owners are still there.

20.   *eele-p*   *žagır-ar*   *er*   *žalıı-zı*   *žok*
own-CONV rule-PRSPRT man young.man-3POSS NEGEXIST

bıdıra-an   *žurt-tan* *žayla-zın*
scatter-PSTPRT people-ABL beware-3IMP

May they beware of a scattered nation without young men to own
and rule the nation.

21.   *ada-zı-n*   *tanı-mas*   *žozun-nu*
       father-3POSS-ACC know-NEGPRSPRT customs-ACC

       kündüle-bes   *baš ulug ool-dan* *žayla-zın*
       respect-NEGPRSPRT head big   child-ABL beware-3IMP

       May they beware of children with big heads who don't know their
       parents and don't respect the customs.

22.   *žurt-tan*   *dez-ip*   *xarın gez-ip*   *gižin-gen*
       people-ABL run.away-CONV adverse wander-CONV nag-PSTPRT

       urug-lar-nan žayla-zın
       girl-PL-ABL   beware-3IMP

       May they beware of girls who renounce the people, wandering
       towards the opposite and nagging.

23.   *xamık-tı bılga-p*   *gabıyaa-nı buz-up*
       all-ACC   do.harm-CONV unity-ACC   break-CONV

       xopšu xoŋša-ar-nan   *žayla-zın*
       gossip spread-PRSPRT-ABL beware-3IMP

       May they beware of those (gossip-mongers) who spread rumors
       and stir (do harm) the whole and break the harmony (unity).

24.   *xaan-nı alda-p*   *xara-nı bılga-p*   *ara*
       Khan-ACC cheat-CONV black-ACC do.harm-CONV among

       gıdı-ır   *iyi söstüŋ-nen žayla-zın*
       visit-PRSPRT two word-ABL   beware-3IMP

May they beware of those two faced who go around cheating the Khan and stirring the common.[25]

25. *žayla-ar   zibe žayla-zın žedi mužora-nan žayla-zın*
     evade-PRSPRT thing evade-3IMP seven evil-ABL   avoid-3IMP

May they beware of the things that should be avoided, and beware of the seven evils.

26. *kož-ar   koža   olur-gan   gožuun eki gabıyaa*
     pair-PRSPRT neighbor live-PSTPRT banner good harmony

     ekkel-sin
     bring-3IMP

May it bring good harmony to the banner (people) who live as neighbors in pairs.

27. *oynı-ır   ölžöy-lüg   bol-sun*
     entertain-PRSPRT amusing-ADJ be-3IMP

May the entertainment be amusing.

28. *gožuun žurt   žırgalaŋ edile-zin*
     banner people bliss   enjoy-3IMP

May the banner people enjoy bliss.

29. *art-göp amguuluŋ   edile-zin*
     people what.has.been.said use-3IMP

The people[26] said: "May what you said be true."

---

[25] *Kara*: refers to the common people.
[26] People here refers to the crowd in front of the person who is giving the speech.

30.   *eki bol-sun kel-ir   gün-ner*
       good be-3IMP come-PRSPRT day-PL

       May the days to come be good!

Conversations

5. 1 Conversation 1

Terbiya and Mongko in Akkaba in September 1995

A.   *se-eŋ   ad-ɪŋ   gɪm*
     you-GEN name-2SG.POSS who

     "What is your name?"

B.   *me-eŋ ad-ɪm   möŋkö*
     I-GEN name-1SG.POSS Möngkö

     My name is Möngkö.

A.   *žeže   žas-ta   sen*
     how.many age-LOC 2SG

     "How old are you?"

B.   *on beš žaš-tɪg   men*
     ten five year-ADJ 1SG

     "I am 15."

A.   *žežinži bän   nomšu-p žɪd-ɪr-sen*
     which   grade study-CONV lie-PRSINDF-2SG

     "What grade are you in?"

B.   *žedinži bän   nomšu-p žɪd-ɪr-men*
     seventh grade study-CONV lie-PRSIND-1SG

I am studying in seventh grade.

A. *se-eŋ   ada-iye-ŋ   bar   ma*
    you-GEN father mother-2SG.POSS EXIST Q

    "Do you have parents?"

B. *aža-m   awa-m   bar*
    father-1SG.POSS mother-1SG.POSS EXIST

    "I have parents."

A. *ol giži-ler   gayda*
    that person-PL where

    "Where are they?"

B. *olar xom-da*
    they Kom-LOC

    "They are in Kom."

A. *olar žüme iš   ište-er*
    they what work do-PRSINDF

    "What work do they do?"

B. *aža-m   taraa tarɪ-p žɪd-ɪr   taraačɪn*
    father-1SG.POSS crops sow-CONV lie-PRSINDF farmer

    awa-m   ög-de
    mother-1SG.POSS home-LOC

    "My father is farming. He is a farmer. My mother stays at home."

A.   *aga-ŋ*   *bar   ma*
      older.brother-2SG.POSS EXIST Q

      "Do you have an older brother?"

B.   *bir aga-m*   *bir žeŋge-m*
      one older.brother-1SG.POSS one older.sister-in-law-1SG.POSS

      bar
      EXIST

      "I have one older brother and an older sister-in-law."

A.   *aga-ŋ*   *ište-er   me*
      older.brother-2SG.POSS work-PRSINDF Q

      "Does your older brother work?"

B.   *aga-m*   *iš-te   baxšı*
      older.brother-1SG.POSS work-LOC teacher

      žeerbi žıl kızmet ište-en
      twenty year work   do-PSTINDF

      "My older brother works as a teacher. He has worked for twenty
      years."

A.   *se-eŋ   žeŋge-ŋ*   *de baxšı ma*
      you-GEN older.sister-in-law-1SG.POSS also teacher Q

      "Is your older sister-in-law also a teacher?"

B.   *žeŋge-m*   *baxšı emes*
      older.sister-in-law-1SG.POSS teacher NEGCOP

ol ög-de
she home-LOC

"My older sister-in-law is not a teacher. She is at home."

A.   *se-eŋ   egiči-ŋ   bar   ma*
      you-GEN older.sister-2SG.POSS EXIST Q

"Do you have an older sister?"

B.   *egiči-m   doy   žaza-an   ö-ö-nde*
      older.sister-1SG.POSS marriage make-PSTINDF home-3POSS-LOC

"My older sister is married and she is at her home."

A.   *duŋma-ŋ   bar   ma*
      younger.brother-2SG.POSS EXIST Q

"Do you have a younger brother?"

B.   *duŋma-m   bar*
      younger.brother-1SG.POSS EXIST

      o-oŋ   ad-ɪ   batɪ
      he-GEN name-3POSS Bati

"I have a younger brother. His name is Bati."

A.   *ol mäktep-te nomšu- ur   ma*
      he school-LOC study-PRSINDF Q

"Does he go to school?"

B.   *ol nomšu-p žɪd-ɪr*
      he study-CONV lie-PRSINDF

"He is studying."

A. *žeženči bän-de*
    which   grade-LOC

    "Which grade is he in?"

B. *bastawšı aldınžı bän-dı   bıt-tir-ip   žedinžı*
    elementary sixth   grade-ACC end-CAUS-CONV seventh

    bän-ge   gır-di
    class-DAT enter-PAST

    "He has finished elementary sixth grade and entered the seventh grade."

5. 2 Conversation 2

Kadir and his wife in Buwirshin county in September 1995

A. *sen bögün eškayda bar-ba-dı-ŋ   ba*
    you today   anywhere go-NEG-PAST-2SG Q

    "Did you not go anywhere today?"

B. *bögün ög-gö   olur-du-m eškayda bar-ba-dı-m*
    today   house-DAT sit-PAST-1SG anywhere go-NEG-PAST-1SG

    "Today I was at home and did not go anywhere."

A. *sen beket-ke   bar-gan-ıŋ   gayda*
    you bus.station-DAT go-PSTPRT-2POSS where

    "What about your going to the bus station?"

B.   *e   beket-ke   bar-ıp   gel-di-m*
      yes bus.station-DAT go-CONV come-PAST-1SG

      "Oh, yes. I just went to the bus station and came back."

A.   *sen beket-ke   žügö bar-dı-ŋ*
      you bus.station-DAT why go-PAST-2SG

      "Why did you go to the bus station?"

B.   *akkaba-nan bir iyi üš mugalım-nar ge-ep   dur irgin*
      Akkaba-ABL one two three teacher-PL   come-CONV stay EVID

      "Two or three teachers from Akkaba had come."

A.   *ol giži-ler-ni   ederd-ip bar-dı-ŋ   ba*
      that person-PL-ACC lead-CONV go-PAST-2SG Q

      "Did you take those people (there)?"

B.   *e olar-nı apar-ıp   gel-di-m*
      yes they-ACC deliver-CONV go-PAST-1SG

      "Yes, I took them (there) and came back."

A.   *ol giži-ler gayda ba-ar   irgin*
      that person-PL where go-PRSINDF EVID

      "Where are those people going?"

B.   *olar ürümži-ge bar-ıp šüübür ber-er-bis   de-p*
      they Ürümchi-DAT go-CONV exam   give-PRSINDF-1PL say-CONV

      ge-ep   dur irgin
      come-CONV stay EVID

olar-nɪ   beket-ke   žed-ir-ip   ga-aš
they-ACC bus.station-DAT reach-CAUS-CONV put-CONV

gel-di-m   emes   pe
come-PAST-1SG NEGCOP Q

"They had come (here) in order to go to Ürümchi to take an exam.
I took them to the bus station and just came back, right?

A.   *o-nun   gedeer ög-gö   baška giži   gel-di   be*
     that-ABL after   house-DAT other   person come-PAST Q

"Did anyone else come to the house after that?"

B.   *olar-nɪ žed-ir-ip   gel-se-m   ög-gö   dee*
     they-ACC reach-CAUS-CONV come-COND-1SG house-DAT that

bir ulug giži   ge-ep   ga-p   dur irgin
one senior person come-CONV put-CONV stay EVID

As I came home after seeing them off, that old man came.

ulug giži-ge   bir šay ber-ip   ɪnža-p   dur-guš bo
senior person-DAT one tea give-CONV do.that-CONV stay-CONV this

bis-tiŋ baza bir giži-ler ge-ep   ga-p   dur irgin
we-GEN again some person-PL come-CONV put-CONV stay EVID

While I was serving tea to the old man, while doing thus these
other people of us/ours came, again.

5. 3 Conversation 3

Jinghua and Turgun in Akkaba in September 1995

A.   *sen aba-ŋ-nɪ   ederd-ip   gayda bar-ɪp   gel-di-ŋ*
      you mother-2POSS-ACC lead-CONV where go-CONV come-PAST-2SG

      "Where did you go taking along (with) your mother?"

B.   *awa-m-nɪ   edirt-ip   bir ög-gö   bar-gaš-tan*
      mother-1SG.POSS-ACC lead-CONV one house-DAT go-CONV-ABL

      xobux-ka bar-gaš-tan iyi üš gün žor-up   o-nun
      Kobuk-DAT go-CONV-ABL two three day walk-CONV it-ABL

      gedeer alday-ga bar-gaš-tan o-nun deskin-ip
      after   Altay-DAT go-CONV-ABL it-ABL stroll-CONV

      gel-di-k
      come-PAST-1PL

      "I took my mother to a house, and we went to Kobuk and spent
      two or three days there, and after that, we went to Altay and came
      back."

A.   *alday-ga žügö bar-dɪ-gar*
      Altay-DAT why go-PAST-2SG

      "Why did you go to Altay?"

B.   *men giži-niŋ   ö-ö-ŋgö   bar-ɪp   gil-di-m*
      I   person-GEN house-3POSS-DAT go-CONV come-PAST-1SG

      "I went to someone's house and came back."

A.   *o giži bar irgin be*
       that person EXIST EVID Q

       "Was that person at home?"

B.   *bis ba-ar-da   žok   irgin*
       we go-PRSPRT-LOC NEGEXIST EVID

       o-nun gedeer erten-i-nde   bar-dı-bıs
       it-ABL after   next.day-3POSS-LOC go-PAST-1PL

       osunda erten-i-nde   bo žer-ge   gel-di-k
       then   next.day-3POSS-LOC this place-DAT come-PAST-1PL

       "(He) was not there when we went. After that, we went again the next day. Then, we came back here (this place) the next day."

A.   *orta žeže   kün žor-du-gar*
       there how.many day walk-PAST-2PL

       "How many days were you there?"

B.   *orta bir kün žor-up   doxturxana-ga bar-ıp*
       there one day walk-CONV hospital-DAT   go-CONV

       teksir-il-ip   em-pem   a-p   o-nun gedeer bir
       check-PASS-CONV medicine-RDP take-CONV it-ABL after one

       kün-nün soŋgaar žan-dı-bıs
       day-ABL after   return-PAST-1PL

       We wandered around there for a day and went to the hospital, got checked, took some medicine, and one day after that, we returned.

A.   *tärbiye gadı   bar-dı ba*
       Tärbiye together go-PAST Q

       "Did Tärbiye go with you?"

B.   *gadı   bar-dı*
       together go-PAST

       "He went with us."

A.   *ol siler-nen   gadı   žan-dı   ba*
       he you.PL-INSTR together return-PAST Q

       "Did he come back with you guys?"

B.   *ol gadı   bar-gaš-tan iyi üš   xon-gaš-tan*
       he together go-CONV-ABL two three spend.night- CONV-ABL

       žan-ıp   gel-gen   bis-ten murun
       return-CONV come-PSTINDF we-ABL before

       He went there with us (but) came back before us after spending
       two or three days.

       dalaš-kaš   gel-di
       hurry-CONV come-PAST

       He came back because he was in a hurry.

       dalaš-kaš   giži-ni
       hurry-CONV person-ACC

       " He hurried people (us)."

A.   *osoonda erten-i-nde*   *ün-dü-gör*
     then   next.day-3POSS-LOC come.out-PAST-2PL

"So you set off the next day?"

B.   *e o-nun üŋ-göš*   *buwuršın-ga   gel-geš-ten*
     yes it-ABL come.out-CONV Buwurshin-DAT come-CONV-ABL

     buwuršın-da   baxıt-dar-nıŋ ö-ö-gö   *ge-ep*
     Buwurshin-LOC Bakit-PL-GEN   house-3POSS-DAT come-CONV

     xon-du-bus
     spend.night-PAST-1PL

"Yes, we went to Buwurshin after we had left there. In
Buwurshin, we went to Bakit's house and spent the night there."

B.   *baxıt žümö gı-p   žor*
     Bakit what do-CONV walk

"What is Bakit doing?"

A.   *baxıt iž-i-n   ište-p žor*
     Bakit work-3POSS-ACC do-CONV walk

"Bakit is working (doing his work.)"

B.   *osunda gayda bar-ıp   gel-di-ŋ   dem-nen beer*
     after.that where go-CONV come-PAST-2SG that-ABL since

"After that, where did you go then?"

A.   *dem-nen beer ög-gö   bar-ıp gel-di-m*
     that-ABL since home-DAT go-CONV come-PAST-1SG

"After that I went home."

5. 4 Conversation 4

Terbiya and Özetti in Akkaba in September 1995

A.   *bod-uŋuz   žönünde xoožula-p ber-iŋiz*
self-2SG.POL about   tell-CONV give-2SG.IMP

"Please tell about yourself."

B.   *mal-ɪbɪs-tɪ   sa-ap   mal   malda-p*
livestock-1PL.POSS-ACC milk-CONV livestock breed-CONV

ɪnža-n-gan   amtan-nar-bɪs
do.that-REFL-PSTPRT person-PL-1PL

xoy mal   bilen dag   daš-ka göž-üp   žoru-un
sheep livestock with mountain rock-DAT move-CONV walk-PSTPRT

"We are people who milk and breed livestock. (We are the people) who nomadize on the mountain and among the rocks with our sheep and livestock."

A.   *ad-ɪŋɪz   gɪm*
name-2SG.POL.POSS who

"What is your name?"

B.   *ad-ɪm   özetti*
name-1SG.POSS Özetti

"My name is Özetti."

A.   *žeže   žaš-ka   gel-gen-siler*
     how.many age-DAT come-PSTINDF-2SG.POL

     "How old are you?"

B.   *käzir aldan bir-lig   men*
     now   sixty first-ADJ 1SG

     "Now I am sixty-one years old."

A.   *gayda žor-up   ös-kön-siler*
     where walk-CONV grow-PSTINDF-2SG.POL

     "Where did you grow up?"

B.   *teginde xanas-ka   žor-up   ös-kön-men*
     formerly Kanas-DAT walk-CONV grow-PSTINDF-1SG

     xanas-tïg-men
     Kanas-ADJ-1COP

     "Formerly I grew up in Kanas. I am from Kanas."

A.   *xanas-tan gel-gen-siler   be*
     Kanas-ABL come-PSTINDF-2SG.POL Q

     "Did you come from Kanas?"

B.   *xanas-tan gel-gen-men*
     Kanas-ABL come-PSTINDF-1SG

     "I came from Kanas."

A.   *xanas-tan di-ger-nen   onsonda bo akkaba-ga*
     Kanas-ABL say-2SG-EMPH here   this Akkaba-DAT

gel-gen-siler   *be*
come-PSTINDF-2SG.POL Q

"Are you saying that you are from Kanas? Did you come to this Akkaba after that?"

B.   *e*
      yes

      "Yes."

A.   *žežentši žɪl gel-di-ger*
      which   year come-PAST-2SG

      "Which year did you come?"

B.   *žežentši žɪl oy utd-up   ga-ap   dur men*
      which   year hey forget-CONV remain-CONV stay 1SG

      nadan giži
      ignorant person

      "Which year? Oh, I have forgotten. (I am) an ignorant person."

A.   *žeže   žaš-ta doy žaza-an-siler   burun*
      how.many age-LOC marry make-PSTINDF-2SG.POL before

      "In the past, how old were you when you got married?"

B.   *burun ba žeerbi bir žaš-ta la*
      before Q twenty one age-LOC EMPH

      "In the past? It was only at the age of twenty-one."

A.   *pa bičii le   doy   žaza-p-siler*
     wow small EMPH wedding make-CONV-2SG.POL

     "Wow, you got married very young."

B.   *e burun ol bičii-de doy   žaza-y   be-er-ge*
     yes before that small-LOC wedding make-CONV give-PRSPRT-DAT

     bol-ur
     be-PRSINDF

     "Yes, in the past it was possible to get married that young."

A.   *bo akkaba-a   ge-ep   doy   žaza-dı-gar*
     this Akkaba-DAT come-CONV wedding make-PAST-2SG

     "Did you come to this Akkaba to get married?"

B.   *e xanas-ta*
     yes Kanas-LOC

     "Yes, in Kanas."

A.   *burun-gu   žayla-agar   gayda-ger*
     before-RELCL summer.pasture.land-2SG.POSS where-2SG

     "Where was your previous summer pastureland?"

B.   *burun bod-ubuz-duŋ   žayla-bız   aldınak*
     before self-1PL.POSS-GEN summer.pastureland-1PL.POSS Aldinak

     aršaan de-p   žer
     Arshan say-CONV place

"Our previous summer pastureland was (at) a place called Aldinak Arshan."

A.   *aldınak aršaan*
Aldinak Arshan

"Aldinak Arshan?"

B.   *e onsunda bo žaylag-ga   gözü-p*
yes after.that this summer.pastureland-DAT move-CONV

gel-gen-nen   gedeer ažay žurd-um   de-p
come-PSTPRT-ABL after   father land-1SG.POSS say-CONV

žor-bus
walk-1SG

"Yes, after moving to this summer pastureland, we are calling it our fatherland."

A.   *dıba-lar dee šag-da ganžap doy   žaza-ar   irgin*
Tuva-PL that time-LOC how   wedding make-PRSINDF EVID

"How did Tuvas get married at that time?"

B.   *käzir-gi šag-da gıdat bo-p   gal-dı*
now-RELCL time-LOC Chinese be-CONV remain-PAST

"Nowadays, (they) have become Han Chinese."

A.   *burun ži*
before how.about

dıba-lar ganžap doy   žaza-ar   irgin
Tuva-PL how   wedding make-PRSINDF EVID

o-nu   bır ayt-kar-nan
it-ACC one tell-2SG.IMP-EMPH

"How about in the past? How did Tuvas get married? Could you please talk about it?"

B.   *dıba-lar doy   žaza-ar-da   mal-ı-n*
Tuva-PL wedding make-PRSPRT-LOC animal-3POSS-ACC

soy-ar   oyna-ar   ırla-ar   tabak
slaughter-PRSINDF play-PRSINDF sing-PRSINDF plate

gag-ar   oylad-ır   dud-ar
hit-PRSINDF chase.away-PRSINDF catch-PRSINDF

kayı žeŋ-gen-i-ŋge   udum be-er
which win-PSTPRT-3POSS-DAT gift give-PRSINDF

"When the Tuva held a wedding ceremony, they slaughtered animals, played, sang, beat (in-laws) with plates, chased and caught them. (They) gave gifts to those who won."

A.   *baza šap   gag-ar   ba*
and   rawhide.strap beat-PRSINDF Q

"Do they also play rawhide beating games?"

B.   *šap   gag-ar*
rawhide.strap beat-PRSINDF

žüstük sug-ar   baš žaza-r
thimble put.on-PRSINDF head make-PRSINDF

"They beat with rawhide straps. They put on a thimble (ring) (playing the ring hiding game) and do their hair."

A. *siler-niŋ   söög-üger   žüžüme bol-ur*
    You.POL-GEN bone-2SG.POSS.POL what   be-PRSINDF

"What is your bone clan?"

B. *söög-üm   soyan bol-ur*
    bone-1SG.POSS Soyan be-PRSINDF

"My bone clan is Soyan."

A. *e dört sumun-ga kelin   bo-p   gel-gen*
    Oh four district-DAT daughter-in-law be-CONV come-PSTINDF

    di-ger-nen
    say-2SG.IMP-EMPH

"Oh, you are saying that you came to the Four Districts to become a daughter-in-law."

B. *e dört sumun-ga kelin   bo-p   gel-gen-bis*
    oh four district-DAT daughter-in-law be-CONV come-PSTINDF-1PL

"Yes, we (I) came to the Four Districts as (a) daughter-in-law."

A. *dört sumun-ga siŋ-gen-bis   di-ger-nen   satkın*
    four district-DAT soak-PSTINDF-1PL say-2SG-EMPH traitor

"You are saying that we have been merged into the Four Districts, traitor."

B. *e   satkın amda dört sumun-men käzir*
    yes traitor now four distrcits-1SG now

"Yes, now I am a traitor. I am (from) Four Banner now."

A.   *žeže   ool-gar   bar*
    how.many child-2SG.POSS EXIST

    "How many children do you have?"

B.   *iyi*
    two

    "Two."

A.   *käzir gayda*
    now where

    "Where are they now?"

B.   *biri-zi   doy   žaza-y   bar-gan*
    One.of-3POSS marry make-CONV go-PSTINDF

    "One of them got married and left."

A.   *urug iyik be*
    girl EVID Q

    "That must be a girl?"

B.   *e urug*
    yes girl

    "Yes, a girl."

A.   *ad-ı   gım*
    name-3POSS who

    "What's her name?"

B.   *ad-ı   oyunčumuk*
name-3POSS Oyunchumuk

"Her name is Oyunchumuk."

A.   *oyunčumuk de-p   urug bar*
Oyunchumuk say-CONV girl   EXIST

"(Do you have) a girl named Oyunchumuk?"

B.   *am biri-zi   kelin-im-nen   bir*
now one.of-3POSS daughter-in-law-1SG.POSS-ABL one

ogl-um   bar
son-1SG.POSS EXIST

"Now the other one, I have a son from my daughter-in-law."

A.   *ol gayda*
he where

"Where is he?"

B.   *ol makdıp-ke gid-ir*
he school-DAT enter-PRSINDF

He goes to school.

A.   *žežinči nomšu-ur*
which   study-PRSINDF

"He is studying in which grade?"

B.   *sezinči nomšu-ur*
eighth   study-PRSINDF

"He studies in eighth grade."

A. *ortalaw-da bol-du   emes be*
    middle-LOC be-PAST not   Q

    "Wasn't he in the middle school?"

B. *e ortalaw-da bol-du*
    yes middle-LOC be-PAST

    amdı šüübür be-er   le   ırgın
    now exam   give-PRSINDF EMPH EVID

    "Yes, he was in the middle school. Now, he is going to take the exam."

A. *ol urug-lar-nı   ganžap nomšu-d-ar-siler*
    that child-PL-ACC how   study-CAUS-PRSINDF-2PL.POL

    "How do you plan to school those children?"

B. *nomšu-d-a   be-er-aan*
    study-CAUS-CONV give-PRSINDF

    gayda bar-sa   žige nomšu-za bol-du
    where go-COND right study-COND be-PAST

    düb-ü-nde   payda
    bottom-3POSS-LOC useful

    "We will let them continue their studies. It doesn't matter where he goes if he studies well. After all/ ultimately, it's good (for him)"

A.   *žeze   duyug inek-ler bar*
      how.many hoof   cow-PL EXIST

      "How many cows do you have?"

B.   *bir on-ža   duyug bar*
      one ten-EQU hoof   EXIST

      "There are about ten of them."

A.   *xoy žeže   bar*
      sheep how.many EXIST

      "How many sheep do you have?"

B.   *xoy-nan   da on-ža   bar*
      sheep-ABL also ten-EQU EXIST

      "There are also about ten sheep."

A.   *žılgı-nan*
      horse-ABL

      "And (how many) horses?"

B.   *žılgı-nan iyi žoon bar*
      horse-ABL two big   EXIST

      "We have two big horses."

A.   *güdee-ger   žüme iste-er   irgin*
      son-in-law-2SG.POSS.POL what   work-PRSINDF EVID

      "What does your son-in-law do?"

B.   *ıstansa-da*
station-LOC

"(He works) at the (power) station."

A.   *kaysı-da*
which-LOC

"At which one?"

B.   *xara daš-ta*
black stone-LOC

"(The one) in Black Stone."

A.   *awdan-nıŋ xara daž-ı-nda   di-ger-nen*
county-GEN black stone-3POSS-LOC say-2SG-EMPH

ay-ı-nda   žeže   deŋge al-ır   ırgın
month-3POSS-LOC how.much money take-PRSINDF EVID

"You say, the one at the county's Black Stone area! How much does he make in a month?"

B.   *bıl-bes-pen*
know-NEGPRSINDF-1SG

üš žüs   dört žüs   al-ır
three hundred four hundred take-PRSINDF

"I don't know. He makes three or four hundred."

A.   *siler-ge   andasanda teŋge be-er   be*
you.POL-DAT sometimes   money give-PRSINDF Q

"Does he give you money sometimes?"

B.   *oy ol bazar-da žibe-zi   bod-u-ŋga   žet-pes*
oh that city-LOC thing-3POSS self-3POSS-DAT suffice-NEGPRSPRT

de-er
say-PRSINDF

"Oh (no), they say that in the city it's not enough for themselves."

A.   *bod-u-ŋga   žet-pes   de-en-i*
self-3POSS-DAT enough-NEGPRSPRT say-PSTPRT-3POSS

siler-ge   ber-be-yin   de-en-i   yoŋ
you.POL-DAT give-NEG-1SG.IMP say- PSTPRT-3POSS EMPH

"(He is) saying that it's not enough for ourselves means that I don't want to give you, right?"

Word List

This section contains words used in the preceding texts. The words in this wordlist are alphabetized as follows: a, aa, ä, ää, b, c, č, d, e, ee, g, x, i, ii, ı, ıı, ž, k, l, m, n, ŋ, o, oo, ö, öö, p, r, s, š, t, u, uu, ü, üü, w, y, z. Each entry contains the following elements: Jungar Tuvan form, English equivalent. Abbreviations of the source of the borrowing languages used in the wordlist are: K. = Kazak, M. = Modern Mongolian, U. = Uyghur, C. = Mandarin Chinese, R. = Russian; e.g., "tüsün- understand, cf. K. tüsin-, saazın paper, cf. M. čagasun, žıŋ true, real, authentic, cf. C. zhen, kawap kebab, roasted meat, cf. U. kawap, pälte overcoat, cf. R[1]. pal'to."

For the Jungar Tuvan forms, when more than one form is given, this means that informants differ or vary in their pronunciation of the word e.g., kara black (see xara). Verbs are listed in their stem form and hyphens are used to indicate the stem in entries for verbs. In some cases, there might be two or three words for one concept. These are cross-listed under each alternate form; e.g., dumžuk nose, see xaay.

---

[1] For those Russian loan words where the Standard Tuvan form is known, the source of the borrowing language is not given.

aal homeland, village

aar heavy, difficult

aarı- ache, pain

aarıg illness, pain, sick

aarıg-doorug illness and disease

aaršı a kind of dried curd-
cheese

aas mouth

aas-dıl argument, quarrel

ab- take

aba mother, see awa

ača bulak Acha bulak
(place name)

ada-iye parents

ada- name, call

adak at the end, end

andasanda occasionally,
sometimes

adaš friend, mistress, lover,
comrade

adaš bol- become friend

aga older brother

agın current, flow

agın sug running water

axırında- slow down

axırındap slowly

aža father

ažay dear father, daddy

ažıg bitter, sour

ažıl work

ažılda - work, do

ak- flow

ak white, pale

ak irgit White Irgit (clan name)

ak köyük White Köyük (clan
name)

ak soyan White Soyan (clan
name)

ak dairy products

ak gut- pour/offer drinks

ak-kök drinks

akkaba Akkaba (place name)

akkaba kıstak Akkaba sub-
village

akkaba gıstaa Akkaba sub-
village

al well, now, but

al- take, obtain, get, buy

al- be able to (do something)

ala multicolored, piebald,
colored, dappled

alagak Alagak (place name)

albatı citizen

alda- cheat

aldan sixty

aldan iyinči sixty second

aldan bešdey about sixty five

alday Altay, see altay

alday awdan Altay county

alday aymaa Altay prefecture

alday xalazı Altay city

aldı bottom, floor, underneath

aldı six

aldı žüs six hundred

aldı žüs žeže six hundred some
aldınžı sixth
aldınžı ay June, see
žaynıŋ soŋ ay
aldınžı bän sixth grade
aldın gold
aldın ken golden mine
aldınak aršan Aldinak Arshan
   (place name)
algıš gratitude
alıškı brothers
almas diamond
altay Altay, see alday
altınča Altincha (personal
   name)
am now, see amdı
ambıl *Ambil* title for governor
   or rank in that time
amdı now, nowadays, see am
amguuluŋ what has been said
amırak sweetheart, lover;
   beloved
amtan human being, the
   common people, living
   creature
amtannar people, populace
anay kid, young goat
andasanda sometimes, once a
   while
anıyag young, young people
aŋ wild game
aŋdar- turn (over), translate

žer aŋdar- exile
aŋgılıg special, particular
aŋžı hunter
aŋna- hunt, hunt wild game
apar- take, deliver
ara place, interval, space
   between, distance
aragı alcoholic drink, liquor,
   wine, vodka
arala- wander round, stroll
aralaš- mix, mingle with,
   associate with, socialize with
aray slowly, barely, hardly
arba barley
arga forest, woods
arga way, means, measure
argaža further
argamžı lasso, noose, lariat
argımak fine horse, steed
arıg clean, pure
arıg sug clear water
arkılı through, via
arnawlı special, intended
art back, backward
   artının later, afterward
   artta kal- remain behind
art-göp people
artık more, better, more than, in
excess of
arzalaŋ lion
as- hang
aš- open, uncover, tear off, lift

(the lid, etc.)

aš- cross (over), climb over

ašı-enži descendant

aškıyak elder, old man

at name, title

at san noun

at horse

   bägige at sal- have a horse race

at- throw, shoot

attıg someone named, called

awa mother, see aba

awdan county

awdandıg (of the) county, county

awdar- translate, turn over

awıldık (of the) village, village

ay hey

ay moon, month

ayda- drive, drive up (animals), see xay de-

ayıl danger; misfortune, disaster

ayırmašılıg divergence, difference

ayla dirty trick

aylık wage, pay, salary

aymak district, prefecture

ayt- say, tell, state

azat liberation cf. K azat

azat bol- be librated

azıl precious

azın- shoulder, carry on the shoulder

azıra- raise, bring up (children), adopt, breed, tend (animal)

   tın azıra- subsist, live

ä okay

ädet habit, custom

ädet-gurpu habits and customs

ädette usually

äkel- bring

äkem my dear

äl strength, power

äle emphatic particle

äŋgime chat, story

äŋgimeles- converse, chat

äreket movement, activity,

ärkandık any, any kind

äytew anyhow

äwöli even

äymen Äymen (personal name)

ba question particle

baalık mountain pass, saddle shaped mountain

bag strap

   sarıg bag a leather ball used for shooting with a bow when playing the game.

bagala- evaluate

bagana pillar

bagay bad, ugly, poor

bagla- tie, bind, bundle up

baxıt Bakit (personal name)

baxšı teacher, shaman healer, shaman

bar- go, go away, leave for

bar there is, exists, present

baran silhouette

barı all, altogether

barıs course, process

barısında during, in the course/process of

bas- press, depress, step on; make (felt)

bastawıš elementary

bastawıš mektep elementary school, see bastawšı

bastawšı elementary school, see bastawıš mektep

baš head, chief, top, beginning

baš žaza- do one's hair, get one's hair done (before the wedding ceremony)

baška other, besides

baškı beginning

baškar- manage, direct, administer, govern, rule, reign

bašta- begin, start, direct, regulate

baštay first, at first, early

baštık leader, chief

batı Bati (personal name)

bay rich, rich man

bayagıda long ago, in the past

baylanıs connection

bayterek Bayterek (personal name)

baza or, and, also, again, more, see basa

bazar market, fair, city

bälendey any particular, certain

bälen-tügön so and so, such and such, everything

bän class, grade cf. C. ban

birinči bän first grade

bäteŋke a leather shoe cf. R botinki

bäygi horse race

bäygi sal- have a horse race

be question particle

beedil condition, situation

beer this way, hither; since, see beri

beesi Beesi (banner name); *Beesi*, prince of the fourth rank in Manchu times. cf. M. *Bees*

beižiŋ Beijing cf. C. **Beijing**

bežen fifty

bežen sesinči fifty-seventh

bežendeg about fifty

beket bus stop, bus station

beldir waist

belek gift, betrothal gift, present, bride-price

belžiir pasture

ber- give, afford

berekeli amicable

beri here, hither, hitherto, since,
   see beer

beš five

beš žüs five hundred

bešenži fifth

bešenži ay May, see
   žaynıŋ orta ay

bešenži bän fifth grade

beštey about five

bet hill side

beti this side

beyin happiness, well-being

biči- write, record

bičii small, little, few, young

bičii-bičii gradually, bit by bit

bičik script, paper

bil- know, know to

bilen with, together with, by
   means of, and

bilim knowledge

bilimnig knowledgeable

bir one, some

bir žüs one hundred

bir mıŋ one thousand

bir žeže several

bir žime something

bir šama somewhat, more or
   less

birak but

birakta however, but

birge together, together with

biri one of them, one of

birinči first, first of all

birleš- unite as one

birleštir- cause to unite

bis we

bister we

bistiŋ our

biš- cut, trim, cut out

bit- end, come to an end

bittir- finish, complete

biy judge, old official title, a
   tribal, clan or village elder
   who judged cases in
   customary law.

biy dance

biyle- dance

bıdıra- scatter

bıdıra shotgun

bıdırandı scattered

bıžıg tight, taut, secure, solid,
   hard, durable

bıžır- cook, roast, boil, bake

bılga- stir, do harm, hurt,
   disturb, soil

bıš- cook, boil, bake, ripen

bıškan cooked, ripe

bıškır- sneeze

bo this, see mo

bo žer here

bo žıl this year

bo žılm this year

bo kıšın this winter
boda- think
bodagan baby camel, camel
 foal
bodal idea, opinion, view,
 thought, intention
bodalınča according to
bodaŋ wild boar
bodum myself
boduŋ yourself
bodu himself, herself, itself
bodunuŋ of oneself, own
bodubus ourselves
boduŋar yourselves
boxda Buddha
bol- be, become
bola- come out this way, go this
 way
bolar these, they
bolat steel; Bolat (personal
 name)
bolat kort- smelt (steel)
bolbaday Bolbaday (name of a
 mountain)
bolbaday daa Bolbaday
 Mountain
bolgayax supposedly
bolšuug way of life
boo gun, rifle
boo-žepsek weapon
bopu bootee
boraan storm

boraan žaškın snow storm
bot reflexive pronoun, self,
 oneself
botpum Botpum (clan name)
bottarı themselves
bottarıŋar yourselves
bottarıwıs ourselves
boyunča according to
bö question particle
bödöge gizzard
bödölge bottle
bödöne quail
böge wrestler
böge sal- have a wrestling
 tournament
bögün today
böl- divide
böl- send, assign
bölek piece, lump, cube, chunk
bölmö room
bölmölüg with ... room
bölüm part, section
bölün- be distributed, be
 assigned
böörüŋke round, spherical,
 globular
börü wolf
budda Buddhist
budda dini Buddhism
bulak brook, stream
buluŋ corner, cf. U. buluŋ
burgan God, Buddha

burun before, see murun
buruŋgaar forwards, ahead
buruŋgu former, previous, ancient, old
buruŋgu kün the day before yesterday
buruŋgu žɪl the year before last
bus- break, destroy
bus- break down (customs)
butkun whole
buwuršin Buwurshin (county name)
buwuršin awdanɪ Buwurshin county
buwuršin xalazɪ Buwurshin city
buyun Buyun (personal name)
buyunbat Buyunbat (personal name)
büdün whole, entire, all
bürün sound
bürün leave
büt- form
büt- end, be finished
bütkün all, whole
bütür- finish, graduate
čala half
čaš- spray, sow, see šaš-
čeček flower, see žežek
čin Qing (Dynasty)
čɪŋgɪs Chinggis (personal name)
čɪŋgɪs xaan Chinggis Khan

čoŋgar Chonggar (personal name)
čuwašilik Chuwashilik (place name)
da also, and, too
da emphatic particle
daara- sew
dadɪg hard
dag mountain
dagɪ- sanctify, perform a ritual
dagɪɪr worship
dagɪn again
dažɪ- carry, transport, convey
dažɪdɪr- move house
daktay board, plank
daktayla- lay board
dalaš- hurry, rush, hasten to, become hurry
dalaš- dalaštan hurriedly
daman sole (of the foot or a shoe), paw, foot
damdɪ drop, drop of water
damzɪ- drip
danɪ- know, recognize, see tanɪ-
danɪš- get acquainted with, see tanɪš-
danɪštɪr- introduce
daŋ dawn, daybreak
daŋ bilen at dawn, in the morning
daŋnɪŋ always
dapšɪ- develop

daš stone
dašta- lay stone
dälde- take aim
de also
de emphatic particle
de- say, mention, name, see di-
dee that, that one
dee žer there, that place
deede-mɪnda this and that
deedis heaven
deedis nobility
deeži seed
deen bilen however
deeš- touch
debiyür fan
dedir backward, reverse, invert,
    back
dedir again, repeat
deg- reach, touch, hit
dege he-goat
degeler they
dežil- make hole in, get a hole
dekpe šay brick tea
dektene Dektene (personal
    name)
dekter note-book
delew Telew (ethnic name)
dem recent, recently, not long
    ago
dem exterior
dem yonder

demalɪs retirement, relax
demalɪska ün- retire
demgi same, specific (one)
deŋ equal, even, same
deŋge money
depse- kick
dere- send
deresin mat, straw mat, see
    teresin
deri skin, leather, hide
des- run away, flee, escape,
    renounce
deskin- stroll, turn in, circles
deš- pierce, perforate, drill, bore,
    make holes in
di- say, see de-
dile- look for, seek
din religion see süzük
dinniy religious
dɪba Tuva, see dɪwa
dɪba dɪl Tuvan language
dɪbaša Tuva, in Tuvan
dɪbalaša- speak Tuva, see
    tɪwala-
dɪbɪš- find each other
dɪl tongue, language, see til
dɪl al- heed, have a receptive ear
    for
dɪŋna- hear, listen
dɪp- obtain, get, gain; find,
    discover, see tɪp-

dıra- comb

dırba- plow, scrap

dırt- pull, drag

dırtta- pull, attract

dıwa Tuva, see dıba

doburak soil, earth, dirt

dogdur doctor, physician, see
    doxtur
      mal dogduru veterinarian

doxtur doctor, see dogdur

doxturxana hospital

doža freeze

doklat report cf. R. doklad

dolga- twist, wring, squeeze,
    turn

dolgaytı Dolgayti (place name)

dom incantation

domak word, speech

domakta- speak

domaktan- speak, converse, talk
    to oneself

domaktaš- talk to each other

domna- treat, cure by
    incantations

don outer lambskin garment
    with wool lining

doŋgur hornless

doora- cut, slice

doorug disease
    aarıg-doorug illness and
    disease

doos- finish

doru reddish brown

doy wedding, marriage, joyous
    occasion, happy event, feast,
    banquet

doy žaza- get married

doyla- feast; arrange a feast

doylık betrothal, gift, bride-
    price

dödö directly

döžö- pad, spread

döžök bed, bedding, mattress,
    sheet, cotton-padded mattress

döžön- pad

dööy alike, similar, resembling

dööy emes different

dörbölžin square

dörbölžinnig square room

dörölži ridge

dörölžü herd

dört four

dört žüs four hundred

dört žüstüŋ üstünde over four
    hundred

dört sumun Four Districts

dörttey about four

dörtünži fourth

dörtünži bän fourth grade

dörtünži ay April, see
    žaynıŋ bašıg ay

dörtön forty

dörtön žetinči forty seventh

dörtönšü fortieth

dörttüŋ biri one-fourth

dörüü dörü tea (kind of tea)

duguruk round

dumžuk nose, see xaay

duŋči verb cf. C. **dongci**

duŋma younger brother

dur emphatic

dur- stand (up), get up, stay,
 live, stay

dura straight, directly

dut- seize, grab, grasp, catch,
 capture, arrest, take, hold, see
 tut-

duyug hoof, measure word for
 domestic animals

dük wool, hair of animals

dül- stew, boil, cook
 et dül- stew meat

dün night

düne at night

düp bottom

dür- roll up

düš noon, midday

düš dream

düš- fall, descend
 kuda düš-   arrange an
 engagement

düün yesterday

e oh, ok, hey

ebeeš little, few, not much, not
 many

ebeešte- decrease, decline,

become few

ebes is/are not, not, see
 emes, ewes

ed- make a sound, utter a sound

et betrothal gift, bride-price,
 property, goods

edek hem, flap (of a skirt), flap
 (of a garment), foot (of a
 mountain or a hill), edge, rim
 brink

eder- follow, go together

edert- lead, bring

edik boot, shoe, footwear

edikši shoemaker, cobbler

edile- enjoy, make use of, take
 advantage

ee owner

ög eezi host, house owner

eedere- become foolish

eemese or see emese

een uninhabited, untended

eger if

egiči elder sister

ežel generous

ežen xaan Ezhan Khan
 (personal name)

ežik door; room (measure
 word), see ešik

ekir- be cured, get well

ekirt- cure

ekeli merit, strong point, virtue

eki good, kind, well

eki bol- get along well

eki gör- like, love

ekilig good deed

ekkel- bring to, bring
along

elbek abundant, plentiful

elder comrade

ele emphatic

elek fun, mockery

elek gıl- make fun of, poke
fun at

em medicine and such

em-pem medicine, drug

emes is/are not, not, see
ebes, ewes

emese or, see emese

emidirel life

emidirel ötküs- spend one's
life

emži doctor, physician

emži-domžu doctor and such,
physician and such

emne- cure, treat

endi then

ene grandma

enir žıl last year, see
ötken žıl

eŋ most (indicating
the superlative degree)

eŋgey face

epteštirip carefully, by any
means necessary

eptig convenient, appropriate

er man, husband

er žedir- raise, bring up

er žet- grow up, mature,
become an adult

eržetken grown up, adult

erdine precious, treasure,
elegant

ereydep barely enough

erge authority, law, order

erge pamper

erkin unconstrained, free,
voluntarily

erte early

ertede in the olden days, a long
time ago

ertem learned, scholarly,
knowledge, learning, science

erten tomorrow

erteninde the next day

erteŋgi next morning

esim noun (part of speech)

eš friend
eži one's friend

eš- twist, spin, row, paddle

ešti- hear

ešik door; room, see ežik
bir ešik ög one room

eštir- take a bath, swim

eškayda anywhere (in negative
sense)

et- make, do

et meat; livestock
et dül- stew meat
et žibe belongings
etik-kep all kinds of
  clothing
ewes is/are not, not, see
  ebes, emes
ezer saddle
ezim forest, wood
gaaŋ aridity
gabıyaa harmonious, harmony,
  unity
gadaŋgır Gadanggir (a place
  name)
gadarlı together with
gadarlıg and so on, etc.,
  together with
gaday auntie, woman
gadı wrong
gadı together, beside
gadı žoru- accompany
gag- lay, put, place, build, erect,
  leave, pave, apply (to a
  surface); hit, knock
  ög gag- build a house
gažaa enclosure, corral,
  livestock pen, barn
gažaa-xamaa barn and such
gak- knock, hit, beat, pound,
  bang, defeat, conquer, assault,
  vanquish, win, throw, leave,
  see xak-

gal- remain, stay, be left , see
  kal-
galži lunatic, madman, see
  kalčaa
gana only, just, see gene
gandıg how, what kind
ganžaar how, in what way; no
  matter how much, how many,
  how much, how it does
ganžalsada no matter what
ganžap how
garbal- seek support
garak eye
gas side, nearby
gatkı laugh, laughter
gatkır- laugh loudly
gatın wife
gayda where, see kayda
gayga to where, whither
gayga- look
gaylap how, where
gaysı which, see kaysı
gayta instead
gaz- dig, dig out
gazırgı whirlwind
gedeer after, until, up to
gežee evening
gežee diligent
geži blessing
gel- come, come here, see kel-
geler coming

geler žayın next summer
geler žıl next year
gene only, just, see gana
geŋ Geng (Chinese surname)
gerbiš brick
gerek necessary
gerel light, sun light, radiance
gereldig light, radiant
ges- cut, slice, saw, see kes-
geš skin
get- wear, put on (clothes or
  hat), dress
gez- wander
gez time, instance
gezde at ... time
gezek charred log
gidis felt
gidis ög felt house, yurt
giži human being, man,
  person, people
giži sanı population
gižin- nag
gir- enter, enroll
girgiz- insert, cause to enter
gıda butt
dıdat China, Chinese, Han
  Chinese, see kıdat, xanzu
gıdır- visit
gıdıg side, edge
gıl- do, make, perform
gıldır as, so that

gılın dense, thick
gım who
gımıyla- live
gımži whip
gır- kill, destroy, slaughter
gırgan old man
gıstak sub-village, see kıstak
gıškı word
gıš winter
gıškı winter, wintry
gıštag winter camp, see gıštaw
gıštıŋ baškay October, see
  on ay
gıšdıŋ orta ay November, see
  on bir ay
gıšdıŋ suŋkay December, see
  on iyi ay
gıžın in the winter
gıšta- spend the winter
gıštaw winter encampment, see
  gıštag
gıy- spare
gıy hail, call
gıy de- hail, call
gızıl red
gožarlaš- form a pair
gožugar small yurt, small tent
gožuun tribe, entity, banner,
  populace, administrative unit,
  region
goldan- use, make use of, apply

gomindaŋ Guomindang, cf. C.
Guomindang
gomindaŋ ökümödü
Guomindang Government
gonžug very, well
goŋgutu Gonggutu (place name)
goŋgutu irgit Gonggutu Irgit
(clan name)
goŋgutu köyük Gonggutu
Köyük (clan name)
gorža- surround, encircle,
enclose, shut in a pen
goržaar fence, circle, pen, fold,
sty sheepfold, small yurt
goržun saddle bag
goš tent, see kos
gozul- agree
göböy- increase
göböy many, much, more, a lot
göbü most
göžö street
göžür- relocate, cause to migrate
gök blue (of sky, eyes, paper,
etc.), green (grass, leaves, hay
etc.)
göktogay Kötagay (a county
name)
göktogay awdanı Kötagay
county
gök sug Kök Sug (place
name)
göp many, most, a lot, more

gör- see, look at, read, watch,
consider; cure
duš gör- have a dream,
dream
eki gör- like, love
görgüzü showing
görünžük mirror, looking glass,
window, see terize
göstür- show
göš- leave, go away, move to
göz eye
göz karas opinion, point of
view
gudu low, down, below, lower,
downwards
gudul- get rid of
gužur Guzhur (place name)
gulak ear
gulgu friend
guŋšo commune, cf. C. gongshe
guŋšo gur- establish commune
gur sash, belt
gur- establish, see kur-
gurga- dry, dry up, become dry
gurgag dry
gurgat- dry, make dry
gurul- be established
gurmustu God of Heaven, God
of Sky, Sky God, see
kurmusdu
gurpu habits
gut- pour, pour out, cast

güdee son-in-law
güdük doubt, suspicious
gümännen- suspect
gün day, see kün
güreš wrestling, wrestle
güreš- wrestle
güreštir- cause to wrestle
gürümži exorcist
gürümnö- exorcize
güs autumn, fall
güsdüŋ bašıg ay July
güsdüŋ orta ay August
güskö mouse
güš force, strength, might
güštüg strong
güzöt- guard
güzün in autumn, in (the) fall
xaak willow, shrubbery
xaan khan, emperor
xaaš cold
xaaš de- get cold
xaay nose, see dumžuk
xaba Kaba (county name)
xaba awdan Kaba County, see
　　xaba awdanı
xaba awdanı Kaba County, see
　　xaba awdan
xabar news
xadax gift
xadar žag dıba Kadar Zhang
　　Tuva (clan name)

xaduŋma relatives, fellow
　　countryman, compatriot
xak- strike, beat, knock, crush,
　　pound, see gak-
　　sigen xak- cut grass, mow
xala city
　　alday xalazı Altay city
xalı- jump, leap, sprint, bounce,
　　run, go quickly
xalıptaš- form
xalžan birth mark, blaze, (horse)
　　with a white blaze on the
　　forehead
xam shaman
xam bolbaday Kam Bolbaday
　　(place name)
xamık all
xamna- shamanize
xanas Kanas (lake name)
xanas awıldık Kana village
xanas gıstaa Kanas sub-village
xanas moŋgul uluttug aalı the
　　Kanas Mongol (Autonomous)
　　village
xandagaytı Kandagayti (place
　　name)
xanıg fluent
xanıg bol- be fluent
xanzu Han Chinese, cf. C. **Han
　　zu,** see kıdat, gıdat
xanzuša in Chinese, Chinese
xaŋgırla- ring

xaŋgırlıg ringing
xar other
xara the common people
xara black
xara daš Black Stone (place
    name)
xara oy Kara Oy (place name)
xaraaža roof ring
xarakan-gurt centipede
xaraal watchman, guard
xaraŋgı dark
xaraŋgıla- get dark
xarın adverse
xay de- drive, see ayda-
xaya cliff, precipice, rock
xayım tie, equal
xayın- boil
xayındır- boil, bring to a boil
xırurgiya surgery, surgical
    department
xıy- cut
xıyır slanting, tilted, inclined
xobux Kobik (place name)
xogam society, see kogam
xol hand
xolu- join, merge, be combined,
    come together
xoluš- join each other, gather,
    come together
xom Kom (village name)
xom gıstaa Kom village

xom sundaarık Kom Sundaarik
    (place name)
xommalga Hommalga (place
    name)
xon- spend the night, stay
    overnight, settle; perch (e.g.
    birds)
xonak guest, visitor, see
    xunaža
xonak bol- be a guest
xonak ög guest room
xonaša guest
xonaša ög guest room
xonuštan- settle
xoŋ after all
xoŋgıray Konggiray (proper
    name)
xoŋgura- jingle
xoŋgurlug jingling
xoŋša- spread (e.g. gossip)
xoočun old lady
xoožıla- court, speak, tell
xoožılaš- converse, chat
xoožu story, tale, see tool
xoožu- speak
xoožula- tell
xoožulaš- converse, be in love
xoor aspan Kooraspan (flower
    name)
xopšu gossip
xorgun fat

xoy sheep

xoy kadar- herd sheep

xoyla- embrace

xoylaš- embrace each other

xoyug rafter (roof poles of a
    yurt)

xörüm better, well

xuuylu law (see zaŋ)

xuburuldu changeable parents
    of one's daughter-in-law or
    son-in-law; relatives by
    marriage, in-laws, see kuda

xuda bol- become in-laws, see
    kuda bol-

xuda düš- be engaged, arrange
    an engagement

xudma Hudma (Mongolian
    alphabet)

xudma üzüü Hudma alphabet

xužat document

xula light bay

xumiy whole

xunaža guest, visitor, see
    xonak

xur over all

xurmustu Kurmustu, the chief
    of the thirty-three Gods

xuškaš house sparrow, skylark,
    see kuškaš

xün sun; day

inek cow

inek kadar- herd cow

irgin apparently, it would seem
    that, evidential particle

irgit Irgit (clan name)

ak irgit White Irgit

kara irgit   Black Irgit

isker dexterous

iste- do, make, work, perform,
    see ište-

iš work, labor, job

iš gıl- do physical labor, work

iš ište- work

iške as- work

iš inside

iš- drink, eat

iš-žüzündük practical

iškıp anyhow, for some reasons

išti inside, within

iškanday any kind, any

iškim nobody

ište- do, make, work, perform,
    see iste-

iye yes

iyi two

iyi mıŋ two thousand

iyik aspect, respect, side, slope

iyilee both

iyileezi both of them

iyinči second

iyinči bän second grade

iyis twin

izde- search, look for
izig hot
izig sug hot water
ıgla- cry
ııt sound, voice
ııtta- make sound, emit sound,
    utter, say
ımdı now, see amdı
ında there (location)
ından from that, hence
ındıg that, of that kind, like
    that, such, so
ındıg bolsa da but
ındıg užun so, therefore, for
    that reason
ındıgı that one
ınža- do so, do that, thus do
ınžal- say so, do so
ınžaarda these from
ınžalsa but
ınžan then
ınžangaš therefore, so, and so,
    thus, then, because
ınžangaštan therefore, so
ıŋga to there, to it, thither
ıŋgay away from, further
ıŋgay always, only
ırak far, distant, remote, afar
ıraktan afar, from far away
ırla- sing, sing the praises of
ıstansa station, electric power
    generating station

ıt- blow
ıt dog
ıyaš tree, wood
ıyaš ög wood house
ıyat- be embarrassed, be
    ashamed, be shy
ža bow
žaa new, tender, delicate
    žaa žıl New Year's Day
žaa just now
žaa enemy
žaagay nice, pleasant, pretty,
    beautiful, handsome, very
    satisfactory; tasty, delicious
žaala- conquer, occupy
žaalaš- become enemy, be
    hostile
žaaš well behaved
žabaa one-year old horse, colt,
    see žawaa
žadak dormitory
žadır tent
žadıra- flourish
žag dıba Zhag Tuva (clan
    name)
    kara žag dıba Black Zhag
    Tuva (clan name)
    sarı žag dıba Yellow
    Zhag Tuva (clan name)
    kadar žag dıba Kadar
    Zhag Tuva (clan name)
žagaa letter

žagaa biči- write letter
žagarı high, top, government
žagday situation
išžüzündük
    žagdayda as a matter of fact
žagır- rule, govern, reign,
    power, conquer
žažıl green
žažır- hide, conceal
žažıra- stew
žažırın- hide
žak- light, kindle
    ot žak- light a fire, stir up
    trouble
    serenge žak- light a match
žaktır- like, approve
žalaŋaš Zhalangash (place
    name)
žalaŋaš naked
žalbar- pray, beg, prostrate
    oneself before the image of
    Buddha, worship Buddha
žalbardın- beg
žalgaš- continue
žalıı young fellow, young man;
    young
žalın- beg
žalpı general, common
žamdık some, several, certain
žamdıkta sometimes
žan- return
žan soul, life, person, people

žan bak- support oneself
žan sanı population
žanada again
žanagaš
    köyük Zhanagash Köyük
    (clan name)
žanžı quiver
žaŋgıs alone, isolated, lone, one,
    single
žaŋnık lightning
žar- split ,break off, strip off,
    peel, stab
žarala- wound, injure
žaralan- be wounded, be injured
žardı thin stick, sliver (of
    kindling wood), chip
žarıl- be broken, be punctured
žarın shoulder blade, scapulae
žarın gör- tell fortune by
    looking at a shoulder
    blade/scapulae of a sheep after
    it has been cooked, practice
    scapulamancy
žarınžı fortune teller who uses
    a scapulae for divination
žastıŋ orta ay February, see
    ortay
žastıŋ soŋ ay March, see
    soŋay
žastıŋ šag ay January, see
    baškı ay
žaš tear

žaš age, year

žaš young, youth, baby

žaš tender

žaš- sprinkle, spray, spill, splash, spurt, pour, spurt, sputter, sow

žaškaar outside

žašta- spatter

žaštıg age of ..., aged

žaštıgı outer

žaštın outer, exterior, outside, surface, appearance, see daštın

žaštında near, along side, side by side, next to, nearby, beside see daštinda

žaštıyık outside

žawaa one-year old horse, colt, see žabaa

žay summer

žayan fortune

žayla- beware, evade

žaynıŋ bašıg ay April, see dörtinži ay

žaynıŋ orta ay May, see bešenči ay

žaynıŋ soŋ ay June, see aldınči ay

žayın in the summer

žaylag summer pasture, summer camp, see žaylaw

žaylaw summer pasture, summer camp, see žaylag

žaysaŋ Zhaysang (place name)

žaysaŋ gölü Zhaysang Lake

žaza- make, do, repair, mend, construct

doy žaza- get married

žazal things that are made of dough to represent genies and devils or Satan

žazın in the spring

žä okay, well

žäne and

žäyit situation

žärmeŋke market, fair, cf. R.

že- eat, see ži-

žedeen huge

žeden seventy

žedi seven

žedi gožuun dıba the Seven Banner Tuvas

žedi žüs seven hundred

žedinči seventh

žedinči ay the seventh month, July

žedinči bän seventh grade

žeen nephew, sister's son

žeerbi twenty

žeerbi beš twenty five

žeerbi aldı twenty six

žeerin antelope, gazelle

žegde narrow-leaf oleaster

žeže how many, how much, several, some
  bir žeže several
  bir žeže žıl several years
žežek flower, see žežek
žeženči some, which
žel- amble, trot
želiš trot
žem food, meal
žeŋ- win
žeŋge elder sister-in-law, aunt-in-law
žeŋges moss
žep thread, string, wire, rope
žer land, earth, place, soil
žer aŋdar- exile
žer žar- cultivate, till, plough (e.g. land)
žergeleš- equal, parallel to each other, walk/go together, walk side by side
žerle- bury; reside
žerlik local
žet- reach, arrive at, attain, achieve
žet- suffice, be enough
žetkilen sufficient
ži- eat, see že-
žibe thing, object, item, article, something, see žübe, šübö
žibe- šibe things and such
žibele- say something, argue

židig piercing
žige correct, right
žime thing
žiŋxua Zhinghua (personal name)
žıg- pile, stack, pile up, heap up
žıg- pick up (from the ground), collect
žıgıl- gather together, assemble
žık area
žıl year
žılga- lick
žılgı horse, herd of horses
žılgıžı horse man, herdsman
žıŋ true, real cf. C. zhen
žırgalaŋ bliss
žırık light, bright, shiny
  ottug žırıgı firelight
žıt- lie down, rest, be situated
  žıdar ög bedroom
žıtkır- lay down, put down
žıyt chirp
žıyt de- chirp
žobat- console
žoguš- fight, brawl
žok no, without, not present
žoktug poor, needy
žol road, path
žon- plane, scrape
žonak saddle flap, wool saddle-pad

žoŋgo China cf. C. zhong guo
žook near, close, beside, recent;
  relatives
žookšula- approach
žookta recently
žoon big, large, massive, think,
  fat
žoor uphill
žor- walk, set out, stroll, move
žora danger
žoru- walk
žoru- converse, be in love
žorun-žozun customs and
  habits
žozun social customs
žozun superstition, ritual, rite,
  ceremony
žozun gıl- perform rituals
žöbüree bark
žön meaning, point, turn, order,
  direction
žönnön as far as, with regard to,
  concerning
žönnünde about, concerning,
  pertaining to
žöp right, fair, express
  agreement
žöp gör- agree, think it's fair
žöreel wish, blessing,
  invocation
žudaŋ poor
žug- wash, launder

žug- throw a party
žugdur- cause to wash
žurt the masses, people,
  homeland, nation, hometown,
  native land, country, yurt
žurtta- live, dwell, reside
žut calamity
žübe thing, see žibe, šübö
žügär woman, female
žügö why
žügür- run
žügürük swift, race (horse)
žük side, direction, edge
  barın žük west, the west
  čöön žük east, the east
  murnuu žük south, the south
  soŋgu žük north, the north
žüme what
žürök heart
žüs hundred
žüstey about a hundred
žüstük thimble, (finger) ring
žüstük sug- put on the thimble
žütülgü consciousness
žüktüülük strong, firm
žüü what, what kind of, which,
  what sort of
žüz face
žüzün colored
žüzün öŋgö a flower name
kaal- be knocked, be shot

kadar- herd, graze, look
after, take care, feed
  xoy kadar- herd sheep
  inek kadar- herd cow
kadı together
kak- blow, see **xak-**
kala city, see **xala**
kalık people
kalıptaš- form, see
  xalıptaš-
kalıptaštır- cause to form
kanas Kanas (place name) see
  xanas
kandıg how, which
kara black (see **xara**)
kara žag dıba Black Zhag Tuva
  (clan name)
kara irgit Black Irgit (tribe
  name)
kara köyük Black Köyük (tribe
  name)
kara oy Kara Oy (place name)
kara soyan Black Soyan (tribe
  name)
kara- belong to, be part of
karak eye
karaŋgı dark, dim, dull
kargıš- meet, run into, encounter
kas goose
katıš- participate (in)
katıš connection, ties
kattır- laugh

kattırıš- laugh at each other
kattıš- stand side by side, link
  up with, join
kawap kebab, roasted meat cf.
  U. **kawap**
kay which
kayda where, see **gayda**
kaysı which, see **gaysı**
kazak Kazak
kazak kıstak Kazak sub-village
kazakša Kazak, in Kazak
kazakstan Kazak
kazı fat under a horse's ribs
kazı- read, learn, find out (by
  reading), proofread
käzir now, at present, soon, at
  once, right away, immediately
käzirgi the present time
kedey poor
keere affection
kek cuckoo
kektaman snowdrop
kelbeerlig shape, having a form
kelekšek future
kelešekte in the future
kelin daughter-in-law
kem river
kem few, less, worse, lack
ken mine
  aldın ken gold mine
kep set, suit, suite, form

kep clothes, clothing

kerek need, require, have need
of, be in need, necessary

kert- carve, see kirt-

kes- cut, slice

ket- wear, see get-

key some, certain

keybir some

keybiresi some, some of

keyin later

kezek time

kilas grade, class

kilometir kilometer

kin navel, belly button

kirelig about, approximate

kirt- cut, notch, see kert-

kıdat Han Chinese, see
xanzu, gıdat

kııra compassion

kıpsı- kindle, light

kıstak sub-village, settlement,
(Chinese administrative unit),
see gıstak

kıškır- shout, yell

kıštak village

kıyat aspiration

kız- burn, blush, turn red

kızıl red, see gızıl

kızıl doru reddish brown

kızıl üyök Kızıl Üyök (place
name)

kızmet work, job

kızmetište- work

kogam society, see xogam

koža neighbor

koŋkabay Kongkabay, a
derogatory term used by
Uygurs when they refer to
Kazaks, cf. U.
qoŋkabay

kos tent, see goš

koš pair, see goš

koš- add, attach something to

koy- place

ködür- carry, lift

köl lake
žaysaŋ köl Zaysan Lake

kön- believe

könö old, ancient

könö türk Old Turkic

könözün food, grain, food
supply

köŋüdü happy

kööl feeling, heart

kööl düš- fall in love

köölge žak- like, please

kööldük happy

körgü beauty

köršü neighbor

köršülös neighboring

köyük Köyük (clan name)
ak köyük White Köyük
(clan name)

kara köyük Black Köyük
(clan name)
žanagaš köyük Zhanagash
Köyük (clan name)
goŋgutu köyük Gonggutu
Köyük (clan name)
kara köyük Kara Köyük
(clan name)
kuda in-law, see xuda
kuda bol- be engaged, become
in-laws, see xuda bol-
kudalaš- become in-laws
kuduk well
kuduruk tail
kupta- agree, support
kur- establish, set up, see kur-
kurmustu heaven, sky, see
gurmusdu
kurul- be established
kuškaš house sparrow, skylark,
see xuškaš
kut- pour, see gut-
külžüŋ Külzhüng (personal
name)
kümüs silver, see möŋgün
kümüs taŋma silver seal
kün sun, see gün
kün day, see gün
kün žayı sun light
kün ötküs- live (a life), get
alone
künde every day

kündölö everyday
kündölügü daily
kündüle- respect
kündüs daytime, during the day
la emphatic particle
lama lama
lama dini Lamaism
le emphatic particle
loymži tape recorder, tape
player, cf. C. lu yinji
magat prediction
magamut stature, height, size,
body
maktıp school, see
mektep, mäktep
mal livestock, animal
mal malda- breed livestock
mal soy- slaughter an animal
malda- breed, herd
maldıg with livestock, having
livestock
malčı herdsman
malčılıg animal-husbandry
malčın herder
mampıy Mampiy (personal
name)
mančiŋ Manchu Qing, cf. C.
man qing
manžay situation
manžu Manchu, cf. C. man zu
manžu čin Manchu Qing, cf. C.
man qing

manžu čin xaan Manchu Qing
  Khan
manžu xaan Manchu Khan
maŋay surrounding area
materiyal material
mädeniy cultural
mäktep school, see
  maktıp, mektep
mäselen for example
meeŋ my
meereŋ Meereng (tribe
  name)
meereŋ gožuun Meereng
  banner
meereŋ *Meereng*: a rank in the
  Manchu administration, held
  by a banner official below the
  Zahiragch, who was a banner
  official just below the
  Tuslagch who was an assistant
  to a banner prince. cf. M.
  Meeren.
mees sunny side of mountain
mege false, lie, fake, wrong,
  sham, phony, artificial
mege ayt- make false statement
mektep school, see maktıp
memleket state, nation, country
memleket dılı state language
men I
menže I think,
meš oven, cf. R.
metir meter

meyge *Meyge* (name of an
  animal or a bird)
meyram holiday, festival,
  celebration, ceremony, see
  meyrem
meyrem holiday, festival,
  celebration, ceremony, see
  meyram
meyren Meyren (one of the
  banner); originally a Manchu
  title/rank.
meyren gožuun Meyren banner
miŋči noun, cf. C. **mingci**
mınaar to there, (direction),
  thither
mında here
mındıg such, like this
mınžap this way
mıŋ thousand
mıŋ bir one thousand and one
  bir mıŋ beš žüs one
  thousand and five hundred
mıŋga to this
mıyak excrement, dung,
  droppings
mıysalı for example
mo this, see bo
mončak Monchak (ethnonym
  and banner name)
mončakta- speak Monchak
moŋ question particle
moŋgul Mongolian, see mool

moŋguliya Mongolia

mool Mongolian, Mongol, see
  moŋgul

mool dılı Mongolian language

mool kıstak Mongolian
  sub-village

moolša Mongolian, in
  Mongolian

morzu Morzu (personal name)

moš seal

moyun neck

mozika music

möndügöy Möndügöy (clan
  name)

möŋ heavily

möŋgü eternal

möŋgün silver, see kümüs

möŋkö Möngkö (personal
  name)

möŋküy Möngküy (personal
  name)

mööre- moo (e.g. cattle)

mör seal, stamp

mörü chance, opportunity, luck,
  success

mugalım teacher

mugat- sadden

mužora evil

mun- ride on horseback, ride a
  horse, to mount, sit on (e.g.
  horse), see min-

munaar on, from now on

munuun from this

murnuu front, southern

murnuu žük south side, south
  part

mümkün maybe, perhaps

mün soup, broth, bullion

naadım Tuvan traditional
  festival

nadan ignorant

nak exact, exactly, precisely

nätiyže result

ne what

negizdel- be found, based,
  established

negizgi main, basic,
  fundamental

negizinen basically

niykim society

niykimdig social

nom book, lesson, instruction

nom ööröt- teach

nom-erdem education

nomna- read, study cf. M.
  nomla-

nomnat- teach, preach

nomšu- read, study

nomšut- teach

nüür conscience, face,
  reputation

odun Odun (personal name)

oglu son, his/her son see ool

oxša- resemble, be similar to,

see okša-
ok bullet, arrow
okka uš- be shot with, get shot
okša- resemble, see oxša-
oku- study, see nomšu-
okuw study
okuw-agartu education
okuwšı pupil, student
ol he, she, it, that
ola- do that
olar they
olur- sit down, sit, settle down,
   live, stay
omdun Omdun (personal name)
on ten
on bir eleven
on beš fifteen
on iyi twelve
on üš thirteen
on dört fourteen
on aldı sixteen
on žedi seventeen
on ses eighteen
on tos nineteen
on mıŋ ten thousand, see
   tümän
onday about ten
onža around ten
onson then, after, also, see
   ooson
onsoonda then

onun then, and
onunčı tenth
onunčı ay October
onzur Onzur (personal
   name)
oŋšu- study
oo oh
ooba dagır sacrificed worship
ool son, boy, child, kids
oola- ascend, rise up, walk
oolgu- adopt
ooŋ his, hers, its
ooršak Orshak (tribe name)
ooson after that, see onson
or- cause to tear, tear up, break
oraa- wrap up, roll up
ornalaš- be settled, placed, be
   located, situated, lie
orta there, than
orta mektep middle school, see
   ortalaw, ortalaw mäktep
ortalaw middle (school), see
   orta mektep, ortalaw
   mäktep
ortalaw mäktep middle school,
   see orta mektep, ortalaw
ortu middle
orus Russian
oson then
osunda here, then
ot fire

ottuŋ žïrïgï firelight
ottug flint
owaa sacred side
owaa dagïïr cairn worship
oy hey, oh
oya low lying
oygur Uyghur
oygur dïlï Uyghur language
oylat- chase away, drive, chase
oyna- play, entertain, see oynï-
oynï- entertain, play, see oyna-
oyun game, joke, prank,
   entertain, party
oyun ötküs- hold game
oyunčümük Oyunchümük
   (personal name)
oy yoy oh oh
ödö very, too, quite
ög home, house, yurt
ög bol- get married
ög gag- build a house
ögbe ancestor
öglön- marry, get married
öglöndir- marry
ökümöt government
öl- die, pass away
ölžöy happiness, fortune,
   good luck, amusing
ölžöylüg happy
ölür- kill
öndürüs production

öŋ color
öör comrade, friend
öörön- learn, study
ööröt- teach
ööru high
ööru mektep high school
öörüg above
öörügü higher, superior
öörügü mektep college
öörün happily
öörüšku happiness, gladness,
   cheerfulness, joy
öörüškülüg joyful
örgün width
örgün skillful
örlö- go up, rise, raise, ascend,
   emit
örögö family
öršeel mercy, excuse, apology
ös- grow, grow up, increase,
   rise, go up
öskölük particularity
öskör- change
öskört- change, cause to change
öskörtüw reform
öskörüs change
öskus orphan
öšku goat
öšku geži goat skin
öt bile, gall
öt- penetrate, get into, leak
   (into), seep (into), pass

(exam), cross, enter (college)
ötküs- pass, live, let pass
  kün ötküs- live (a life), get
  along
ötküs- hold, put on
  oyun ötküs- hold game
öy time, season
öz self
özü himself, herself, itself
özetti Özetti (personal name)
pa wow
park difference
paš bowl (iron), kettle, pot,
  cauldron
patča emperor, king, czar, tsar
payda profit, useful
paydalan- use, make use of,
  utilize
pälte overcoat, cf. **R. pal'to**
pižiu beer, cf. **C. pijiu**
pırasent percent
poburuk woolen cloth, cf. **R.**
  fabric
pozitsiya viewpoint, standpoint,
  attitude, manner
pozitsiya bildir- express one's
  opinion
pukara masses, people,
  populous
saam time
saat watch, clock, hour, time,
  see **sagat**

saat resin, tree sap, used as
  chewing gum
saattıg pregnant
saattıg bol- be pregnant
saazın paper, cf. M. **čagasun**
saba- strike, hit, see **sawa-**
sag- milk
sagat watch, clock, hour, time,
  see **saat**
sagıš intention, mind, feeling,
  purpose
sakta- keep, protect, maintain,
  preserve
sal- put, place, apply, release
salgın gentle breeze, wind
salım fortune, fate, destiny
salt customs
san count, number, numeral,
  numerate
sana- count, consider
sanatoriya sanatorium
sarakayla- tighten
sarıg yellow
sarıg žag dıba Yellow Zhag
  Tuva
sarıg a leather prepared from
  goat-skin or sheep-skin, rough
  leather, cf. M. *sar's.*
sarıg bag a leather ball used for
  shooting with a bow when
  playing the game.
saruul Saruul (banner name)

sasın letter, paper
sasın biči- write a letter
sat- sell, sell out, betray
satkın traitor
sawa- strike, hit, card, see saba-
säbet soviet, USSR, see söwet
seeŋ your
seere- better, improve
sekiriw leap
   zor sekiriw the Great Leap
   Forward
seleme sword, saber
semis fat
semis bol- gain weight,
   become fat
semiyä family
semont cement
semontta- cement, put cement
sen you
sen- believe
sendir- convince, make believe
sener you all
senim trust, believe
sereŋge matches
sergeleŋ buoyant, cheerful
ses eight
ses žüs eight hundred
sesinči eighth
seske sieve, sifter
sestema system
sezen eighty

sezen üžünči eighty-third
sezenči eightieth
sezendey about eighty
sidik urine
sigen grass, hay
sigen xag- mow
siir tendon, sinew
siler you all (polite form)
siŋ- absorb, soak up, be
   absorbed, be assimilated
sıınak fawn
sıkta- cry
sımıran- whisper
sın- break, be fractured
sıŋsalıx Singsalik (personal
   name)
sır paint
sır secrete
sırakayla- tighten
sıralıg pine tree
sırgak ill, sick
sırgabul *sirgabul*, a long tapered
   pole used as part of a yurt
   frame
sırla- paint, cover with paint
sırla- gallop
sıtalin Stalin
soguna onion, green Chinese
   onion
sokta- beat, strike, hit, pound
soluŋgı Sonlunggi (personal
   name)

sonda there, then, after

soŋ end

soŋunda at the end

soŋgaar backwards, back, after

soŋgu northern, last, past, recent

soŋgu žük north, northern side

soŋgu kün day after tomorrow

soo agree

sook cold

sor- keep in the mouth, suck

soy- slaughter, butcher

soyan Soyan (one of the
   banners), clan name

soyan söök Soyan clan

   ak soyan White Soyan

   kara soyan Black Soyan

soyul culture

soyulda- civilize

söök bone, clan

sös word

sös žok certainly, definitely

söwet soviet (see säbet)

sug water

suglug watery

suk Suk (clan name)

suk- insert, put in, put on

suk- hide

sumun district

sumanlaš- live in the same
   sumun

sunda extensive

sundaarık Sundaarik (place
   name)

suŋ Song (Chinese surname)

sura- ask, inquire, request

surax question

sügünžü pursuer

süt milk

süzük religion

šabax basket

šag time, time period

šagaa the New Year, the
   Chinese Spring Festival

šagın small

šagıš time

šažın religion

šak- strike fire (e.g. from a flint),
   kindle

šala inadequate, half, lacking,
   incomplete, insufficient

šala-mužuk inadequate, half,
   lacking, incomplete,
   insufficient

šamanan approximately

šanagaš Shanagash (clan name)

šap rawhide, strap

šap- gallop (on horseback), run
   (of a horse)

šaŋ award, price, reward, cf. **C.**
   jiangshang

šar tsar, czar

šar patčazı Tsarist emperor

šar- tie, fasten, bind, bundle up,

wrap
šarana placenta
šaš- sprinkle, spray, spill, splash,
   scatter, see čaš-
šaš- sow
šay tea
šay ber- serve tea
šay xayındır- make tea
šeberle- clean, make clean
šegärä border, frontier,
   boundary, border area
šegäräli bordered, having
   frontiers
šegin- retreat
šen rank
šerig soldier, army
šiawžaŋ head of a school,
   headmaster, principal,
   president, chancellor, cf. C.
   Xiao zhang
šigi like, alike
šimi milky
šimi aragı milky drink
šimže- move
šinžiaŋ Xinjiang
šinžiaŋ yišöyuan Xinjiang
   Medical College, cf. C.
   Xinjiang yixue yuan
šiŋgil Shinggil (a county name)
šiŋgil awdan Shinggil county
širikte- smooth out
šiwžinžuyi revisionist, cf. C.

xiuzheng zhuyi
šıda- endure
šın true, real, genuine, actual,
   authentic
šındık truth, truthfulness
šınında actually, as a matter of
   fact
šolak short
šoor traditional wooden flute
šoorla- make a flute
šuunžı exam
šuluun fast, quick, rapid, right
   now, immediately
šulmus devil, demon, witch
šuŋgur Shunggur (clan name)
šuŋkur Shungkur (place name)
šuŋkur awıldık Shungkur
   village
šübö thing, see žibe
šüübür exam
šüübür ber- take an exam
šüüt chores
taar- rebuke, bawl out,
taart- emboss
taart- rebuke
tabıžak lined or lined outer
   garment with wool or cotton
tabak dish, plate, see tawak
tal willow
talap request, demand, wish
talap gak- request
talaptan- seek, demand, require,

request
talay many, quite a few
talay ret many time, quite a few
    times
tamaša wonderful, perfect
tanı- know, recognize, find out,
    get to know, identify, see
    danı-
tanıg known, familiar
tanıš- get acquainted, be
    familiar, be acquaint with, be
    familiarize with, see danıš-
tanıš acquainted, familiar
tanıštır- make acquaint,
    introduce
taŋdı Tangdi
taŋdı dırba Tangdi Tuva (tribe
    name)
taŋdı ooršak Tangdi Oorshak
    (tribe name)
taŋma brand, seal
taŋsa ballroom dance
taŋsa oyna- dance
tap class
tap- find
tap al- find
tapta- trample
taptıg sweet, honeyed, tasty,
    delicious
taraŋkay Tarangkay (personal
    name)
taraa grain, flour, wheat, kernel,

crops
taraa tarı- grow grain, farm
taraačın farmer, peasant
taraančı farmer, peasant
tarbagan marmot
tarčı three-year-old marmot
tarı- plant, grow
tayжı *Tayzhi* crown prince, and
    also a title of nobility held by
    the descendants of Chinggis
    Khan. **C. tai zi**
taylak 1 or 2 year-old camel
    foal
tärbiye Tärbiye (personal name)
teginde before, in the past,
    formerly
tegindee the previous one
tegis flat, smooth, even
tegiste- make even, flat, smooth
tek only, just
tekser- check, exam (medical)
tekseril- get check, see a doctor
temeki tobacco; Temeki (place
    name)
temeki awıldıı Temeki village
tenek fool, foolish
teŋ equal, same, equally
teŋge money
tep- kick
terek poplar
terekti Terekti (village name)
terekti awıldık Terekti village

teresin splendid achnatherum,
  feather grass, grass mat
teyle- beseech
tik- sew
til tongue, language, see dıl
tildeš- confide in one another
tiwiy physical training center C.
  ti wei
tın life
tın azıra- subsist
tın azıran- live
tınıŋ gir- come back to life
tınıŋ gıy- spare one's life
tırısšaŋ hardworking
tıt larch tree
tıwala- speak Tuva, see
  dıbalaša-
tıyım prohibition, restriction
toluk full, senior
toluk orta senior middle school,
  see toluk orta mektep
toluk orta mektep senior
  middle school, see toluk orta
toluksuz mektep junior middle
  school, see toluksuz orta,
  toluksuz orta mektep
toluksuz orta junior middle
  school, see toluksuz
  mektep, toluksuz orta
  mektep
toluksuz orta mektep junior

middle school, see toluksuz
  mektep, toluksuz orta
ton fur line coat, overcoat,
  traditional garment
tool story, tale, folk tale, epic,
  see xoču
topta- amass
toptaš- be concentrated in,
  gather, assemble
torga woodpecker
torgun Torgun (personal name)
tos nine
tos žüs nine hundred
tozan ninety
tozan üžünči ninety-third
tozančı ninetieth
tozınči ninth
tozı personal seal, signet C.
  tuozı
töbe roof
tödö all
tödübüs all of us
tögöle- surround, encircle,
  gather round
tögörök round, circular, wheel
törö leader, chief, ruling nobility
töröön relatives
törü- give birth
töz all
tözübüs all of us
turgun Turgun (a village name)

turgun awıldıg Turgun village

turmuš life

turmuštan- get married

turmuštug of life, daily

tut- seize, grab, grasp, take,
hold, hold up, support, see
dut-

tutkıš holder, handle

tutkıštı with a handle

tuwırga wall

tuwralı about, concerning

tük any, whatever

tür variety, kind

türk Turkic

türlü various, different, assorted

tüsün- understand, cf. K. tüsin-

tüsündür- explain, cf. K.
tüsindir-

udazın thread, string, wire

udu- sleep, spend the night, stay
overnight

udum gift

ugaan wisdom, mind, memory,
thought, intelligence, intellect

ugundur- explain

užun because of, for, for the
benefit of

uk- understand, comprehend

ulanbayır Ulanbayir (personal
name)

ult nationality, see ulut

ulu- howl (e.g. dog, wolf)

ulug big, huge, great, major,
older, elder, senior, adult,
grown up

ulug aga older brother

ulug bičii old and young, old
people and children

ulug ulus senior, elder, adult,
grown up

ulus nationality, nation, state,
people, see ult, ulut

ulut nation, nationality, see
ult, ulus

uluttug nationality

uraŋxaa Uriangkhai, see
uraŋxay

uraŋxay Uriyangkhai, see
uraŋxaa

urpak descendent

urug child, girl, daughter

urug-murug girls and such

urug-tarıg family members,
descendent, children and such

urtu length

uš- fly

okka uš- get shot

uškar- carry in front of the horse

uštu- dredge up

ut- forget

ut- win, beat, beat, gain

utdup kal- forget

uušta- knead, limber up, rub
with hands, shell, peel, pare

uygur Uyghur, see oygur
uzun long
üžön thirty
üžünči third
ülö- divide, detach, distribute,
    assign, shuffle (card, etc.)
ülögür tale, story
ülögörü for example
ülös- follow along, catch up
ülözör- convergent
ülüg turn, share, portion, part
ün- grow, sprout, come out
ün- go out, enter, go into,
    emerge, move (out), exist,
    leave, depart
ündüsüden nationality,
    belonging to a certain ethnic
    group
ünübey dumb
üŋgö- crawl, creep, climb,
    scramble, get up
ür- blow, exhale, blow on (e.g.
    soup, tea)
üren fellow
ürösün seed
ürümži Urumchi (capital city of
    Xinjiang)
üs butter, fat, oil
üs-müs oils and such
üsdü top, above, top of, see üst
üsdünde above, on the top
üst top, surface, upside, see

üsdü
üš three
üš žüs three hundred
üy hey
üylösör- convergent
üytkönü because, the reason is
    that
üz- tear, rip
üzdür- be broken
üzük break, rupture, gap
üzük letter, alphabet, word
üzük Üzük (place name)
    soŋgu üzük Northern Üzük
wayke surgical department, cf.
    C. wai ke
wınžaw cultural and education,
    cf. **C. wenjiao**
wınžaw žü cultural and
    education bureau, cf. **C.**
    wenjiao ju
yišö yuan medical college
yoŋ emphatic particle
zaman time, era
zan station, frontier station
zasık government
zertte- research, do research
zor big, hug, great, enormous
zor sekiriw the Great Leap
    Forward
zorla- force somebody to do
    something
züldö soul

Bibliography

Anderson, G. D. S. and K. D. Harrison. 1999. *Tyvan*. Languages of the World/Materials 257. München: LINCOM-EUROPA.

Anderson, G. D. S. and K. D. Harrison. 2003. *Tuvan Dictionary*. Languages of the World/Dictionaries 28. München: LINCOM-EUROPA.

Cheng, S.L. et al. 1997. *Tujue bijiao yuyan xue* 突厥比较语言学 (A Comparative Study of the Turkic Languages). Urumchi: Xinjiang People's Publishing House.

Cheng, S.L. 1994. Xinjiang Aertai shanqu de Tuwaren 新疆阿尔泰山区的图瓦人 (Tuvan People in the Altay mountain region). *Zhongyang minzu daxue xuebao*. 5: 39-42.

Clauson, G. 1972. *An Etymological Dictionary of Pre-Thirteenth-Century Turkish*. Oxford: Clarendon Press.

Golden, P.B. 1992. *An Introduction to the History of the Turkic Peoples*. Wiesbaden: Otto Harrassowitz.

He, X.L. 1984. Guanyu Aertai diqu minzuxue diaocha baogao 关于阿尔泰地区民族学调查报告 (Research Report Regarding the Ethnography in Altay Area) *Xinjiang shehuikexue yanjiu*. 11: 1-7.

He, X.L. 1988. Aertai Wulianghai shehui lishi shuliue.阿尔泰乌梁海社会历史述略 (A Brief Narration of the Social History of the Altay Uriangkhai). *Zhongyang Minzu xueyuan xuebao* 1: 36-42.

Mawkanuli, T. 1988. *Tujueyuzu zhu yuyan yuying xitong de bijiao* 突厥语族语言语音系统的比较 (A Comparative Study of the Sound Systems of the Turkic Languages). Unpublished M.A. thesis, Xinjiang University, Urumchi.

Mawkanuli, T. 1999. *Phonology and Morphology of Jungar Tuva*. Ph. D. Dissertation, Indiana University.

Mawkanuli, T. 2001. The Jungar Tuvas: language and national identity in the PRC, *Central Asian Survey*, 20 (4): 497-517.

Mawkanuli, T. 2003. Jungar Tuvan-Kazak-English Lexicon. In preparation.

Mawkanuli, T. 2004. A Grammar of Jungar Tuvan. In preparation.

Nadeljaev, V.M. et al., eds. 1969. *Drevnetjurkskij Slovar'*. Leningrad: "Nauka".

Chen, Z.Z. et al., eds. 1990. *Zhonguo Tujue yuzu yuyan cihui ji* 中国突厥语族语言词汇集 (China's Turkic Language Family Dictionary). Beijing: Minzu chubanshe.

Song, Z.C. 1981. *Tuwayu yanjiu* 土瓦语研究 (A Study of Tuvan Language). Unpublished M.A. thesis, Zhongguo shehui kexueyuan yanjiushengyuan, Beijing.

Song, Z.C. 1985. Tuwayu gaikuang 图佤语概况 (A Brief Account of the Tuvan Language). *Minzu yuwen* 1: 65-80.

Su, B. H. 1986. Xinjiang Aertai shanqu Tuwazu de laiyuan he xianzhuang 新疆阿尔泰山区土瓦族的来源和现状 (The Origins and Present Situation of Tuva in Altay Mountain Area). *Xinjiang daxue xuebao* 3: 41-49.

Tenishev, R. ed. 1968. *Tuvinsko-russkij slovar'*, Moscow: Sovetskaja Enciklopedija.

Wu, H.W. 1999. *Tuwayu yanjiu* 图瓦语研究 (A Study of Tuvan Language). Shanghai: Shanghai Yuandong chuban she.

www.ingramcontent.com/pod-product-compliance
Lightning Source LLC
Chambersburg PA
CBHW060330100426
42812CB00003B/940